MY BELOVED WAGER

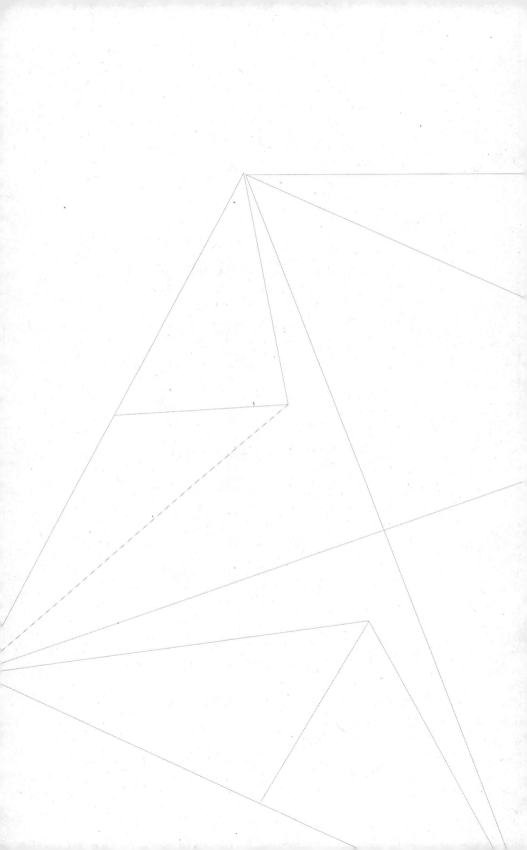

ERÍN MOURE

my beloved *wager*

ESSAYS FROM A WRITING PRACTICE

NeWest Press

COPYRIGHT©ERÍN MOURE 2009

All rights reserved. The use of any part of this publication reproduced, transmitted in any form or by any means, electronic, mechanical, recording or otherwise, or stored in a retrieval system, without the prior consent of the publisher is an infringement of the copyright law. In the case of photo-copying or other reprographic copying of the material, a licence must be obtained from Access Copyright before proceeding.

Library and Archives Canada Cataloguing in Publication

Moure, Erín, 1955-
    My beloved wager : essays from a writing practice / Erín Moure ; Smaro Kamboureli, editor.

(Writer as critic ; 11)
Includes bibliographical references and index.
ISBN 978-1-897126-45-5

    1. Poetics. 2. Poetry--History and criticism. I. Kamboureli, Smaro II. Title. III. Series: Writer as critic ; 11

PS8576.O96A16 2009   808.1   C2009-902344-X

Editor for the Board: Smaro Kamboureli
Cover and interior design: Natalie Olsen
Cover image (red shoes): Vida Simon, "Walking in Russia" (2005), vidasimon.net
Author photo: Erín Moure

NeWest Press acknowledges the support of the Canada Council for the Arts, the Alberta Foundation for the Arts, and the Edmonton Arts Council for our publishing program. We also acknowledge the financial support of the Government of Canada through the Book Publishing Industry Development Program (BPIDP).

trañsCanâða NeWest Press also thanks Transcanada Institute for
—INSTITUTE—   its contributions to the publication of this book.

NeWest Press   201, 8540-109 Street
Edmonton, Alberta T6G 1E6
780.432.9427
newestpress.com

No bison were harmed in the making of this book.
We are committed to protecting the environment and to the responsible use of natural resources. This book was printed on 100% post-consumer recycled paper.

1 2 3 4 5 12 11 10 09
printed and bound in Canada

In memory of my mother, M.I.M.: Mary Irene Mouré, 1924–2007; and of Robin Blaser, 1926–2009.

11	PREFACE
13	READING NEVER CEASES TO AMAZE ME
17	AND POETRY

19
'TWAS THIS BEGAN

21	THE ANTI-ANÆSTHETIC
35	IT REMAINED UNHEARD
41	DEEPER THAN ANY SILENCE: BRONWEN WALLACE (1945–1989)
49	BREAKING BOUNDARIES: WRITING AS SOCIAL PRACTICE, OR ATTENTIVENESS
59	POETRY, MEMORY, AND THE POLIS
69	THE MEDIUM

71
A NEW BIRD FLICKER, OR *STOOKING*

73	NOTES ON POETRY AND KNOWING
79	*I LEARNED SOMETHING ABOUT WRITING FROM YOU IN THE SPORTS PAGES OF THE* MONTREAL GAZETTE
87	MY RELATION TO THEORY AND GENDER
89	FOR SCOPING GIRLS
97	SPEAKING THE UNSPEAKABLE: RESPONDING TO CENSORSHIP
103	*A FRAME OF THE BOOK* OR *THE FRAME OF A BOOK*
113	A NEW BIRD FLICKER, OR THE FLOOR OF A GREAT SEA, OR *STOOKING*

119
RESPONSE TO LIGHT

121	*THE CAPITULATIONS,* A TEXT BY, FOR, AND THROUGH THE ART OF LANI MAESTRO
127	THREE NOTES ON LANI MAESTRO'S *CRADLE*
131	A PAN OF QUAIL
135	MORNINGS ON WINNETT: *TRUST MEDITATIONS*

143
AN EX*H*ORBITANT BODY: CITIZENSHIP, TRANSLATION, SUBJECTIVITY

- 145   POETS AMID THE MANAGEMENT GURUS
- 151   PERSON, CITIZEN: SOME CUES FROM A POETIC PRACTICE
- 163   THE PUBLIC RELATION: REDEFINING CITIZENSHIP BY POETIC MEANS
- 173   THE EX*H*ORBITANT BODY: TRANSLATION AS PERFORMANCE
- 179   SUBJECTIVITIES: AN APPROACH THROUGH CLARICE AND FERNANDO
- 187   FIDELITY WAS NEVER MY AIM (BUT FELICITY)
- 195   TRANSLATION AS ABSENCE, BOOKENDED AS GIFT

201
STAKES, POETRY, TODAY

- 203   STAKES, POETRY, TODAY
- 217   *RE*-ÇITING THE CITIZEN BODY
- 223   ONE RED SHOE: NARRATIVE AS A PRACTICE OF POSSIBILITY
- 235   CO-TRANSLATING "NICOLE BROSSARD": THREE-WAY SPECTACLE OR SPECTRE DE TROIS?
- 245   CROSSING BORDERS WITH A GALICIAN BOOK OF POETRY: TRANSLATING A REALIST POET
- 261   SHAGGY MAMMAL INTERVENÇÃO
- 271   *O CADOIRO:* THE CATARACT
- 279   STAGING VERNACULARS
- 301   THE POLITICS OF PRACTICE: ARTISTS AND INSTITUTIONS (MY ASSIGNED SUBJECT)
- 307   A CODA—BEACONS

- 311   NOTES
- 329   WORKS CITED
- 337   ACKNOWLEDGEMENTS
- 343   PERMISSIONS
- 345   INDEX

PREFACE

▌ *My Beloved Wager* stems from the propulsion to speak out, albeit restlessly. In this collection of essays, "essay" is not pronouncement but the fraught terrain of a practice, an *essai* or *try* articulated from inside the work of poetry. Essaying is part of the work of poetry, part of my practice of writing and reading it.

This practice is influenced by feminism and has a stake in it. And it's influenced by asthma. By allergy. By sexuality. By the somatic. By all that can't be ignored, on pain of numbness or loss of consciousness.

Even so, it is not a recommendation or map for another's writing or reading practice, for the path of any one practice is always necessarily fraught or frayed by small decisions, tumults, absence, absent-mindedness — processes that open the mind's weave, the movements of small animals (feline) in domestic space. The trajectories of thought are as strings of a harp: all present, but only some plucked at any given moment, while the music is written as the plucking occurs. Startlingly, we can pluck some strings only by breaking them and, eventually, we must cast down the harp, for thought is not a stringed instrument at all but an organic passage within and through the forces of nervousness, of dilemma, of

> *reason's gloss*
>
> *hieratic echo*
>
> hostis hospes *"wherein host/guest's configural."*

This record of a practice might indicate what a writing and reading practice *can* be, show the kinetic and lapidary nature (*rature*) of it. The insist*in*ence. All assembled here in the hope (one hope) that some may find nourishment in the world

> more curiously,
>
> having read it.

READING NEVER CEASES TO AMAZE ME

▍Whenever I go outside, it seems, I always go out with a book. I just *want* one with me, even when I know I'll have no time to read. A book, to me, is the possibility of reading. I learn from it, even if I can't open it, simply because I desire it so strongly. It's smaller than a computer, less complex than a toy. Yet just carrying it opens me up to riches.

Fact is, reading never ceases to amaze me. Little squiggly ants on the page, no pictures: nothing or no "thing" — *aucune chose* — is presented for me ready-made on the page. Reading itself constructs what is there. I love every part of words, their syllables, their repetitive formations, their letters, their attributes and modes, declensions and cases, their antiquity and renaissance, their infinite juxtaposability, their combinatory effects, and the languages they bring to me.

Above all, for me, reading is where thought risks. And more: reading is where thought risks concatenation with that which is exterior to it. That which isn't yet in the head and has never before been called to mind. Yet reading's concatenation of thought and circumstance is nothing in itself. It is not ever for anyone in particular. Rather, it is to be seized by those who would seize it, for it is the seizure that characterizes reading. Not seizure as grabbing something to settle it down, but as a force (perhaps external) entering and breaking apart the organism, the organism's complacency, its complicities with the status quo.

For reading is potentially a place that brings challenge to old structures, including that droll old structure, the self. To get to this place of curiosity and challenge, one must — I think — confront the difficult and not shy from it. As Pierre Macherey wrote about reading Spinoza's *Ethics*: "There's nothing to do but throw yourself into the water, confront the text without being discouraged by the resistance that it puts up, and try to penetrate the content little by little, even if only partially. This confrontation is indispensable" (38).[1] It is indispensable because the resistance is not only in the text but in the way that the reader is structured by society.

Challenging the self leads to seeing where self is constructed, recognizing where thought's wires act as stop signs. Challenging the self is learning to walk past those wires, learning that the borders in one's thought are but seams. There's cloth past them, too, and fields, light, birds —

Early in his *Negotiations*, Gilles Deleuze (one of my favourite *provocateurs*) says there are two ways to read a book:

> you either see it as a box with something inside and start looking for what it signifies, and then if you're even more perverse or depraved, you set off after signifiers. And you treat the next book like a box contained in the first or containing it. And you annotate and interpret and question, and write a book about the book,

> and so on and on. Or there's the other way: you
> see the book as a little non-signifying machine,
> and the only question is "does it work, and how
> does it work?" If it doesn't work, if nothing comes
> through, you try another book. This second way
> of reading's intensive: something comes through
> or it doesn't. There is nothing to explain, nothing
> to understand, nothing to interpret. It's like
> plugging into an electric circuit. (7–8)

The first kind of reading is the way reading is taught in classes, in schools, in institutions. The second way of reading is what I call writerly. It finds ways forward or sideways in what the book itself essays; without trying to box it into explanations, it finds ways out of the box. Openings. Curiosities. Glimmers.

That's the kind of reading I can best recommend for anyone. Read your way out of the box. Read what you don't already know, plunge in. Read widely across domains and epochs, across intentionality, across languages too, their particular and haunting sounds and formations. You never know how thoughts may come back and re-entwine in the present; thought itself is always haunted by prior or anterior incarnations, by apparent misreadings, by folds and convergences. Even outmoded philosophies can help us read contemporary surfaces and depths in new ways.

All of which is why I go out, always, with a book.

It is not me and I am not contained by it.

It is small but it bursts "me" open.

I am carrying it with me. Soon I will stop to read it: in the gym, on the bus, in a store line-up or a café. Or I will just carry it close to me as my risk, my wager. For I am a being open to reading, and this is the most inviting way of being of all.

AND POETRY

▎My method? If anything, a kind of accretion. Sounds attract feelings and aches, and vice versa. Sounds and words attract each other. They attract, too, ideas and worries. And dreams. And they shudder a thread of remembrance that knits the self over and over again. It's preposterous; it's hard to keep up with, do justice to, keep track of. The world is imbued with language and linguistic possibility, with bad and good expression, with hopefulness, but with manipulation and trickery as well, with rationalizations and silences and gaps. All of these alter, slowly, the structures of thought in the head. Poetry laughs at all of this at the same time as it confronts it, because poetry is entirely useless and owes no debts. It's a weightless possession that nevertheless bears the weight of responsibility and forgiveness. It's an object that is first a noise, then a resonance of words that alters noise over and over in the head, breaking through the pallor of the image and the self.

I revise a lot, and listen and learn when revising. I try consciously to push words forward and make them tumble, to work through my own perceptual failures, to create a space and duration in the marks that are words where differences are possible, multifaceted articulation is possible. Even if this pushing breaks down the construct of the self — the seeing self, the self as un-self-conscious observer in the poem, as poetic voice, as stability steering the poem.

To me there's a relationship between physical processes, presence, and voice that is articulated, constituted only in relation to other beings. I'm more interested in those links we have to each other, so well buried by the social constraints built into our speech and perception, and in the movement of those links, than in objects or conclusions at either end. If you damage or conceal the links (as we do in damaging the earth or in underfunding AIDS hospices and medication, for example), what are the consequences for the individual? I believe they are grave.

The structure of the poem? To me, absolute structure is motion. Being is always in excess of this structure; it *endures* while motion is already past. Shock of that. Here we are. The body requires motion for memory and to interpret context. Memory is one part of the construct of a present context, which is to say, of the plausible. The brain puts forward these plausibilities by selecting neural paths we have previously travelled. Concomitantly, the neural paths murmur to each other. The paths alter themselves in response not just to outside data, but also to this murmuring. Recontext, then, as new context. Never the same. In the midst of the murmur, we must be attentive and moving in order to receive outer stimuli, whether identifiable or unknown, familiar or strange.[1] Attention is that burst of light. Burst of speed. *Furious*.

Poetry is a limitless genre. Its borders are only in ourselves and we can move them, in our lifetimes, if we dare to.

'twas
this
began

THE ANTI-ANÆSTHETIC

▌The framework — can we avoid it? Can we speak outside a framework? *A guide or friend? A restraint on vision?* Can we ignore it? Can we say "pure sound"? "I am a woman is full of consequences" (Nicole Brossard, but now everyone knows), for we are part of a representational system, a system of behavioural laws, of social conditions that have privileged the (male) gaze.[1] Thus what I have to say is necessarily tied with social and linguistic conditions, and with the gaze through which femininity has been defined. (In the work of some philosophers, when the notion of the gaze is questioned or displaced, not only femininity disappears, but also women. The discourse of privilege is infinitely absorptive. The relational vanishes. There are versions of the postmodern, too, that wear this privilege.)

Here, though, I just want to propose some notions and musings on the idea of poetic structure. Structure, not form. And the social consequences of structure. We normally talk about form as one side of the content/form binary, the side that contains structure. Yet, for me, they are different; structure deals with the stresses and forces in materials, in the relationship between materials and in the proximity of materials, whereas form is a cultural artifact, a presentation, "a principle giving unity to the whole," and "the shape and structure of something as distinguished from its material" (*Webster's Collegiate Dictionary*). It's materiality that interests me in writing poetry: words and the force of words, sounds, and signification, as well as the relation between the parts or particles, the interrelation of parts in the whole. <u>This sense of structure I refer to as "the jewel."</u> What intrigues me is how this structure relates to our bodies and physical presence and, thus, to the social order. I won't deal here with events or content or histories. My thoughts are purely of structures, forces inside forms, forces and order. And privilege.

JEWEL

Because words can't entirely convey our desires, because a gap between desire and expression is implicit in language and also because language carries the baggage of the social and metaphysical order, the poem is a physical presence whose structure, outside the surface meaning of its words, can and must resonate (desire) in and through the reader. In a non-verbal way—like painting does, according to Francis Bacon, but not a flat surface. Because if you use a word, or a sign like a word, a hieroglyph, relying only on semantic meaning, you are back to that gap between desire and expression where "something" is lost. A heat loss, entropy. This makes memory essential because without it we would risk total heat loss; we would spontaneously combust. *But memory also is a structure framed by social order.*

<u>The poem itself is the jewel, a knotted space made out of the world.</u> A planar fold, not flat: a set of foldings. A relation of light, and not the flat mirror of the "specular" gaze. Closer

to the speed of light, the jewel is those spoken sounds whose mass increases and becomes a tracing, visible. Coalesces in a linguistic order. Density and cadence. Sound. The fold. Place of memory and desire. The past and future tenses in us, acting, as we look upon and consider their tension. (As in "The Acts" in *Furious*.)

The jewel is an enactment of linguistic sounds in which the relational (a folding?) pushes at order (the gaze?). Enactment, of course, presumes a subject enacting, or through whom something is enacted. The speaker appears, or has always been there. Identity becomes apparent. Yet memory here — for a speaker has memory — is not a stable telling of *I remember when*. Vasyl Stus, a Ukrainian poet imprisoned by the Soviets (who suppressed all manifestations of Ukrainian culture) until his death in 1985, wrote in Perm labour camp: "Memory, the sound of the Dnieper."[2] Sounds unlock memories which precede the laws of social order. Sounds that precede words. The sound is where memory coalesces in the poem.

Not *sound*, but *sense*, you insist? Sound *is* sense, a truer sense, undercutting surface commerce and ideology. When we rely too much on the surface meanings of the words we are in danger, for the surfaces are always full of commerce; the meanings and neurological thought processes they evoke and provoke are those of our social and economic culture, and convey those values, perpetuating them, using our words as their icons. But sounds are not surface; they endure in the brain longest of all sensory information. Psychologists have shown that in a train or plane crash what is etched most deeply in the brain is the sound. In recovering from disaster, people can eventually reintegrate the visual — the sight of torn bodies or burning people or people being shot — but sounds veer up, deafen, overwhelm years later. I was in a train wreck in 1980 and can still hear the exact grinding of the sleeping car bending around me, the gravel roar of the roadbed underneath and shredding of ties, rivets popping out of the paint inside my roomette. The long-term psychological wounding stems concretely and precisely from the neurological scarring made by the sound tearing electrically inside the skull. How can any of us write again without considering the sound of what we do?

Of course, we can't speak about sound without admitting the presence of the speaker, that socially structured being who enacts it. Vasyl Stus, for example, was the speaker or subject in whom every kind of enactment had been exhausted and sickened except this: the sound of a river existing ever and irrevocably in proximity, though it was not near. Through this proximity (not coincidence or prescription) of sound, the self makes its fierce sketch that coalesces in the *now* of the poem.

RELATION/TERMS: DISRUPTION/RECUPERATION

When Julia Kristeva talks of two types of signifying process at work, the semiotic and the symbolic, within any production of meaning, I hear an echo of the jewel. Kristeva relates the semiotic to the (Platonic) *chora*, a space anterior to space/time/law, a structure imprinted in relation to the maternal body (*Revolution in Poetic Language*). The entry into the symbolic is an entry into sign, syntax, the Law of the Father (the social order, the republic, the polis). From sound to sign. Memory becomes possible, for memory is known to us only as it becomes structure.

Poetic language, Kristeva claims, comes from the semiotic *chora*. It's a return to the mother, to that unspeakable, non-extensible hole from where we are descended. It contains *that* memory. It contains the unspeakable. It enacts. It is an enactment of what can't be said in words or forms. It consumes its form in order to enact, but can do so only through the sign, through the Law, by disturbing the sign in its own soil (Derrida, *Of Grammatology*). It is a leak out of meaning and a folding back on meaning, an excess, not a complexity of meanings but the way that new meaning occurs, as doubling, redoubling, but not of "the same" (Irigaray). It is "the expression of longing, in and among the collapse of social systems" (*Furious*).

Yet the relational does require *terms* to make sense. The semiotic *chora* is not simply relational; it is not the absence of terms but the non-identity of terms prior to space/time. It is non-extensible because infinitely extensible, and duration does not apply to it because it is unlimited in duration. That unspeakable hole is not translatable. In a curious paradox, we can speak of its *relationality* rather than its *terms* only because the symbolic aspect of signification always contains and privileges *terms* (though it still contains relations). To truly privilege the relations, then, requires the creation of a structural slippage, but this process holds only for a moment because to privilege the relational (since it requires terms) means, ever, a slip back into terms again. In addition to causing the force of the terms to slip momentarily, the terms themselves must be examined and our relation as speakers who are subject to those terms must be laid out. At times, even laying out the terms acts to disrupt the law. On the other hand, to ignore the entry into Law, and think we can define ourselves through slippage alone, is dangerous. It perpetrates a social order.

Entry into the Law (at Lacan's mirror stage, when the Ego is formed) has an advantage: it reduces anxiety for the organism. Its binding is painful but reduces anxiety. Quite efficiently.³ Provides the coordinates of space, place. But for some people, the ones who later realize they are absent (women, blacks, First Nations, lesbians, working class, immigrants, combinations of all these), the ones who are not centred in but are at the edge of society's privileged markings, the Law increases anxiety to a sometimes unbearable level. How can this anxiety be alleviated? Well, there is an alleviating force at work: a pull toward the centre. An anæsthesia. A centripetal force to lure us and make us forget, or repress, or define ourselves in terms acceptable to the order. If we don't accede to that pull or drift, if we resist it or do not love it, something often breaks in the organism. People are carried off by smallpox, by tuberculosis, by alcoholism. And we all know the history of women who have put stones into their pockets, or who have shut themselves into their rooms.

Poetic structure does not come solely from the semiotic, from some undifferentiated place related to the mother; the relation of the speaker to social order is also part of poetic structure. The entry, the flash of a mirror. Poetic structure has to reflect this, too. Even if it can't stop or hold it, it's there as a fold.

RHYTHM

A poetic structure is a linking that may not be a completion, a final thing. (Until it is recuperated or absorbed as marginal into the social order, of course, where poetry is received as completion and thing.) It's a collection of stresses, of rhythmic steps, an interplay with the reader.

Cadence, the extension of rhythmic sequences over space/time, extends rhythm or sound beyond the word, beyond the sentence. Sound and rhythm, cadence, are bases of meaning, too. We need more than the dictionary meanings of words. These are just legal traces of meaning (and not the important ones) that privilege certain speakers and ways of speaking in the social order.

What I long for is the gaps that make the body present as a reader, and make it impossible to be satisfied with a surface that alleviates anxiety: the oh-what-a-beautiful-poem representation and effect. Instead, I want the words to make a context of sound that envisages the folds and flashes, the gaps in words, where time is ready to reverse if the tracing can be visible, audible enough. Defying the entropic process. Visible: but folded, faceted — thus, THE JEWEL.

COMMUNITY

To consider social ordering, we have to consider how our bodies, our sense of ourselves as physical presence, fit into this context of sound, this semiotic field, these gaps. I think of neurologist Oliver Sacks, in *The Man Who Mistook His Wife for a Hat*, describing cases of brain damage to show that even when the sense of self as memoried and present Cartesian individual is damaged, a core self can still assert a kind of presence *in relation to* the community of objects and individuals, *in relation to* the interlinking, even when objects and individuals themselves can no longer be identified. It is as if relation itself becomes present or privileged in the (not absence but) non-identity of terms: a folding redoubled many times. This relationship is rhythmic, each part of it forming a beat: Sacks described people with brain damage who use musical rhythms almost as prostheses to help them perform tasks such as walking and dressing. He tells of the man with neurological damage to the frontal cortex who would mistake his wife's head for a hat and who, in order to get dressed and put his shirt on instead of the chest of drawers, sang himself little songs about the objects. It is songs — the creation of narratives — that help the body function despite the damage. Sound and rhythm give the objects and our actions meaning, allow our bodies to establish their own physical presence and capacity, and to constitute, on some level, the self. Clearly, to keep the self intact, to *identify*, is in some way an acknowledgement of the otherness and multiplicity of the non-self, of what is outside the self, an acknowledgement the body makes automatically at a pre-social level to retain its own sense of body, of presence, of equilibrium.[4] (To speak of eliminating the subject, then, is a bit of a cover-up.)

This acknowledgement is the building block of community and self. It's also very tentative and has no root in what is called basic experience. It *is* rhythmic. As if the interlinking (the jewel) is what keeps us in the world. It precedes (by the flash of a mirror, thus an inversal-precedence, a blur) the inclusion of the self as "subject" in a system of representations. Which could be why women have insisted on it so urgently: because the system of representation, once entered, covers over, as Irigaray says, the economy of women's desire. It's hard to make an identity-discourse out of women's desire — that economy of "touching" or contiguity where "nothing" is visible — because its terms slip; they are not privileged, so they never reassert themselves over the relation in the same way. There is always a return to the terms but they are unstable, and for women there is always this radical instability of terms.

That first rhythmic interlinking, tied to community, is a linking that creates the self without any teleological end: without transcendence, and not containable in words. How does language account for this relationality? It devalues it, says it's meaningless unless turned into visible representations, where the terms themselves predominate. My poem "The Jewel" (WSW 15–19) struggles against this, tries to focus on the interlinkings, dehierarchize the visual, not just in its use of the image, but in the existence of the beginning, middle, and end of the poem, and in the title, in the very location of the title. The poem breaks up the gaze and specular knowing, breaks up self-presence, when it is read.

But "to move the force … even for a moment" only "held for that moment" (*Furious* 98). This breakdown of the gaze breaks up the logos as self-evident meaning. Still, "the tendency toward the centre breaks down the fucking organizm"[5] because *even the breakdown of the logos is buried in the logos.*[6] The discourse of privilege (that privileges speech, the speaker, and the speaker's position in the social order) is infinitely absorptive. The reduction of anxiety is a pull in the organism, in the cells. The tendency toward the centre, the centripetal force, is a paradox: necessary to reduce anxiety, and deadly because it involves one's own absence. The anæsthetic. Æsthetic, from the Greek word *aisthetikos* (of sense perception), had ties to the word that became, in Latin, the root of the word "audible." We've gradually lost the sense of sound in the word "æsthetic." Anæsthetic comes from *anaisthetos* (insensible), not-perceiving. If we are not perceiving the audible, the sound of the Dnieper, the sound of the womb, we are anæsthetized; we become citizens of the Republic.

How then to maintain or urge a shift to the relational? How to not let the slippage stop, and pull us toward the centre again? Is it memory itself *slipping* (because memory is a social structure, a linguistic order)? If so, it would *have* to stop, or we would spontaneously combust (we as identity, our *"us"ness*). Is the slippage the evidence of time reversing?

The end, therefore, of entropy? The end of decaying orders is not so simply arrived at! If we speed up, time moves faster, but we can't pass the speed of light because, when we do, time reverses. Thus, such a passage is not permitted: as we approach that speed, mass increases and we slow down, creating a trace that is audible, visible. We can't just speak of slippage of meaning, but slippage of whole structural relationships. Which only holds for a moment, otherwise our "us"ness is too threatened. Mass increases and we slow down. We arrive at a kind of individualism that is a set of terms privileged over the relational presence that is our first notion of community. *What we call community — the Republic, polis — exerts this kind of privilege, has this power.*

There is a parallel moment in metaphysics: to posit Being as transcendent privileged "substance" of which we are made, or in which we think, is to obscure the sound of the Dnieper, obscure our origin out of our mothers from whom, physically, we are descended. The word *descent*: its ancestral connotations seem to indicate we are descended from our fathers. But descent: downhill, slippery, descent into hell, into the gutter. And being rises. *A tree rising! A tree inside the ear! The family tree? The father? The baron in the trees? The tree on which the Son was hung up & pierced in the side, androgynous, his vaginal wound?*

Literally, we flow out of our mothers and are made present. We are slippery. We are slimy. We enter into the world by turning inside out the place we were in. The womb just becomes more extensible when we are born; we don't start to distinguish from the *Mother* who is not a person, object, but rather an extension-without-end, a phase-without-duration. As we start to distinguish space differences, durations, and ourselves mirrored, we enter into the polis. We distinguish sounds. In us is imprinted the Law. We are. We recognize ourselves.

The I of the (liberal humanist) individual is the figure caught in the "Platonizing drift" toward the centre, that centripetal pull, which requires suppression of certain noises, pulses, and beats that cannot be located or identified as "in" or "out" of the body. This drift also places origin outside the body as transcendent, claiming we resemble "God," instead of locating origin in our mothers. Even if we do not recognize these standard social representations, they will still try to represent us. For women, they can mean an erasure of ourselves, of our bodies. To avoid this, we must take risks, and engage what coalesces, refracts, folds, enfolds, multiplies, and digresses. The cadence in the sounds of words, in their interlinkings. We must risk imperfection, so-called "flaws" in expression, that are flaws only according to the Law which seeks to uphold the Republic.

> Look you, child, I signify   three hundred years in
> swarm around me this thing I must   this uneasy
> thing   myself the other   stripped down to skin
> and sex   to stand   to stand and say   to stand
> and say   before you all   the child was black and
> female and therefore mine   listen you walk the
> edge of this cliff with me at your peril do not hope
> to set off safely to brush stray words off your face
> to flick an idea off with thumb and forefinger   to
> have a coffee and go home comfortably
> Recognize this edge   and this air carved with her
> silent invisible cries
> Observe now this harsh world   full of white
> works   or so you see us

> and it is white   white washed male and dangerous
> even to you full of white fire white heavens white
> words   and it swings in small circles around
> you   so you see it   and here I stand black
> and female
> bright black on the edge of this white world   and
> I will not blend in
> nor will I fade into the midget shades   peopling
> your dream
>
> ❙❙ Claire Harris, "Policeman Cleared in Jaywalking Case"
> (*Fables from the Women's Quarters* 38)

DEFYING ENTROPY: STRUCTURE AND SOCIAL ORDER

Poetry is protest, for it opposes, even as it uses, ordinary speech where the gap and heat loss *are* entropic. Poetry's fold is a disruption of order, which is really a disruption of disorder, because entropy is the constant tendency to disorder, measurable as heat loss.

If there is no need for poetry in Plato's Republic it is because it would be a fissure, a gap where entropy falters, and there is thus no need for the Republic. It is what the Republic fears most, because it is a fetishistic construct that covers up a blind spot (I can only describe it with an oxymoron). The jewel—which is a faceted relationship, a folding, and not a sum—cannot be co-opted by the terms of a political or any other structure. Because of its disruptive capacity, the jewel will always be suppressed by the centre, if not by censorship, then by privileging other speakers, or by covering over the relation of the speaker in the text.

"Not to question the Republic" reduces anxiety. But if we merely reproduce the forms of the polis without questioning, directing our energies on neural paths already well established, we reproduce oppression. This is especially apparent to me as a woman, and lesbian; I ride that balance of reproduction every day. Every day, I reproduce both my own privilege and my own oppression. The Republic acts as an organism that has a collective will to maintain itself. And this happens regardless of what kind of Republic it is, or what kind of group gets together: even a world of feminists would begin, without certain applications of heat-awareness, to act like a Republic. Maintenance of the collective body (the polis) is easily compatible with anæsthesia of the cells. Without a kind of stress applied to the cells (or the individuals), the cells lose mitochondria: the cell parts that digest, and which feed the cell. When there are fewer mitochondria, the cell can't store glycogen as easily, and thus begins to lack endurance. It is therefore part of the entropic order of the whole. The whole, the Republic, the social body, and the human body seen as entire are — at any given point — processes of falling apart. The drift toward the centre is a redoubled fold — the coalescence of falling apart. The fetish of Being tightens the bounds around these processes to alleviate our anxiety at being nowhere at all.

If poetry just privileges the author's voice, without self-questioning, or if it tries to make the subject vanish, it fails to take into account this social and linguistic condition (which includes, as well, the edges, folds, and contradictions that feminism, radical feminism, blacks, lesbians, the working class, and the poor are talking about), and if it fails to take into account the dynamic between the mainstream and the marginal, it will fail to deal with how information is conveyed, and fall into the Order created by the Republic, thus perpetuating it. As Derrida notes: "'Everyday language' is not innocent or neutral.

It is the language of Western metaphysics, and it carries with it not only a considerable number of presuppositions of all types, but also presuppositions inseparable from metaphysics, which, although little attended to, are knotted into a system" (*Positions* 19). This system is — or risks being — an anæsthesia (non-perception). The discourse of privilege is infinitely absorptive. Engaging poetry or poetic structure as enactment can help us defy the second law of thermodynamics, that is, disturb the organism and apply stress to the cells (for it is the tendency to the centre, to stasis or anæsthesia, that destroys the organism) even to those cells called feminism or feminist writing. Because these too are terms.[7] Yet when we speak, we have no choice but to use the terms, putting the relational at risk. Since we need the order to express the relational, we have to face the risk, and create questioning folds in the order: enactment.

This defiance is not a battle or destruction, to me, but a cherishing. To cherish entails "the expression of longing, / in & among/ the collapse of social systems" (*Furious* 98). And if we are to free our memories, our desires, we must take up the wager offered us by this longing, and refuse to *restrain ourselves*.

IT REMAINED UNHEARD

▌That we integrate the visual more easily than we do sound, calming it and quelling it, so as to feel remote or separate from images, means that television is a perfect method of social control. The screen can show us any atrocity — napalm burning children, black South African policemen in fatigues shooting blacks, the RCMP in riot gear called in to prevent New Brunswick woodcutters from blocking the road to the Consolidated Bathurst pulp mill — depriving us mostly of the sounds, just giving us the visual and the voice and head of the newscaster, maybe a bit of background noise but the newscaster is always standing in a safe place, in a studio or to the side. After all, their equipment is expensive. We can be *shown* anything and integrate it into our lives and feel only sympathy. Which is the perfect corporate emotion. It protects and isolates the self. It has no sound but is mimicry — no sound of its own. Even the sound of the TV is not ambient but sets us up as "viewer" of a screen, provides a binary context which excludes "us" from "them," secures us in an economy of "the same."

But for the woodcutters who saw the police advance, banging billies on their plexi-shields in an intentional show of fierceness — long after everything else departs, there will still be that sound. When they hear it in their minds, they'll be able to smell the trees again, the dust on the road, the isolated branches and light shining, oh, through clouds let's say, the cigarette smell of their comrades, smell of jacket-wool, tiredness. All this because of the sound of those clubs. *Memory, the sound of the Dnieper.*

Our bodies, with our proprioceptive sense of our selves as physically present, fit into this: a relation between rhythm and the body is crucial to self-identity, as Sacks noted. This relation is clearly one that is taut with an outside world, with community; it is a *skin* or integument that relates without "dividing." The two sides of it may not be commensurate but may, fleetingly and persistently in repetition, correspond.

I believe *narrative* is tied to interlinking, to correspondence, to rhythms, and not just to temporal order. The importance of an event as *meaning* is in interlinking, in its *événement*, its *coming to be*, in the contiguity of sound(s), image(s). Interlinking *is* narrative structure, and (re)presents the desire (our inner mode for the future tense) that slips in the words themselves.

Sometimes what I long for are the torn edges where we can't or won't grab on to the image as singularity (it's a construct anyhow), yet something powerful coheres in our reception. We receive not an image but a shape that coalesces out of movement's very intensity. I believe that when the structure *does* resonate in this way, as shape or sound, that even if the poem is in a foreign language, we can capture the resonance by reading it aloud. Thus, I sometimes try to read Neruda in Spanish or Ritsos in Greek. I remember hearing Yevtushenko in 1979 at the ICA in London reading "Dwarf Birches" in Russian and me, in the sound of his voice, finally understanding the structure of that poem. His words existed in a context of sound that envisaged the gaps *in words,* where time is ready to reverse if the tracing is visible, audible enough. Defying the entropic process.

This is one way that poetry fissures, or can fissure, oppressive structures. Because of this possibility of fissuring, poetry will continue to be suppressed by some governments and some social structures, if not through censorship, then through some kind of *smoothing*: by not broadcasting certain types of poetry on the CBC, for example, claiming it is too difficult. The Olympic Arts Festival in Calgary in 1988 was a case in point for me; there, talk about poetics was funded, but as part of an event sponsored by business and government to give bobsled runs and other sports facilities to Calgarians. Also part of this event, a spirit of First Nations life was celebrated by the Glenbow Museum, when the reality in Alberta was and is that some First Nations people — the Lubicon Lake Cree — didn't and still don't own their own land because the government, which is all of us, forces a certain definition of "negotiation."

Under such circumstances of questionable justice and "smoothing," some people believe poetic theory is best not talked about, and should be discussed in another framework. Those who accept invitations to talk about poetry at such events are co-opted, as I was, or was in danger of being, for I was invited and was present at that arts festival. But it made me uneasy. If structure is *in* the interlinking, then what I was saying was linked with that bobsled run. What were *my* motives for being there? For appearing as "poet"?

I knew and know very well that to work on a poem is to displace oneself as "poet" at every possible turn. Appear as a "poet" often enough and you will start to behave like one, and write things. The essential is the other way around:

don't write things, and avoid as much as possible being a poet, before, during, and after you are writing. Talk about the language as if you participate in its strictures and structures irrevocably, and not as if it is just "you" "speaking." Talk about the social representations, the systems of representation that, if you do not recognize them, will try to represent you. To do it and not be precious, you will have to risk failure and listen to the cadence in the sounds of words, in their interlinkings: the places where "noises" "touch," where they extend to "interlink" and "fissure," which is no place. You have to risk imperfection, the flaws in expression that are only flaws according to the Law that upholds the Republic. Where some of us are not heard, or are "marginal," or "non-mainstream," or fail to accept the meaning of words like "negotiation."

Yet why did I not *say* these things? The Olympic Arts Festival was clearly not set up for serious discussion about writing. Though I'd prepared a talk on these precise subjects, when I discovered that neither of my two panel companions had prepared anything, nor had had any questions posed to them in advance (nor was there a moderator), I didn't present what I had prepared. The panel would have been too lopsided, and I would have stood out as ungrateful or unruly, I felt. Our mutual talk, instead, regrettably, fell into the personal, anecdotal mode that addresses nothing and perpetuates everything.

The actual purpose of the Olympic Arts Festival still confuses me twenty years later. What was it? To bring variety to Calgarians? To entertain? But whom? And why? Why was the set-up beyond criticism? Why was any protest or defiance referred to, as was the Lubicon petition in a *Calgary Herald* article, as detrimental to future funding? Is to disagree to cut oneself off from funding? Is funding destined to cow us?

At the event, I felt very much the unease of being funded. The funded are supposed to be glad to be there. But I felt the same unease I had felt some days when at work in the bureaucracy of a large corporation, a benevolent and good corporation at that. I had the uneasy thought that I was accepted into the social order as marginal in order to perpetuate the order. Even though "the marginal" is a fiction of the centre, it is part of the social order, and this order restrained me in Calgary, and I acquiesced. I turned my back on the fissure, and I felt bad about it. I stood in a safe place, miming safe people, as if my equipment was expensive. I admit it; I wanted to fit in that day, and — to my peril — I made only safe sounds. =7 not poetry

DEEPER THAN ANY SILENCE: BRONWEN WALLACE (1945–1989)

DEAF EARS

▌What it came down to was the desire for the words to be "natural," as when they are present in the skull and spoken out loud, the shudder of that, the way women look up at each other startled but still listening, listening, adding their own viewpoint only where necessary, where the thread means they should add urgently, add a few words, the story of children or anxiety or fear. We are all one story and the narrative voice of the poem is a thread carrying us through and past meaning, to burrow deeply into the fear and its wellspring or ignite, its flail upward. All this in a rural Southern Ontario that is claustrophobic and stilted to those of us not from there, is incessant and inturned. It doesn't look up and outward to a flat prairie, for instance, so there is no or little space in which to move. As if people born there can never quieten the stubborn centrality of themselves. As if it's mountains or prairies that make one shut up, and articulate with silence and gestures.

What it came down to, on those scraped stones of the

Shield, was the expression of women's lives because they had to be spoken, had been spoken but no one was listening. History didn't hear them; history had money; history was busy; history had deaf ears.

KOKO

As if we are people whose inner light glows through the veil of the surface. To write: "*Bronwen Wallace wrote out of a transcendent longing and would not witness its dismantling.*" She nurtured it through the stories of women and of her own family, through incredible bits from sources like *People*, the *Guinness Book of World Records*, *National Enquirer*. It was the same dream and craving for wholeness: *Koko the gorilla naming her pet cat All-Ball, Philippe Petit climbing out the top of the World Trade Center, the grandmother with the breast removed in an operation on the kitchen table,* transcendence complete and turned from us, not quite reachable but still present.

Neither would she witness the breakdown of prayer, of this thing "prayer" which is necessary even without gods, because our own stories crave others; our own lives are illuminated by the guttering light of the other. The women's feeling of community: this was the prayer she yearned for.

Like Diane Arbus, whom she once quoted, "I work from awkwardness. By that I mean I don't like to arrange things. If I stand in front of something, instead of arranging it, I arrange myself" (*Newsweek*, March 20, 1987). Bronwen worked from the everyday language, never shirking that surface. As if the act of "standing in front of something" were to her the pure act of prayer, she wrote as if things were not always already "arranged." "What I try to do," she said, "is to recreate their voices, their view of things, their way of telling a story. When I do this, I am 'facing the question of language.'"

Even if the voice of the poet telling the stories were "a liberal, bourgeois lie" (WSW 84) this by itself did not reduce the necessity of speaking, but increased its urgency.[1]

For Bronwen, the current order was a place in which to be heard; there was a legitimate public sphere and a place in it for poetry, a place for women's stories. To me, the thought of a legitimate place was a dangerous shoal. "What if, under the surface is not depth, but another surface" (*Furious* 90). We never answered that.

INSISTENCE

The twin beams of stubbornness and privilege
the ability to see beyond them
to a kind of totality we call wholeness
without cynicism
to be brave or hurt
to step forward with an "opinion"
which is also privilege
that step

without faltering
with the usual and unusual prayers
most of which have been invented
suddenly
anyhow

The craving for love
The ability to see it there

or there

in the rootedness of all the stories

in the way all stories grow from the same root
exposed to light
as deer have been, caught on the fence wire and eaten
or exploded by their own parasites
yet the light of their bones is their only proof
So we must remain

rambling
rambling here

insisting on the taproot
insisting on the depth of the jaw wherein the bone
resides
quiet

so we must remain
in sight of this
straining to listen to each other

such wholeness

because it is listening not the noise
that is the shape, our words

THINKING ABOUT

Thinking about Bronwen's poetry made me think a lot about narrative. Somehow her poems were baldly narrative but at the same time were doing something else that intrigued me. Her narrative was different than other people's narrative. As if (then) she wanted to take the narrational surface and show how each detail of its depth, and each nuance in us as readers that we mistake for personal confusion and doubt, is present in the surface and in fact constructs it, a surface deceptive in its smooth realism. As if one story *is* recognizable amid the babble because even the strangest bits are held in common and are thus coherent.

So I thought about narrative content and how that content is also a form for speech, not just a form of speech. Narrative order. What comes first in the brain and how it's entangled with other things. How any one thing has its story and how we make ourselves present with these bits of stories, bits of the thread of the voice.

Jacques Derrida pointed at voice as indicative of the construct of self-presence (most significantly in *Of Grammatology*), but for women there is no one voice that makes the self present. Bronwen's relationship to voice was like that. The author's voice didn't matter in itself, but mattered for what it pulled together, echoing gently other voices. The problem for me was the socially structured nature of all discourses. Given this nature, is integrating the voice of others in one's own poem even possible without appropriation or distortion? Is there not a risk of perpetuation of the dominant ideology and structure?

At the same time in those days in the mid 1980s, I was teaching supervisory skills to adults in a corporation, and learning for myself the powerful role of stories in integrating information. I heard my students tell stories to me and to each other in order to absorb and take ownership of new data. As a result, I became interested in the brain and how memory and perception work on the mechanical level. How is any one bit of communication absorbed? What change does it make on the individual (who is ever only part of a community)? How can it enable or disable the creation of new grammatical chunks (chunks of memory) in the head?

Grammar and memory are buried in each other, and connected on the same plane as well. And there is a physical grammar — proprioception — that keeps us continually located and present in the world. Without this grammar, the world goes awry. "The perfect flatness of ordinary language, our ordinary saying of it." "The surface content is not content in the same way that we normally use the word 'content.' It can be form as well" (*Furious* 88). I was thinking about how, in Bronwen's poem about the hand (85), the story/description of the hand is not merely content but form, the way hands are forms, holding what they hold: death in life, life in death, what makes us go on and why we do. "There are nineteen small bones in the hand/ and nineteen small muscles" (87).

Added to Bron's stubborn veneration (perhaps) of a certain narrative order or presence was a kind of moral urge. For Bronwen it was important to validate ourselves, find ourselves not just in our own stories but in the stories of others. It was as if the shape of us were not in the noise that words make but in the listening, and she wanted to catch the shape of listening, of women straining to listen. To her it wasn't that women have been mute in history but that no one has been listening. They have been talking incessantly, yet no one has been listening. To catch the shape of what it is to listen! This was Bronwen's way, and she fully believed in the power of women's stories to enter history. Though she did not question the very discourse of history and how it is structured, what unifies discourse itself and makes things presentable to us, this aspect did bother her in some way, as she did like to argue about it with me, who insisted always on looking at the structures. As if the hands could exist apart from the language in which they are spoken!

She didn't ruminate upon and publicly think out her method. When asked by *Fireweed* to talk about it in an issue in 1986 on Canadian women poets, she quoted Flannery

O'Connor to say: "I write because I'm good at it" (61). She didn't offer explanations of how the surface content alters perception, or of how a narrative form could work to make content into a form too, in the way that form can say something absolutely apart from the story being related. The bare-bones power of stories—funny that it should be found in poetry, using anecdotes as triggers, clues to a larger existence, clues to wholeness and love. Yet, though stories are repositories of public and collective meaning as well as private action, they can lull. How do we overcome that? "The illusion of wholeness captivates us, as a kind of slavery" (*Furious* 60). How do we overcome the ability of discourse to recuperate all dissent into its own order? Into *history*? How do we overcome the fact that its noise is just emptiness turned up loud?

Sometimes I wonder if Bronwen heard the poem's inner pointing at the structured nature of discourse, and chose to turn from it in order to write stories instead, in order to stand in front of something. Even when she faced and acknowledged the terms of discourse, they still didn't seem to her the place from which to ask questions when there were so many problems already in the world. Her work wouldn't fully face the possibility that personal validation is a class- and culturally bound way of framing narrative, one that perhaps comes from a need for the belief in a transcendent order, a need than shuns the silences and warps in speaking, and that therefore subsumes differences and protects—however hesitantly—ideas and beliefs at the roots of the status quo.

We never worked that out, Bronwen and I, that tentativeness and the point of contradiction we both struggled with. And I wonder now who will take up the discussion, who will listen—insist on wholeness, and listen.

*The Berlin Wall is nothing
compared to the boundaries we carry inside of us.*

BREAKING BOUNDARIES: WRITING AS SOCIAL PRACTICE, OR ATTENTIVENESS

▎Writing is always and forever a social practice. The varying discourses in a society either shore it up or challenge it. And discourse isn't something we walk away from when we set down our pen.

In fact, the way we *conceptualize* (i.e., how we organize the world through the categories and connections in our thinking) affects the way we *perceive*. We don't perceive, then interpret. Interpretation is an instantaneous shutter. The world is simultaneously perceived and framed. Seeing and hearing are never pure, never objective. These great tools of the writer are not, in themselves, unproblematic. We're not as open to the "new" as we think we are. And, yes, the way we conceptualize is affected profoundly by language, its habits, norms, and structures, which then affect the way we see and hear.

For example, take an adage that's often tossed out: "Art and ideology don't mix." This phrase is an outward symptom of the internalized concept that "art" expresses an inner personal urge, albeit made universal, while "ideology" is an outside force, a constraint. As if the language of the "inner urge" were pure, and didn't carry significance from the dominant ideology, from the social order! Curious that this argument, this adage, comes mostly from those whose norms are most transparently reflected in the social order (middle-class, white, male—or others who tacitly accept these norms). The argument that art and ideology don't mix acts to shore up this order, keep it that way, keep everyone in line.

Yet, as Julia Kristeva wrote in *Language, The Unknown*, her critical overview of language and linguistic practice: "A discourse bears and imposes an ideology" (287), and "every ideological content finds its specific form, its language, its rhetoric" (282). Which is just to say, words bear ideology. The naive use of them does not change this fact. The act of telling the story, telling the "truth" about peoples' lives and articulating the self, also reinforces an ideology and transmits the weight of the social order, validating it. This is fine, I suppose, if you believe that the social order serves everyone equally, but what if you hesitate in front of such a belief?

Because if ideology is bound up in rhetoric and discourse, any kind of social transformation (or change in ideology) is going to rely on discourse as well. So it's in the interests of the status quo, of the constraining structures that we accept without question, to censor, prevent, scorn (whatever) discursive play or challenges. Kristeva writes: "One can understand why a dominant class has its favourite languages, its literature, its press, its orators, and why it tends to censor any other languages" (287). Thus we get little mottoes to live by, such as "art and ideology don't mix," which cover up completely that they're always and already mixed. We are carriers of ideology. Still, I can understand *why* the scorn is there: after all, mixing art not with ideology but with a *different* ideology makes people uneasy.

At this point, a writer could feel uneasy too, and say: "Yes, but I just want to write the truth about peoples' lives. If you look around the world, we're doing okay here, we don't need social transformation. A little tinkering, maybe, but we're basically okay. So why should I challenge my own discourse, my own use of language? Besides, readers don't want to hear this. The text should be transparent. The good story is all."

As a woman, I have to say that *that* position makes me feel very uncomfortable. The social structure values some people and not others; it maintains the power and constructs the way of seeing of a certain class, a certain sex, a certain race. It maintains fairly strict boundaries within certain categories of thought and feeling: "right," "family," "good," "true." And social and economic structures back up these discursive formations. In our society, some people ("racial minorities"—excuse me, but it's a fraught term, First Nations people, gays, lesbian families) are still less-thans; they can still fall outside the dominant discourse unless they accept the position assigned to them by that discourse. But they're not just outside a discourse; they're outside in economic and social senses as well (health-benefit plans, pensions, clean water, housing, etc.). And sometimes their position is actually life-threatening; if you're a black male in Toronto or Montreal, for example, and don't make visibly exaggerated gestures of submission when stopped by a police officer, because of certain thought processes of the police, it's more likely the officer will draw a gun, and more likely he or she will fire it.

It was in understanding the constraining role of (social) structure that I, for one, became a feminist. My awakening to feminism took time. Because the individualist ethos of our society is blind to structure, I couldn't at first trace the unease I felt back to a structure, so—like many—I tended instead to think there was a problem with *me*. Flipper thinks he just has a headache, when all along he's been running up against the side of the pool!

Discourse, then, has to be questioned, turned over, or it shores up what is, for me, an oppression and silencing of others. It shores up my own silencing! It is a tacit agreement with the status quo. Every word we write can do this, fall into this tendency, or it can be attentive and can subvert it, reveal its seams, push it sideways. This oppressive tendency, remember, is not solely an outside pressure imposed upon us by the world of ideology and consent; it's inside. We carry it within us. You can't easily see a structure from inside. Yet focusing on the language can help us find its boundaries, rub up against them, and see what changes, what enters.

Being attentive, after all, doesn't mean direct frontal attack (which would be not only boring but problematic as it just doubles the problem: an authoritarian ideology, the same one unquestioned, can lurk even in a discourse called radical). There are other ways: in poetry, concentrate not just on a surface message, but on the rhythm and sound in words, between words, echoing through words.

This rhythm and sound are part of the meaning. Kristeva, again, says the rhythm and sound are not ornamental but the vehicle of a new signified superimposed on the explicit signified. In fact, they press on that explicit signified. This can work both ways. Rhythm and sound can be called up, nurtured in order to disrupt, question, focus, trip, dispel. Or they can be imposed to lull and forget: an iambic pentameter, for example, in most hands, or rhyme not necessitated by the text, or the discourses of Ronald Reagan (or any head of state). The novel, too, can question narrative practice, can pull it apart, push on its tendency to flatten thought and feeling into a chronological line or lines (which neither life nor thought follow, for we are a jumble of memories, connections, and relations that remake themselves and alter constantly in us, because they exist only as relations and not as things). We have to give up the idea, I think, that we can tell the truth about people's lives, because we can't witness the lives of others anyhow. As witnesses we take up so much space, the original voices are no longer present.

The truth, in any case, is a problematic category that can shift (for it depends upon who is in power), though it pretends to be stable—we want it to be so. The idea of telling the truth is often tied by writers with the idea of accessibility and communication. I can't break down constraining structures in discourse, they say, because I want to "communicate and reach out." Stéphane Mallarmé said, of communication: "The best of what takes place between two people always escapes them, as interlocutors."[1] In other words, the communicative function of language is not the only function, and it's probably not the most powerful or important. The poetic function—the function that ties rhythm, the body, our mothers, the unconscious (which does not fear contradiction)—bears us hard up against the boundaries of the communicative function, allows us to push it further, to break past it. The sound of words can release and loosen images and connections by which we live but which aren't readily apparent to us. As physics shows us, evolution and change occur as a result of disruptions, anomalies, and contradictions, not as a result of a continual line of order (if the latter were the case we'd still have lobed hard shells, and ten legs). It's the same thing in writing.

And when you are attentive to language, you'll find that it's not true that your hair falls out, your tongue turns into spaghetti; it's not true that your limbs fly off. It's not true that you'll start spouting gibberish. Rather, you start to see how ordinary communication is the real gibberish. And because language affects perception, you won't be able to perceive again in the old way. It's not a cure, of course, for blindness, for we recreate the blindnesses that help us live, recreate them out of the material we have at our disposal. But maybe, through attentiveness to language, we are better equipped to take off the blinders we are constantly acquiring. The process of shedding blinders is continual.

But what about the audience, some say; we should be attentive to the audience! I sense that old stick rising: accessibility. I call it a stick because it's most often used to beat people into submission. What is accessible to people is precisely what they are used to, what reflects back their own prior values as readers (though it may not reflect their social values, it is still consoling to have your readerly values reflected). The accessible is merely a way of reading. We are taught one way because it benefits the state that we can read — what? — the *newspaper*. So we can *follow*, and enter commerce, because newspapers are about advertising. The accessible, by not questioning reading and language, ends up simply leading us to comfort. This is the real escapism, for it uses our energy in a way that is static, that changes or reveals nothing, and is thus not threatening to the currents that inhabit popular, accessible thought and action: capitalist, overly governed by police control mechanisms, homophobic, racist, misogynist, anti-immigrant, simply greedy. The accessible image acts as a kind of comfort zone, whether it displays itself as powerful, or harmed, or as the target of powers out of its control. It isolates itself. It fails to recognize those it oppresses, or those its memories oppress, or where its memories are.

To see the seams in language, we have to question our readerly selves. And, as writers, we have to expect our readers to desire the text, to be willing to read and let go of their fixities. We have to permit them to admit that more is accessible to them than they thought. It's accessible in a different way. Some of it won't go away or be simply explained. We'll make some people uncomfortable, of course — those who read for comfort and to be lulled, those who need their values reinforced, who crave a reinforcement of the status quo because they want to believe it represents them. They want to be reassured that if the stories feel funny or uneasy, it's themselves personally, not the social order, that is the source of the unease, thus leaving the order intact, human beings divided, and the earth dying.

To change the traces words carry — to enact — is to alter the possibilities of human seeing, and this change affects even those who will not read. In my own teaching at VIA Rail years ago, I saw that many people do not learn by reading; they learn by dialogue with others. Sounds and sight. Sparks, incomplete. People need to forge their own narrative relation and not have it given to them ready-made. To open up linguistic possibility within the poem frees others to think, even if they do not read poetry, or much of anything else. Conversely, to reinforce linguistic commonality and structure imprisons others in an order that does not love them, whether they read or not.

All of this is meant as a challenge. It's not a prescription. Accepting the challenge means challenging preconceptions, taking a chance with poetic structures, with using sounds and words to call those deep and senseless images and connections out of you. A whole world of possible and as-yet-unimaginable results opens up. And those of us who would rather reject the challenge? They're free to. It's each of us, remember, who creates, and then realizes or ignores, the boundaries.

As for me, I'm going to try consciously to push words forward and make them tumble, to work through my own perceptual failures, to create a space/duration/marking where differences are possible, where a multifaceted articulation is possible. Try to break down the construct of the self, the seeing self, the self as un-self-conscious observer in the poem, as "poetic voice." To me, the risks I take in language honour those with whom I work, and honour our struggle, a struggle that includes the facticity of paper itself, the surface of the page. Because when I put my ear to paper, I hear guns and money, the thoughtless oppression of women, of labour in the third world by we who wear its clothes, the death of bees and songbirds, the loss of wetlands, the rising of the great Antarctic shelf as the ice that holds it down melts away. Phooey on the poetic voice. In my work, I'm moving (trying, leaning) toward a dislodging of the purity of the image, the purity of expression, dislodging the invisible seams that cover up how language works to support the dominant order and how the expression of one person creates the silence of another, how ideas and dreams and love are separated from each other.

The point of writing as act is a point of risk, for me, a point of great uncertainty. The thing is to get that point to endure long enough to listen to. It's not easy. We tend to pull back from feeling, repress connections, want to diminish anxiety. Even our childhoods are largely hidden to us because of this necessity. What is outside the structure of our language can and does escape us. And what is inside the structure confines us. But I can only say, as I have said before, that the borders of poetry can be moved, in our lifetimes, if we dare to. For the borders are not only subjective, they are *subjectifying*. We can act to cultivate a kind of curiosity that wishes the world bigger, and discovers and enacts a world that is *more* striated, *less* constrained.

POETRY, MEMORY, AND THE POLIS

1

▌ We live in an age of civic despair. The City — Polis as social organization — is entropic. We know this, especially those of us who have been born in North America since the beginning of nuclear testing. The process of decay through low-level radiation, some say, is worse than certain higher bursts.[1] An article in the conservative and ruling-class British journal *The Economist* in early 1988 described results of research about US death rates and milk radioactivity that indicated the effect of the Chernobyl disaster in North America might have been worse than in Northern Europe. This research was dismissed by others, but one still wonders. We've seen an increase in diseases associated with the autoimmune system (not just since Chernobyl): twentieth-century disease or total allergy syndrome, other allergies, increased toxicity reactions to chemicals in food, in pesticides, even in the food chain (the chemicals we ban in our country return to our organisms in meat, fish, and vegetables from other poorer countries where these chemicals are still sold), AIDS, and diseases we now know to be faults/failures of the immune system: cancers, diabetes, multiple sclerosis, asthma. Deaths from these diseases more than doubled in the ten years up to 1988; the rate is three to seven times higher for the black population than it is for whites, and up to double for women.[2] It seems that, because entropy is the organizing law of the City, what we perceive as order is actually a continual process of decay—the same for the City as it is for cells.[3] The City too is an organism; *the Law, too, its "fixing" of points in time, acts as an organism in spite of what we claim of it.* Any threat to the City means an increase of its order, thus of entropy; immunity is exhausted or altered; the cells are blinded, perceive differently. The organism dies more quickly, and, in this process, is paradoxically revived. Sometimes to threaten the civic order only makes the order more pernicious and invasive.[4]

Poetry, I think, is a structuring (an action rendering visible, audible) of memory that can undo the Law of the City, because it both precedes and passes through that Law: it precedes it, for poetry is yet unsettled, and passes through it, for even poetry can't avoid the Law. Not even memory can. *"I never thought I'd write a line about the woman's curls"* (WSW 114). The way we remember, have remembered, the way we structure memory, is mediated by language, by the conceptual frameworks buried in language, as use values. If we're not careful, the structure of our work reinforces these frameworks.

Poetry's sound precedes the forms acceptable to the Law: representation, meaning, codification. Yet if we merely use it to oppose the Law, we risk being defined once again by the terms of the Law. Opposition alone just leads back to sameness. Our voices have to leak out *before* the Law settles, or have to keep unsettling it.[5]

This is not a call for giving up on "meaning." By just defying linguistic and semantic organization, we would be saying that our memories are unintelligible. Which is not true. They are intelligible but not in this organization, this order. They are intelligible but not free of anxiety, especially. This anxiety is a resistance to *anæsthesia* of our memories: *not hearing sounds.*[6] Anæsthesia: the force that pulls us toward the centre, centripetal. To make us forget, or repress, or define in terms acceptable to the order.

The poem precedes and passes through, but also contains the Law, and must therefore be subject to watchfulness. Because a poem reaches out to and contains a social order (a set of terms), even if it's not overtly admitted. Thought, unwatched, tends to resolve itself in a binary way, a natural leaning toward decreasing anxiety in the organism: leading to poetry<->women's poetry, women's poetry<->lesbian poetry; women's poetry<->working-class women's poetry. A mimicry of norm and difference. There is so much that tends, even in new movements, to perpetrate or reinforce such structures. What we call our "difference" doesn't save us from this dynamic. "Difference" itself contains the law it opposes, for articulation of "the same" is needed to make difference comprehensible. And "the same" is that which is *the norm*. It reduces anxiety, stress on the cells. Since the concept of the norm has been used to legislate (in and out of legislatures) against certain groups or classes — women, gays, First Nations, others — for a long time, we know already what tyranny it is. We should seek to avoid falling into it when we write. Avoid falling into difference as mere opposition. It's the *same* thing. And one reinforces the other. Perpetuates the civic order, the *Polis*.

"Identity" too must be questioned in the poem. For even at the level of our cellular identity, our blastular memory, we are being altered by changes in our environment, in the very earth we inhabit. The DNA patterns in our cells are deteriorating as a result of nuclear and other poisoning, and by what we insert into the food chain. As well, in any case, the body's sense of individuality and community, *of congruence and of non-congruence*, are intertwined — making "identity" suspect. A word-play. It's language and naming that presume and codify "identity."[7]

To me the notion of identity contains a preceding notion of *community* (whereas in the dictionary, the word simply relays a sense of self-contained commonality or sameness). The structuring of community, I believe, has its seed not in likeness but in the non-identity or non-congruence that the child begins to realize — not experiencing itself as identity (as the mirror-stage would have it) but experiencing some "other" as being non-congruent.[8] The sense of community contains an elemental sense of non-congruity. A focus on the mirror-stage as glad entry of the Ego erases and blinds us to this foundational non-congruity, for the Ego has but two planes and one space-time: self and non-self. Congruous. This forced sense of congruity is the Law speaking. The desire to close or diminish anxiety. What holds "community" together has to be a notion other than same-difference: a sense of the elemental non-congruity of things, and the beauty of that. *The sense of "with"-ness, "joint"-ness that conveys no hierarchy of terms.* Which is how our community can and must exist. "Among-many." Not reproducing those hierarchies of the "same" (i.e., hegemony of the correct feminist) or of many "sames" (fragmentation).

This process is not easy. And it's anxious. And it takes attentiveness.

2

Every night I come home at six o-clock and I cry.
Then I go back up the hill to picket.
Red Deer nurse on the sixteenth day of the strike of the United Nurses of Alberta against the Alberta Hospital Association, February 8, 1988

Attentiveness. What does this mean for writing poetry, for women remembering, for validating our acts of memory and affecting the social order, the *Polis*: acts which surely are of value? Displacement is important, but to displace *how*?

Irony — a tool of modernism — hasn't helped us too much. It is so often part of the unified system of meaning of the literary work and does not breach it. And irony has a strange way of highlighting the figure of the author as standing above the circumstances and manipulating language (without affecting the speaker and the speaker's own vocabularies); it shores up a kind of stasis. If irony does not honour the contingency of language, and the aporias that this contingency might open, it can act merely as a way of distancing author and reader from the problematic raised, leaving it unaltered, acceptable. Making us feel good about ourselves, as if we have risen above circumstances. When devices like irony are not used to make the conventional untenable, absolutely untenable, showing its folds and creases — requiring that readers act to alter their own vocabularies and thus their lives, they support the status quo, and defuse energies. Irony can let the observer walk away from genocide.

Re-creation or reappropriation of myths or words hasn't helped us get out of this civic order either. Our "memories" are just called upon in the same metaphysical terms. The same mirror/order and civic space. This re-creation only works for those who would see themselves as separate from the civic order; it works because when they turn their backs, they no longer see that the mirror still bears their reflection.

I think, therefore, that, since it's impossible to precede the Law completely and without ambiguity, we must reflect upon and acknowledge the Law's interference in our work, and peel it back to reveal its brokenness, the non-congruity behind it. We must look for the point, no, *gaps*, where we can leak out of the Law. Yet even the word *excess* refers to the Law, the norm! It is no easy thing "to inhabit freely the civic house of memory I am kept out of" (*Furious* 91).

The fear in writing is this: to reflect on the Law is to increase anxiety of the working process. Memory is difficult. Memories are not things, but processes. The danger is that in order to alleviate the anxiety, we are tempted to create fixities that act as a new Law. A new congruity. A *self*-congruence extended outward. For example, when we write of other women, create memories for them (concept of writer as witness, as resuscitator of the past, of invisible women's history), we tend to create them in our own image, out of our own class and cultural background, our own values and processes. Wearing our shoes. Perpetuating our own Law. Our own privilege. Thus placing these women of whom we speak in a double silence. And every re-creation of the Law takes the same form: Law = "same" + a notion (albeit hidden) of "ethics." We end up acting in relation to the Law even if the Law is not something articulated. Yet even this acting-out is a behaviour that is linguistically tied.

In my own work, I thought at one time that the simplest line was best. Yet when I wrote anecdotal-conversational poems without reversal (which is to say, without the language confronting itself and its assumptions in the poem), I suppressed both my feelings as a lesbian and my concerns as a woman. My poetry was supposed to reflect my life, especially my life as a worker, and these things were suppressed in that life. To write the poems, then, perpetuated (unknowingly) my own pain at being invisible, and left my desire silenced or screened. As if I could belong, by force of will, to that *sameness*, that *anæsthesia*.

By speaking (because I must use language), I risk reproducing the Law, perpetuating the civic order. Or (since I write poetry, since I am lesbian) being recuperated as marginal into the civic order. Or being perceived as antagonistic to the order, the Polis, and then disqualified as a serious writer, *a serious commentator on the human condition.*[9] This dynamic of perpetuating the Law can happen even in the community of feminist writing. Much writing by feminists has focused on notions of the body and speech, the body as difference, as house of memory, without focusing on the bodily context: the City. Community as elemental non-congruence. Or, if focused on the City, the writing has often retraced those same myths, used the same tropes, that is, it is preceded by the Law. Either literally or conceptually, perpetuating the same order.

Relying on work on etymology alone is also problematic, for beyond being a momentary tactic of displacement, it lulls. It can so easily divert attention from the privilege in our speaking voice, in the present tense. Etymologies of words trace dominant meanings, as recorded by makers of dictionaries (who already "leave out"); though they are incredibly useful to locate aberrant traces and sounds, as well as turns that led to disappearances, it can be difficult to have them leap the distance from the trace to women's everyday lives. More is needed. The notion of the "holy lesbian," too, the positive role model in the poem that some feminisms keep insisting upon, the utopic fantastic woman — when taken beyond a certain context (i.e., it's mentally healthy to be positive, and to internalize positive images of oneself), can turn into a transcendent ideal, or a kind of heroic essentialism.

So, then, how to displace? Displacement as tactic. The brokenness of the lien that has always already been broken. Sutured. The ribbon looser now. Our excess. Not ecstasy yet.

> What I brought back to poetry from my job was a stutter that replicated surfaces imperfectly, like the television screen with the vertical hold broken, no story possible, just the voices
>
> heard again & again without image. Those dark voices. & I wrote, not into the book's heart, but out of fear, to make the image come back to me. Any image. My coat & shoes. My faint moving at the edge of the screen, blood in my head not moving but the room moving & the blood still... so that to move the force <u>for a moment</u> only <u>held</u> for that moment. (The word "held" a stillness, relational, not a motion...) (the word "moment" not a thing...) The preposition so relational it could not hold a <u>value</u>, & could hardly keep from vanishing.
>
> (*Furious* 98)

There are views of writing that tend to accuse writing-that-displaces of being academic, of being inaccessible to most women's experience. But accessibility can be reductive: the lowest common denominator of the possible. Literalist uses of the accessible don't help women and working-class people for they act to reproduce their place in the social order that diminishes their capacities. It's the cannon-fodder mentality. What is accessible is what can be read by agreed-upon methods. And who agrees here? The class for whom "reading" and "the book" have the greatest value: the white, middle class, the phallocentric order, and those who have internalized it. Accessibility unconsciously promotes what-already-is, the comfortable. It reinforces the rhetoric of the already-powerful. This rhetoric infects all of us, variously. Consider the whiteness of the woman who is writing these words, and who was employed for years as a corporate communicator.

Writing, however, is capable of dealing with the biological forces that underpin the conveying of information, forces tied with anxiety and its alleviation in the organism, tied with the organism's compulsion to anæsthesia. Even management systems in corporations are attentive to this information order when they communicate; how can poets ignore it? Poetic silence on this count is complicity with the existing order.

It's memory that keeps us in the world. That is the past in us. Structured by language. And by the Polis. And if one function of language is to harbour coherence, or social identity (Kristeva, *Desire in Language*, affirming Husserl), then our writing must admit and deal with this social identity, which means with our privilege, as well as with our silence. We have only the symbolic to give us the terms to discuss what precedes its laws.[10] A pre-linguistic memory, the memory of the mother, is unpresentable without its trace in words, in writing. The Law is hidden in these traces, the Law that privileges some of us. Yet the trace of words can also show us those gaps in language where maternal non-sense is. We have to query *those* traces in our writing, through the act of writing itself, because the social function of language marks our civic place and civic memory. For women, and for men, too, these marks are a structure of anæsthesia. Why frame our writing in this order?

THE MEDIUM

▌The medium is not poetry but language itself. An electro-connection in the brain, culturally identifiable.

>Because language affects the way we perceive.
>
>Because perception is all we know of reality.
>
>Because the surface and density of the words affect our seeing, even if we don't believe.
>
>Because the surface of the words has been damaged by commerce.
>
>Because meaning is a cultural artifact designating a perception of the dominant commerce.
>
>Because I think therefore I am is also culturally specific.
>
>Because the camera of expression therefore leaves out.
>
>Because there are values embedded inside words that affect the way our brains interpret light reflected on the retina.
>
>Because the eyes see.

Because each cell sees.

Because the cells exist to reproduce themselves.

And therefore, without embedded value, cancer is a success story.

Because the surface of commerce of words is all there is.

Because this is not true.

Because "the opposite of truth, which is untruth, may not be a lie."[1]

Because the surface commerce of words maintains the status quo of power, deprivation, and economy.

Because the individual is sanctified by the surface, yet does not exist.

Because even buildings are held up by stresses in their own structure.

The medium is not poetry itself but language and I choose language. Because the surface commerce hurts me I choose language at its densest edge.

Poetry, because the sound of words is perceptible as meaning. Because the sound of words makes my heart ache and I love the density of a single word. Poetry because of density. Poetry because a word's density can alter even DNA. Poetry because of its picture on the page.

Because of light—that blue. Because I am womanly, by the sound of words. Because the sexual is present in speaking. Because I am responsible. Because I have been in love.

a new bird
flicker, or
stooking

NOTES ON POETRY AND KNOWING

1. *provisoire*
Before we can talk about poetry and knowing, I think we have to come up against the possible untenability of any kind of knowing, that much knowing is *provisoire*, subject to change upon the intrusion of new data, subject to change when the model is changed too (the paradigm, if you like), the glasses through which the ostensibly objective factors are viewed. As well, knowledge can be, to some degree, merely subjective (both in terms of the individual's perceptual apparatus and in terms of socialization, and in sheer terms of availability of information as well). It's also subject to change through the model of the body, its fundamental notionality regarding itself, for the fabric of words is constructed through the body: what alerts the basal ganglia and what does not, even awake, even in dreams.

2. *materiality*
Then there's the materiality of the language fabric itself, the adhesion of word to word, or the forces of repulsion in a line, how the line works the forces of repulsion, of noise, more so

than the paragraph which works the forces of compulsion and propulsion, all these pulsions releasing the reader to the fundamental opacity of the word (to which the only response, at times, is laughter, it so wobbles, that sound).

3. tenacity

And that's before we come up against the notion of poetry. Poetry? It's clearly untenable if treated as separate from these issues. Though how tenacious it is as a notion! What, then, makes the notion of poetry endure?

> Sound
> The effect of sound on the organs of the body
> Rhythm
> Drumming
> The womb ("obrigada, we have reached you")
> Frank Auerbach — "style is how you respond in a crisis"
> vs.
> Poetry as it is taught in schools, reduced to symbol and theme
> vs.
> As it is experienced by people (one out of three, it is said, write "it" at some time in their lives)
> *all this, plus*
> The grooves of neural impulse in the brain, its possibility for change and shimmers that alter former pathways

4. *chora, sort of*

My take on poetry's place in the world and links within the world is somewhat Kristevan. I believe that sounds and visual presence of words can provoke more than denotative sense. By this "more" I mean something materialist rather than transcendent, yet something that grapples with abstractions such as the sense of evil, the failure of tenderness. That words as material are dense and cluttered, constructed: this is clear enough to me. So how to shine a light on us humans without the writer being the homunculus in the machine (there is none, nor is one possible), the little poet looking in from outside the poem as if at Creation? yoya· TRANCENDANCE

5. *matters*

One of the matters of language (here where language matters) is to disrupt at the edges of what we claim to know; this is one of the functions of poetry, quite apart from the functions "to lull" and "to reinforce what already is." In the same way as new discoveries in science often come from the edge. Pushing the boundaries.

6. *limits*

There is still poetry born out of the love of the familiar, of the status quo: poetry that limits possible questions and possible answers, that accuses anything outside itself of being inappropriate, of going too far. As long as this attitude exists in the world outside poetry, and it does, it will persist in poetry as well. Poetry is no different than other forces already in the world; in many ways, the tendency toward conservatism and stasis is not new, nor is the tendency toward poetry as a kind of entertainment or solace.

7. *community*

Our notions of communication (thus of poetry) are linked to notions of the self, identity, and self-identity, and require community. Whatever the brain "knows" is relational, web-like. Poetry requires and feeds off the world.

8. *experience*

Experience is a construct. We construct it or enact it in "whatever" ways; there is no one approach or solution. But to say poetry must "reflect experience" is just an empty phrase. What experience? Whose? Good writing problematizes experience, lays bare the seams and switches. Why bury consciousness of the construct? To do so is to turn away from the seams and give in to the centripetal forces altogether, give in to banality. All new discoveries are made at the edge and in what we today call "disorder." Accepting this does not mean embracing an approach that ignores human emotion, but embracing one that accounts for it without quashing its contradictory manifestations.

9. *generation*

Any political system or nexus, be it communism or the university, will die if it restricts information generation and information practices. This is why capitalism continues to function, in spite of its obvious material inequities and iniquities: it tolerates generation of information and disjunctive information practices and in fact feeds off them, feeds off artists, feeds off its own disruptions. Even as states and corporations endeavour to control information flow and interpretation, capitalism lets it leak out. There *is* a possible movement in this, as yet unharnessed by progressive (human) forces.

10. *university*

The university can be a problematic place for a writer because, in general, liberal arts departments mostly feed off the "already written" and fear the generative edge. Moreover, they instill fear of the generative edge. They need to ensure stability of social and cultural codes, and writing as a practice is always toppling the barriers of these codes.

11. *technology*
It's easy to see that technology is altering the human brain's ability to absorb and condense information. Even if the technology that brought this about were dissolved or were to vanish tomorrow, our brains would still function differently than in the past (for the brain is biogenerative) and would construct new bridges.

12. *theatre*
These days, the brain can move and generate extremely quickly. After a certain point it's not even dependent on elaborate external stimuli, which are merely theatre. Perhaps the only two significant remaining acts are poetry and theatre. Theatre at least keeps the body in the picture, presents the body full-face, and achieves its full textual power only in the relation between the speakers. So it is, and is not, material. Theatre is also gestural: it moves air, alters in time and light.

13. *body*
Poetry also keeps the body in the picture, because of sound and how it is absorbed by the body, by different parts of the body. Again, there is the pull of the relational, and the material texture and opacity of the language.

14. *readings*
We have to deal with language as a material that does not just create but resists readings too. When language is at its most powerful, resistance is most palpable. Resistance is not something to shun or despise, but a matter to work with. Sounds and disjuncts are generative of meaning too; it is not just syntactic and denotative continuity that does this.

15. *act*

What if I said poetry as an act, the act of poetry, to act *in* poetry, is a *way* of knowing? And a way of shuddering. It pulls *closer* to some word-hungers, and goes out to the edge, touching the tripwire.

So touch it and trip it. Even as others might want to pull *away*, or lull.

I LEARNED SOMETHING ABOUT WRITING FROM YOU IN THE SPORTS PAGES OF THE MONTREAL GAZETTE

A CONVERSATION WITH JOSHUA LOVELACE,
SEPTEMBER 28, 1994

JOSHUA LOVELACE: In the last section of your book *Furious* entitled "The Acts," you develop several ideas "about" poetry that have become indicative of your work. How have these ideas developed?

ERÍN MOURE: In WSW (*West South West*), in *Sheepish Beauty, Civilian Love*, and in the work I'm writing now, the thinking is integrated into the work, whereas in *Furious* the thinking parts in "The Acts" are separated from the rest of the poems. The notions that form is another content, or that no meaning exists outside of context, still inform my work. It is also informed by the idea that when we consider reading and accessibility in a too-narrow sense, we end up disinformed as citizens or incapable of informing ourselves. I feel less and less the desire to be 100 percent complicit with the conventional ways in which language means. By writing, we create context, a context where meanings "operate," not necessarily something that "means" something. So much of political and economic meaning is created not through straightforward language, but through other processes. So unless we attempt to be aware of all the forces operating, how can we really function as complete individuals or as part of a community?

JL: In your poem "Corrections to the Saints" in *Sheepish Beauty*, do the words "this" and "that" operate to establish context?

EM: If the sign fails to mean, leave it out. Or, just have *this* and *that*. Who says we always need real images or real references? For me, leaving the referent out shows the referentiality *between* things. When you're talking about *this* or *that*, *here* or *there*, you dissolve the actual referent and you heighten your own positionality. So many poets pretend that they don't have a position, or that the one they do have is not important and has no effect on meaning.

JL: Does *this* then allow the world into your poems? How important is establishing some kind of connection between the signifier and signified in your poetry?

EM: There's a connection. There has to be a connection. The signifier calls attention to the fact that we can identify something from numerous aspects. One of my favourite examples is "chair." [Erín stands and picks up a chair.] The human brain can see it like *this*, but if I come back and show it to you like *this* [she changes the position of the chair], you're still going to identify it as a chair. Our brain situates the parts of the chair in relation to each other. If there was no connection between signifier and signified, or too direct a link, you or I could show up wearing a different shirt and nobody would know what we were wearing, or even be able to identify us as ourselves.

JL: A lot of your recent writing is preoccupied with the workings of the brain.

EM: It's one of my favourite things to think about. I find it interesting how the frontal cortex has developed in humans and how the boundaries of thought are in your own head, that you can think past them and make your brain make new connections. In my poems, I work especially at challenging the mind's conventions. I try to disrupt conventional ways of reading, knowing that the brain will connect (as it always does) and arrange things. I want the reader to pick up little things that aren't necessarily allowed to be "meaningful" in other types of works that concern themselves with achieving a totally smooth surface.

JL: You have your critics like other poets. But because you don't necessarily demand a smooth surface, your poems set themselves apart by opening up spaces that often include the voices of your critics. What is this all about?

EM: That's more me just being funny. I've been blasted in various journals. I guess everyone gets blasted. It's legitimate. I have no problem with that. But I figure that whatever a critic can say, well, I can write *another poem*! Whatever you say, I am going to write other poems. [Erín picks up *Furious* to find a passage in "The Acts." The interviewer leans over and apologizes for having marked the book, even though it is his. Erín says it's okay.] But with *Furious* it was mostly academics who were disgruntled. Curiously, a few of them took umbrage at: "I want to write things like *Unfurled &*

Dressy that can't be torn apart by anybody, anywhere, or in the university" (*Furious* 92).

JL: Elsewhere, you've said that you see an affinity between your poetry and painting. What exactly do you mean?

EM: A lot of people say poetry is closest to music. I see it as closer to painting and I like the idea of words as material in the same way that paint is material. When you paint you don't mystify or glorify the paint. It's the material. Whereas with writing, readers tend to mystify words and create these mystical—like, you don't mystify brush strokes, but in writing you have similes and metaphors and all these things which are then mystified. I guess colour is mystified to some extent. But I like the idea that words are simply material. I can pile them on like thick brush strokes or move them apart. It's also important that painting and poetry work with visual space: the flat surface of a canvas or page still opens up infinite possibilities depending on the pressures you bring to bear on it. By stressing certain parts of the space, for example, you can then illuminate another part or push things forward or back or whatever. Again, what interests me is proximity, relationality, and bringing different elements together.

JL: In *wsw*, you develop spatiality independent of a "directional" frame in which things have coordinates, etc. Instead, the points "west" and "south and west" are like layers. How do you see space and time? Is it something you create in your poetry?

EM: I think you create it. It makes me think of Hélène Cowan, a woman from Quebec who played on the basketball team in the 1994 Commonwealth Games; I was reading an interview with her in the sports pages of *The Gazette*. The questions covered what she was thinking on the court, and what made her so effective as a player. She zeroed in on what was important to her: she said you have to create space. And said something like: "In order to be successful, in order to get this far, you can't wait for space, you have to create space. You create it for yourself and for your teammates. You have to pull it out of thin air." So her whole idea of the basketball court is as a place where space does not exist prior to its creation. Which creation is an act. Space only *looks* like it is there already. And where does she get this space? Not from a prior and stable existence, but out of *thin air*. I thought: *Hélène Cowan, I've learned something about writing from you in the sports pages of the Montreal* Gazette.

JL: How does time fit into all this?

EM: Well, time. We have this notion of forward time — whatever it is, the second law of thermodynamics, entropy — because things decay. Voilà, you have linear time. Isn't that lovely?

JL: Is that the answer?

EM: Sort of. What's most interesting to me is not only that we measure forward time from the "fact" that bodies and materials decay, but that it also relates directly to the processes of consciousness and advanced consciousness. To understand that something occurs before something else and that something took place in the recent past or in the further past is what makes us different. Animals with primitive consciousness don't conceive time and space that way. They exist in a little "present" bubble that moves forward even though they don't acknowledge that it is moving forward. They just exist in it. To us it's moving, because time is passing, etc., but to them it's just a little bubble of "present." That's why, in "The Acts" in *Furious*, I say that the past and future are in us as memory and desire. These things enable us, in a sense, to be conscious in the present tense.

JL: What about humour and irony in your work?

EM: I play with jokes a lot. I think things are funny. But, with irony, I'm always suspicious. Irony often diffuses energy. You can take things that are frightfully off-kilter, and then it's just "how ironic." Irony allows us to accept or reconcile things that shouldn't be reconciled, instead of railing against them. But some things you just have to laugh at. It reminds me of Baudelaire reportedly saying: "They left two things out of the Declaration of the Rights of Man — the right to make a fool of yourself and the right to leave." I retain the right to make a fool of myself; it lets me stretch further.

JL: That reminds me of "Seebe." [seeb]

EM: Seebe. [seeb-ee]

JL: Sorry.

EM: You wouldn't know unless you'd heard.

JL: There in "Seebe," you make a fool of yourself. [Erín frowns.] Well, I mean, perhaps that's not it. Towards the end of the poem, you let it fall apart.

EM: At the end, the poem *did* fall apart. I couldn't figure out what I was trying to do. I realized that I was trying to make some kind of relationship apparent between *this* and *that* and being — and it fell apart. All I was doing was describing the event. Then suddenly I had this image of this kid who is experiencing the event, looking around. It was as if there were a veil between our experiences of the event, where we came from, and how we had come to this point—and I was laying my world across his. So what was there to describe? He could stand up and say "what the hell was that?" I thought *I'm just inventing a bunch of bullshit here.* If I'm going to invent something that he can't possibly agree with, then there's a problem. And I knew, just from his look when we picked him up and went into the train: you could tell he'd never been in a train before. So then it's just me constructing something. And for what, to make me the author of the piece? I realized that I pulled him into the emptiness of the poem. The poem was the real emptiness.

JL: Does that mean that experiences within a community can be the only real context of a poem?

EM: I don't think it's the only context. It can't be. But it's something that bears questioning. We have to live with ambiguities and contradictions. You have to let other people be who they are, in order to begin addressing words to them. All I can do is present points of challenge—points of opening—and maybe for that person those points *aren't* points of opening. To me, it's important to keep the discussion open. Otherwise, things degenerate into backbiting or separate camps. That doesn't advance things. The potential for poetry is virtually untapped. We have just started to understand a little bit. I just see it that way. But different people have to bring different thoughts to bear. For some people the view I hold represents a loss of control. It means that they can possibly contribute only a small bit. They think, *I want to contribute the whole thing.* You can't. Some people like to think of themselves as sitting atop a big pyramid with all the people they like. *This* picture is called "literature." For me, rather, it's like there is this little hole in the veil and we are about to tear past it, into something. That's literature. We haven't got there yet. And who knows where *there* is. But we have tools and we have markers from the past. We have forces intersecting in the present, economic underpinnings, relationships that are global, really. It is within these things that literature has to exist. As I keep saying, writing is always and forever a social practice. You can't pretend that discourse doesn't affect you or that it exists severed from you — *out there*. It's impossible. Writing must be, always is, engaged in some way.

MY RELATION TO THEORY AND GENDER

▍The work I do is all about being hurtled or suddened, or a combination, trying to get some of the confusion about feeling into the material of the poem. Yet things never work out simply. And I'm not always capable of admitting how I feel, even to myself, in case it just produces more difficulties. Or more material. That being said, theorizing the work is part of getting it done, part of my distrust of the "said" or "saying," my distrust of the finality of saying any word, which is never what was meant, anyhow. Years ago, when I wrote *Furious*, I included the thoughts or anxiety, the "minutes" of the poems, at the end, as part of the book. Since then, my work tends to interrogate itself as it is being written, within the work itself: as soon as a single word enters, the line changes, right as it is being written. And words themselves are already socially and culturally charged. So the picture changes beyond my grasp as an individual: where can I locate myself now? What is locatable? What is location?

The relation with theory and my gender is this: I have never been spoken by conventions of theoretical or critical thinking, conventions that I see as separate from and parasitic on the work. Some of them ready to shut you up, shut me up. My own seams — the borders between inside and outside where everything is susceptible to shift and illumination — are not spoken by the conventions. To me, theory is *not* those conventions, not a thing-to-obey but a process of thinking right inside the work that helps push the work where it otherwise could not go or would refuse to enter. I prefer to call it philosophy. This process is both rigorous and aleatory; it does not make for nice poetry at all times, and it irritates nice poets.

I write as a woman writing and will not silence the consequences of that, but I don't trust too easily the process of setting down, and being the author of, writing. And I don't want to, for there's too much co-option already by the social order. Too much restlessness in the words themselves, which don't want to mean and are always in danger of being co-opted at any point by economic or poetic authorities, or the authorial voice, their internal representative.

The body is melody, and its melody is how we keep track of our selves; it is wordly. I am just trying to keep track of the movements and processes. I definitely write as a woman writing, though. Mine is not a universal view because the universal is just the suppression of anxiety, anxiety of difference. Which betrays the body and is a lie, finally.

And so I am badly behaved because I must be. Unruly, perhaps.

"Now run for cover," she thinks.

FOR SCOPING GIRLS

1

When asked where my own writerly concerns coincide with thinking about the visual image, I realize that my answer is anterior to current discourses about the gaze and its relation to images. For me, a seminal question precedes the image: What is a trait or mark? What is a line?

A delimitation of space, a contour. For me as a writer, a line is not, you might say, the same line as is meant in art. A line of poetry is not a drawn line, a trait. But what if I approached it in that way? What if my line too were a physical mark on the page? Directional. A (possible) contour. Possibly torsional.

2

What then would representation be? A step away from that figurative mode which tells its story in the baldest narrational way, thereby reproducing a certain order? But how to get out of that order without merely reproducing a discourse of art on the margins? This kind of discourse merely fortifies a social structure wherein art is a harmless discharge device for non-compliant energies, instead of a constitutive device that actively has an affect/effect of alteration on public space. As poet Lisa Robertson says, I/we must admit complicity with the social structure, and this admission, to me, is to divulge and admit our stake, for somehow we still have one, in forces that would constitute us as separate, clearly bordered, self-enclosed.

In this vein, I cite Robertson's "The Device":

> What are the terms of our complicity?
>
> We cannot definitely know, for
>
> reasons of faulty appearance and mis
>
> managed debt...
>
> Nor do we want simply to reverse the
>
> narrative, placing a cultural
>
> organ at an ethical height from which
>
> "we" devolve, plying our giddy nostalgia
>
> for the fragment.   (84)

3

US American poet and theorist Barrett Watten wrote that "statement builds in the conditions of its reception" (36). But does it? I want to disagree with according such autonomy to the statement; the context also builds conditions into the statement, conditioning both its creation and its reception. Shonagh Adelman's "statement" in the form of photographs, on the other hand, acts to *interrupt* the "conditions of reception" with which our culture encodes images of the female body. Her statement's job is, in fact, interruption: it appropriates images and interrupts them. It interrupts the habit of the gaze, but not rhetorically.

By foregrounding haptically insistent surfaces of incongruous textures, such as tree bark, that poke fun at the haptic gaze while provoking it (or overprovoking it), and that cross the boundaries of corporeality between tree to human, Adelman calls attention to the surface qua *surfact* even as she represents or *figur*ates bodies. What makes us/our bodies different from other mechanisms anyhow? Like bark? Biotic systems are communication devices like any other, as Donna Haraway has said. Bodies are coding devices. As Wittgenstein says in *Tractatus*, "The subject does not belong to the world: rather, it is a limit of the world" (5.632). Adelman goes further than manipulating texture, though, by flattening conventions of chiaroscuro with overlays of abrupt colour and, in a defiant textualization, including words that are at odds with any voyeuristic absorption of the images.

On the other hand, Watten's statement *applies* somewhat, and Adelman takes painstaking care to ensure "different" conditions of reception for the images, thus ensuring that her work provokes a discourse decentred from (at the sides or margins of) the common public discourse of "porn" or "titillation" which is compliant with and to some extent even regulates imperial figurations of the feminine.

4

But to return now: what is a trait or mark? This is a question critical to writing, especially in poetry, which is not a transparent use of language. Surface (text or any mark) *is* a prime consideration in composition here too.

For me, writing is an incorporated act. It is not signs for what goes on in the head but comes out of the hand, is mediated by the hand. The hand meeting/marking such a surface. The hand is productive. I want to say, too, the hand is also a sex organ. If you don't believe me, look how it proliferates in photographer Shonagh Adelman's imagery. Her photographs are traversed by the presence of hands, those organs of power and insistence, organs of tactility, *le toucher*. Organs that write.

Here I want to evoke Deleuze's sense of the haptic gaze (*Francis Bacon*): the gaze that touches, rather than the optic gaze. The trait or mark must work with the haptic, and even provoke it, which means provoking sensation in more than the eyes, as touch is a sensation.

What possibilities are opened by such a view of writing practice?

5

I might as well say it at this point: lesbian sexuality. *Where does lesbian sexuality figure in all this?* We exist in a world of images and stories and methods that represent the eerie construction and oppression of the feminine, that institute the definition of the feminine in patriarchy or in a phallogocentric system so that it forecloses other definitions. How to frame an image, then, so that I, as lesbian, can inhabit it, so that the coding as lesbian is clear to the reader? How to build in conditions of reception, even as the culture itself has already marked conditions I cannot avoid?

The whole public debate in the 1990s around the pornographic was another way of codifying discourse that foreclosed other possible definitions and ways of looking at images. What is really pornographic to me is not certain images, but what reproduces this cycle of power. But how can we get out of it? And how can we do this without getting caught in banal and transparent images of women's bodies, of their acts together? How can we make the trait count haptically, even in writing?

In short, how can we be true to the way the brain works? For the brain, the fragment is not a part broken off a whole, but is the way the brain sees, absorbs, and codifies information, in a way that parallels, curiously, today's information environment in the world external to the body.

We also need to look at what is culturally and racially determined, and look at other uses of the body in and by power: the piles of wasted bodies in death camps such as Auschwitz, for example. If there is an impossibility of writing lyric poetry after Auschwitz, is there not also a severe problem with using these images of the human body?

What is an aspect? What is a racialized aspect of a work or process? What is a cultural aspect? What is a lesbian aspect? What is the Whole? All these questions arise for me from my initial one: what is a trait or line?

6

Maintenant on regrette beaucoup le temps des escargots pestilentiels... Dit ficelle et fiche le camp. Ficelle! Ficelle!
‖ Matei Vișniec

I believe it is important for women to seize the *informational moment* in which we are living at the turn of the twenty-first century, with its formation of discourses and technologies. It is a time when discourses and ontologies are shimmering against each other, where the *sujet-femme* constitutes herself across various boundaries, seems fragmented from an old perspective, but it is really not so. To ignore this moment of change in human articulation and absorption of information of all types is to lose the informational moment, lose the chance to articulate a womanly space, women's desire for the world and for each other, women's exploration of their own bodies and desires outside commercial commodification of the *woman-object*. My narrative strategies in poetry are my ways of seizing this moment.

This is what I tried to do in *A Frame of the Book* (aka *The Frame of a Book*) in exploring problems of designation and figure, exploring the mechanisms of act and consequence and how they function in the person, in human beings singly and in relation to one another, and to others. This involves sex, too. Of course, as a lesbian I must be talking about sex! Yet I'm also criticized at times for not being clear enough in my imagery, for not purveying a "lowest common denominator" of imagery of women as if it could be sufficient and adequate for describing the complex *tournures* of the sexual charge between us.

But I am just *not* the girl for that job. What the reader finds in my work strays far from the conventional images of sexuality adopted in much lesbian poetry: I want to go beyond utopic portrayal or distopic or atopic portrayal (all of them meaning "not a place") to what I call, wonderingly, *to-pic*. For me it is important to free oneself from the banalization of images that occurs as a result of proliferative excess; the problem is how to evoke a lesbian imaginary that *acts across boundaries* without falling into the utopic or the banal, an imaginary that, as well, resists commodification, and works without slipping into a solipsistic version of tenderness. Here it is critical to consider the body not as self-enclosed and complete but as a coding practice, to understand, as Donna Haraway does, that what constitutes an organism or a machine is in fact indeterminate. They are coded by culture, oh yes, but there are ways to have agency and code back (Adelman's images do "code back"); I think we have to demand that of an image.

I am concerned, then, with material subject to abrasion, deformation, collapse, and passages, which is to say: with words, enacting a poetry that contends with the figural pictorially, and thus does not operate as representation but as designation — an *act* or continual coalescence — of being, that both counters the grain of power and recognizes, as Robertson does, its complicity with and in those structures.[1] A poetry wherein persons live, move, love. Lesbian persons. Feminist persons. I call the reader's attention in my work to missing words, repetitions, misspellings, and jarring representations — or not representations but designations: machine struggles, coalescences, constructing selves that collide, molecularize, pine, adopt, enjoy, and confront a wide range of emotions and desires. I have no easy answers; I don't even look for ease.

poetry of the baby; a topic poetry of place a poetry going somewhere - a destination

SPEAKING THE UNSPEAKABLE: RESPONDING TO CENSORSHIP

▌It is true that sex has imbued much of what I write. I don't *direct* myself toward expression of sex, but it always risks coming out and often does, though mostly entwined with other concerns. I do write from a sexual and sexualized body, and it is from this body that I receive the world.
 The view of the body most akin to mine is Spinoza's, which I first encountered via Gilles Deleuze. Spinoza defines a body in two ways, which work in simultaneity: first, as composed of particles, an infinite number of particles in motion or at rest, thus defined not by forms but by velocities; second, as a capacity for affecting or being affected by other bodies, so that part of a body's it-ness is its relationality. To me, there's a clear marker here for *community*—broadly speaking, all other beings we are in contact with—as an indispensable part of our definition of who we are as individuals.
 When I think of the body, it is as massed forces or condensations of forces: velocities and relationalities. Libido, then, is invested everywhere: chairs, tables, cats, fish, fishing,

eating, looks, motions, words, sounds. Sexual investments define my relationship with what I experience as the world, and I write them, write through them.

How, then, might censorship of sexual representations by our government's border-sanitation edicts[1] affect my writing practice?

First of all, I create in the medium of poetry, which is so little circulated in this country that censoring me overtly would have little effect on my production. My poems first circulate among a few friends who are my most passionate, rigorous, helpful readers. By responding to me, they make me feel I am alive and that these writing acts are possible. To be Spinozan about it, their velocities affect mine. Beyond that, I have a kind of fatalistic attitude. I send out book manuscripts and will continue to do so as long as they continue to be published, and I harbour the naive belief that they will, but it is more important to me to *do* my work than to be published. And because poetry has a small readership in Canada, crushing poetry for purported crimes of sexual speaking wouldn't really produce that much more public silence: I mean, how far a fall is it from the sidewalk to the gutter? Because my artistic practice does not always use words conventionally, I am more inclined to be criticized for being "difficult" or dismissed for purveying "rhetoric and jabberwocky,"[2] which criticism, in fact, gives me more freedom. If I'm already denominated as difficult, it opens the door to being "more difficult" without provoking any worse reaction. If what I write is already gibberish, it frees me to explore. Having already been called names is kind of liberating!

My work relies on my capacity to force the borders, and concentrate the density of language as "material," to be attentive not only to the surface levels of meaning, but also to the convulsive, torsional power of words, of transcription, of syllables as marks, of "sounds like," of "means." In this attentiveness, I find myself every time, no matter what I start writing about, to be confronting the linguistic order with a kind of sexual, phenomenological order, foregrounding an extremely insistent carnality that infuses all acts, all potential for human affection and responsibility. The body, as Michel Serres has written, *mimes the future participle* (30).

Bald images of girls *in flagrante delicto* is not what you will find in my work. Yet I still do explore and move forward into the wreckage of being, in and out of my sexualized, lesbian body, which to me is not marginalized but the locus of any possible coalescence/configuration of a "me," any possible utterance or inscription (which are also relationalities, velocities), and this locus is contiguous with the "me"s of others. Contiguity is critical to me as a conscious being: this relationality is part of what defines me as a body, as present in space, as conscious, as imbricated.

My main interest these days in my writing is in how subjectivity works and how we are persons: how our being is socially and culturally constructed, and constructed in and through technology(ies) that flatten and twist notions of space/time, making any conventional notion of presence, self-presence, or corporeality virtually untenable. I am interested in how we tend to act our relationships out of these constructs, to a great extent unconsciously, because to do or construct otherwise produces too much anxiety in the organism. I insist on exploring these things without constraint, and I do so out of a lesbian body and sensibility.

Nevertheless, I do at times experience a kind of censoriousness that I want to name here: the expectation (too often, but not always) coming from other writers or artists that presses me to write more explicitly about sex. *When are you going to read sex poems?* someone once said to me after a reading. *I just did read them*, I said. Of course there's a place for this comfortable and recognizable kind of sexual imagery that mimics and repeats what people are used to, but an insistence that everyone produce *Just This* is, to me, a kind of "dumbing down" of the possibilities of imagery, of explicit speaking, that shuts down thought and visibility for work that questions sexual identity and positioning. It narrows the horizon. I find that there is a definition of "lesbian work" that bears the same kind of insistence of the old left on social realism. I object to that. In my case, it is important to embody women, and my own sense as a woman, as a lesbian woman, without reinforcing boundaries that are false, and without utopizing a naturalized boundary or definition or reification of the body. The libido is invested everywhere; I know this, so I cannot merely let myself be coded by demands of the culture that render me invisible, or by demands of a sector of the lesbian community that wants bordered images, straight narrative, clarity of a sort that does not exist and is actually harmful. I refuse to be made invisible in my own community of artists because I don't produce obvious images that accord with conventional notions of accessibility. I want to work at the boundaries of what is possible and extend that range, not just fall within the rules, no matter whose rules they may be.

    Another, less pernicious, form of censorship is that it seems possible to read my work and ignore what is lesbian in it, because the work has so many other presences. My work has had a kind of mainstream presence and has thus been subjected to a mainstream kind of commentary in places like *The Globe and Mail*, or in literary journals, which often tends to sanitize my writing. Yet the consciousness of being lesbian informs my work at its deepest levels (if I can speak of such things as "depths" and "levels"). This form of censorship is less pervasive because younger critics are noticing and speaking of the lesbian conjunctures without the fears once held by "family newspapers." As well, the Internet is a much more open environment, without the guiding eye of "daddy" over what is published, without the same old strictures. The Internet proliferates all kinds of dubious information and garbage, but can also create space for speaking otherwise.

The question for me is how to build conditions of reception for works that insist on being read as lesbian (without wanting to assume at the same time that there is an a priori or even prior definition of the word "lesbian"), works that can be placed within a sexual identity, however flexible and permeable this identity may be, while taking into account that as a woman and a lesbian my body is already read in a certain way by this culture, and that this reading can "harm" me.

As regards the Internet and hate proliferations — always the next question when it comes to censorship — I believe we can't censor, we can't stop. I know that the pumped and primed organs of censorship will end up being used against me, to suppress representations of my sexuality, to suppress sexualities that are unruly and refuse control by the social order. I think that, rather than censor, we have to insist on the necessity of unmasking what exactly it is in our social order that makes hate possible. We must proliferate for ourselves, and for each other, the widest possible realm of images that reflect otherness. Censorship is only another method of maintaining the status quo by preventing thought, discussion, and availability.

And, yes, I think that we have to watch all the time that, in our lives and work and relations with other artists, we don't reproduce the structures of censorship in our own communities, for we also are at risk of replicating the same oppressive forms in our discussions with each other. It is critical that we encourage an openness of ways of reading work that will expand everyone's access to images, to artistic expression, to language. And thus, to joy, to human possibility, to febrility and astonishment, which are there, in spite of the wreckage.

A FRAME OF THE BOOK
OR *THE FRAME OF A BOOK*

▌ Poetry has always been haunted by concerns that press upon the ontological. In my body of work over the years, I've been haunted too, pursuing such questions as: what does it mean to love, to exist, to communicate? how does the social framework influence us or limit us? what are the limits of the person, of tenderness, of grace, of honesty, of speech? how do we situate ourselves as beings in civil society?

Through the years, in the course of writing more books, I have found fewer certitudes in the poetic, and in life itself. *Search Procedures* closed with a poem that presents simultaneously an image of human birth and a declaration of the beauty of thought — beauty not of *sense* but of *sounds* and *signs*: "a r yp al oi." This line brought me perilously close to silence, to being unable to continue, to a wall in the search, a necessary wall, meant — as all walls are — to be breached.

"We like this. We go on."

1

A Frame of the Book (aka *The Frame of A Book*), the book that followed *Search Procedures*, was directed toward a deeper exploration of human responsibility: act and consequence, judgment and circumstance, ardour and grief. The poems attempt to uncover and articulate the mechanisms of all these forces, and their ways of operating in the human organism, "the person," their sensory aggregate. There are, in short, forces that link us, that make us "persons" and not simply organisms. These forces compel and hold me.

What is the place/role of the skin in all this? Does the skin mark the body's limit? How can one rethink the skin? Does the skin still demarcate the borders of identity when we work with a computer, when we no longer see our interlocutors? What is the effect of distance on the human body, on a woman's body, on relations between women? Is distance also an inevitable effect, thus a fact of the text? In what ways does the text act like a skin, like a libidinal band (after Jean-François Lyotard)?

We don't see each other, my readers and I; what is it then that constructs us as individuals, as "acts" (a word I used in *Furious*)? What are the limits of individual consciousness? Where are the borders of memory, of the construction of the present, of the past and future?

As neurologist Gerald Edelman says, "More is involved than a brain-state" (213). This brings me to Donna Haraway's notion of the body — that the body's boundaries are socially constituted, bodies are communication practices, coding devices.

> If it were ever possible ideologically to
> characterize women's lives by the distinction

> of public and private domains... it is now
> a totally misleading ideology, even for the
> purpose of showing how both terms of these
> dichotomies really construct each other in
> practice and in theory. I prefer a network
> ideological image, suggesting the profusion
> of spaces and identities and the permeability
> of boundaries in the actual personal body
> and in the body politic. (170)

And, further: "organisms are not special natural entities, whether they are fetuses, plants, or bacteria; they are particular technological solutions to a production problem."

For me "the permeability of boundaries in the actual personal body" is a fact; much of selfness comes from contextualization with or through the other, from this play between autonomy and other. Even the notion of will to me is a flux force between bodies and not a static though insistent expression of the individual (à la romanticism).

This project is traversed by the urgency of desire, because the skin in itself is a "desiring integument," and even the cartography of the skin in the cortex alters in response to tactile stimulation. "The maps turn out to be dynamic in that they reflect the interaction of the individual with its tactile environment. Body maps are dynamic over time, are functional constructs not structures."[1] The "libidinal economy" delineated in my work is always traced as well by political economy, by the economic forces that hold us in the present.

The body itself is a geography, and an economy. Spinoza's views of the body as an assemblage and confluence of particles (which have motions and rests, i.e., velocities), and as relational with other bodies (affecting and being affected by), are pertinent here. The boundaries of selfhood shimmer; in fact, it is not even proper to speak of boundaries that shift; so-called boundaries are just shimmers, constantly shifting. This shimmering occurs outside the body too because your friends change, you change landscapes, animal presences, beings, lovers, tactilities; all these things alter who you are as an incorporated being, and change you differently, differentially. Because touch alters the brain and alters the way that the brain maps the relationship with the body's shape and extremity, these things affect you internally as well as externally. Depending on touch, your brain's maps of your body can change up to 10 percent. If you were to move the boundary of Alberta westward to include the Kootenays, you'd have a pretty good correlation for how much the brain's mapping of the self changes. It's in motion all the time. As such, the skin *desires* to be presented, both inside the brain, in those maps, and outside, in relation to those others, to another, *that other*. The inside configuration(s) in fact partly rely on the shimmer of the outside, where touch comes from. In a sense, inside and outside become reversible; the inside is a kind of outside, and the outside is necessary to make the inside realize it is an inside, a configuration that evokes Lyotard's libidinal band. It's not exactly clear what a self is or what you could be without that relationality with other people.

Personal identity is, thus, libidinally invested everywhere, in and through a series — a clamour, really — of relationalities.

The brain, in fact, does not make a value distinction between body/mind, outside/inside; it seizes information without regard to source. The voice speaking on the screen is still a voice. We are extensional over virtual spaces; with computers, localities themselves are extensible over and through what we know as the old boundaries of physical space. Economic globalization and digitization are obviating national boundaries in different ways, and changing the nature of localities. Yes, we still inhabit and are coded by national and local territories. But space and the idea of boundaries are changing rapidly, and can't help but affect, reverberate, and reconstitute the body's boundaries as well.

The brain maps information, reads it in parts, overlapping the parts. To see what is in front of our open eyes we need dynamic brain processes/structures for movement, for edge, for colour, for shape, for sound. But nowhere in our brain is there a site where a picture is assembled. We beings are shimmers, coalescences, coalitional, but not fragments. If everything is a fragment, if everything in the brain works in so-called fragments, then we no longer need this word *fragment*, which merely reflects a nostalgia for the notion of a wholeness. If everything is a fragment and the whole is illusory, it makes no sense to talk of fragments. In the corporation where I worked, playing with the information environment and teaching managers to manage others, I watched how people absorb information: not in whole fashion, but partially, by connecting what they can of it with their own culture/upbringing. Both information and the connecting process were affected, as well, by noise interference from other communicative endeavours in their environment. In other words, information absorption is consistent with a network or coalescent model, not with any model that relies on visions of a whole structure.

Our interactions as persons, as women, are changing through technology and through socio-economic shifts. How we think, locate, and combine information is changing, has changed. Important aspects that I noticed:

107

- We reproduce bits of information from various sources and recombine them in ways that create faults, unbeknownst to our conscious minds.

- The receiver of information can alter the message.

- We draw or link diverse forces by proximity, not logical progression.

- It is impossible or unnecessary to view, account for, all the information before moving on.

- "Knowing" does not have to be data in your head, as in older models of knowledge retention: it is a locational and recombinatory device and keeps data both inside the head and outside it.

The creation of ourselves as subjects takes place continually, is part of a continual *actactact*. What was a fragment may prove to be sufficient to open us up to another space, an altered coalition of conditions. It's this space that I seek in poetry.

2

In my texts I want to play with the notion of a figure that can emerge from data that are, or appear to be, non-figurative. The work of portraitists, along with the history of portraiture (from the Etruscans onward), interests me and underpins my poetic research on what constitutes a figure. For me, as for the painter Francis Bacon, "the figure itself lies beyond the figurative," and "sensation is, rather, the effect of borders, of context, of difference" (Buci-Glucksmann 54). As usual, what propels this play is the encrustation of words on the page, their thickness and surface porosity — this, and the body not as container but as complex-implosion-traces linked to other complex-implosion-traces and taking its identity from this flux and from the *imprévisible* (the unpredictable, the unaccountable) always present in and around ourselves.

The path this poetry takes or wants to take is not that of ordinary narration. Because conventional narrative order tends to suppress emotional or designational "matters of fact"—to use a Deleuzian term—I sometimes have to work by damaging narrative possibility, denting it, in order to expose what is painted just behind its surface. The word-material enables creation—or accretion—of torsional scenes that are figures, as the page itself is a figure. I'm looking above all for ways to *figurate* being, human relationality, relationality especially between two women, between women as figures or beings who have been formed with great fear, with loss, who are coalescences of old griefs, who crave sweetness, and for whom the great imperatives of physical proximity or distance bear emotional weight. The resulting work in *The Frame of a Book* can be responded to viscerally as sensation, almost spatially, despite being rejected as non-coalescent by cortical processing. At the same time, it can't be entirely rejected, for it haunts or aches in ways that speak a kind of facticity for the human person or girl and what holds us intact while at the same time letting us change. I work with boundaries in the head and the worry there, the extreme worry that alters boundaries and is processed below consciousness, because thinking is not only a conscious act but is also a coding practice transversed by other coding practices both in and outside of the head.

The lines of the poems in *A Frame of the Book* put particular pressure at times on parts of speech, above all on the article, on definite and indefinite articles, to create an effect of zones swept of certitude, insisting thus on a more global reading of the text (as in Latin, where the role of each word and what it designates is not fully evident until one reads the sentence "globally"). In fact, the scenes that emerge, particularly in the long poem "Calor," work upon and within a problematic of reading, a problematic of designation, searching for the "ressemblance qui surgit comme le produit brutal de moyens non ressemblants" (Deleuze, *Francis Bacon* 75). That this is an identity problem, as well as a human problem, a gender problem, and a person problem, is evident to me. What can words, phrases, and their junctures designate of *us*? That there is some instability here, and where it isn't easily legible, putting pressure on designation can make it evident.

Francis Bacon said about painting that it "directly touches the nervous system" (Deleuze, *Francis Bacon* 28);[2] I believe that this can be equally true of poetic form. Recent neurobiological research indicates that it is the unconscious that interprets sensory data, that anticipates and determines the organism's next moves; very little of this process manifests itself, even at the final steps, at the conscious level. And the material substrate of the unconscious is, in effect, the nervous system, that extension of the brain everywhere in the body.

This work on language, because relational, also broaches notions of civil life, of what one has in common with others, and notions of justice; it explores how our beings are socially, culturally, constructed, and constructed as well in and through technology(ies) that render conventional notions of presence untenable. As the French philosopher Jean-François Lyotard said, "Justice here does not consist merely in the observance of the rules; as in all games it consists in working at the limits of what the rules permit, in order to invent new moves, perhaps new rules and therefore new games" (*Just Gaming* 100).

3

In *The Frame of a Book*, I tried to write a book of poems where the texts take on the questions and aims I've mentioned, a book that pushes and disturbs the limits of poetry, where a bodily pressure on words and form is evident. It is a poetry not exempt from narration, but for which narration is a textual strategy among others, poetry that works with the figural from a pictorial point of view, not as representation but as torsional designation of a being. These are things I must explore without constraint, out of a body and sensibility that is sexualized, that is specifically lesbian (though all the possible consequences of that site are not defined but open), that is gendered *female*, and that is socialized as *female*. Out of these explorations, I believe, can come new ways of seeing sexuality, sexual imagery, and sexual feeling, along with civic responsibility and civic being. My wish is that this poetry contributes to a community of such endeavours so that multiple refractions, questions, and reverberatory echoes are possible.

bring a "being" out of fragmented poetry

A NEW BIRD FLICKER, OR THE FLOOR OF A GREAT SEA, OR *STOOKING*

▌That small flicker in the far grass scrub. What is it? The eye moves with it. There is no fixed point the observer can occupy in such a landscape. The her grass flickers; it is a the bird. Her eye, too, her bird eye. A phenomenology here, the chiasmic imbrication of the visible. "I" am pulled in. Part of a planet's integument. But not just that.

What if I said: I grew up on the floor of a great sea. *Would that be your Alberta?* I could insist: for I have always looked out and seen *that* sea. I still write at my desk near a fossil fish: it is the endurance of a life in the brunt of momentous physical dislocation. A life as a mark made by the body, a kind of writing. From this mark we read politics, social arrangement, heritage; from this mark — a corporeal trace — we extrapolate belief. The effect of chemical interaction on stone. In effect, a chimæra.

The floor of such a sea. My Alberta is both prairie and mountain: even as landscape, it is not singular. "Alberta," on the other hand, is a social collectivity that exists for administrative purposes; as such it is relevant only if you are among the administered, which I am not. If you want to render Alberta completely irrelevant, all you have to do is leave. Because I left so many years ago, I can't talk about a current Alberta. My Alberta has more to do with a childhood relationship with place or landscape, with sounds. When you're just eighteen, as I was when I left, you're still not quite administered.

Can my Alberta be a context for talking about relationality and the formation of sexual identity? What might *that* entail of place, be that place Alberta or anywhere? In fact, I think that place is probably more exactly situated in plants beside a river than in units that exist for administration. Though even there, wet-legged in the new-grown sedge, we are part of, and subject to, the administration of those grasses.

When I first read the two words "geography" and "sexuality" together, my thought was *the body itself is a geography*. Yet if we are geographies, we are not fixed ones: our internal velocities, and affects or relationships with other bodies, mean the boundaries of selfhood are always in process. One example of this is the geography of grief. When part of the body goes missing, the cortical map that held that part still endures, until other touches replace it. The phantom limb syndrome is explained by this. Also grief at the loss of a partner or a close friend to death or sudden separation. The process, the physical dis-orientation, the "un-Easting," of grief, has even been observed in geese.[1]

Sexual identity grows out of all relationality, is not sited just in sex but in our relationship with tables, chairs, grasses, people we don't have sex with, birds, winds. The social structure, of course, does enter into it, delineates what is permitted, the modes of thinking and the cultural threads that are available. Thus the administrative unit, the structure in place when and where we grow up, clearly influences us. But it does not necessarily determine our identity per se, because bodies are seekers (or have that capacity, a capacity that exceeds what is administered) and will seek their own equilibrium in spite of what administrative units are trying to do, and despite the pain we may or may not feel at our contiguities and the choices our psyches lead us to.

Still, we have to resist administrative structures in order to make choices other than those offered as norms. These administrations want to make us into their "subjects" when we crave to be "predicates" or "future participles," answering with our own extensiveness another extensibility, leaning into the next phrase or point, crave to be responsive and respond.

One of those extensions, extensibilities, is our relation with landscape. Clearly there are ways in which we don't ever leave the landscapes of our childhood — the first places, those grasses, stones, light, our first contiguity with a world outside our primal envelope, the skin. Our first touch. In some ways we extend out into that landscape or streetscape or apartmentscape, stuccoscape. Theirs are neural pathways that are always present to us. And if that's the case, I've never left Alberta, because the inner maps of my body and my geography extend into all those landscapes. They are visible in my work even though I've been gone from Alberta for decades and not a single cell of my body is the same as any that I had when I lived there.

Can landscape be read directly by the nervous system? What is a neural structure? Really it is not a structure, but a configuration of neuronal pathways that have fired repeatedly over time. There are signs in the Albertan landscape that persist today of that ancient sea. The dendrite glow of childhood in the head, its relation with the social construct "Alberta," with "feminism," with "race," with "origin." Who am "I" if I remember? Am I the I remembering or the remembered? And whose falseness do I perpetuate? And how must we speak? Skin and neural maps. Touched by humans. Also touched by what we see. Uttered.

These days I am suspicious of such an "I," of any stability of such a construct, for the stability is often determined by administrations, blinding other constituent factors. Still, I know we do not lose the landscape of our childhood. Years ago in Vancouver, a stranger cited poet Georges Brassens in my notebook in his strange French handwriting: "I pity the poor people who were born somewhere." We all have an uneasy relationship with that *somewhere*, and we recognize and dislodge its social arrangement in the self only after arduous questioning. Which means: departures.

But can departures echo back and alter place? Can we get out of the dynamic or lure of opposites, of "here" and "there," wherein we can be (to evoke Lyotard) but litigants? What does this have to do with language, if the body also *writes*, if its unEast-ing, its un-Northing, also disengages sounds from the cacophony, puts together word configurations?[2] Perhaps poetry offers a compositional possibility, an errancy at the edge of word-sense-conjunct (that cannot be turned into a rhiz-o-mat).[3] If only we could just cease to look at poetry in a surface sociological sense, trying to find in Alberta-born writers only images or sentiment that reflect Alberta!

As a writer I see possibilities in the words the same way a stroke of paint can declench and divulge to a painter, the way a colour and the thickness of a metal in solution can divulge to a painter. In general, my work constructs texts whose lines are "planes" or "planar components" linked proximally in scenes that act in turn as a kind of figure, which itself often repeats, backtracks, jumps, is partial, twists, impedes. Alberta's topographies of immigration, the restlessness of a rural, religious society that became urban and secular only during my childhood, still trace me. Parts of its landscape still inhabit and compel me. I still remember "stooking." I still want to say: "the stooks of yellow barley" as if everyone will nod at what I am saying.

But I can't live in Alberta. Its social organization rejected me as a lesbian for so long, rejected my humanity, continually had difficulty with it. My insistence on living as I do, though, prevails beyond its or any laws. Denying me work or housing or funding — as occurred to people in Alberta in a quite recent past — won't stop me. I write each day in a terrible urgency, against death, I write, literally, so as not to die. I write as an allergic person and as a lesbian, as a woman whose greatest fondness is directed toward other women, whose skin feels theirs, but also as someone whose trajectories do not seek transcendences or ways out, but ways in, sonorities, complexities, febrilities. My landscape is one of desire, a geography not "fixed" because boundaries must change and seek new predications, and do so outside the order of capital, the order of consumption and product, and outside the administrative plan.

Thus, not a subject, but a shimmering predicate. Leaning already into the next field, the future participle. Shifting already the frame of any prior arrangement. Maps, landscapes. What we bear in us of an ancient sea. Her body, too, is also a landscape, figural, infinitely absorptive.

Read directly by the nervous system. O but I am glad.

response to light

THE CAPITULATIONS, A TEXT BY, FOR, AND THROUGH THE ART OF LANI MAESTRO[1]

*

The disturbance of light in a room
(How to make a story palpable without letting the viewer fall

for "the liberal, bourgeois lie")[2]
to enact the palpable, or repetitive-caress-of-material
while knowing that, by "nature," "art" is "spectacle"

the relationship of sound, movement, and gesture
embodied
(that theatre which gives lie to intentionality)

so that the artwork, in fact, cannot be viewed
in its entirety

breaking, thus, with any notion of "entirety"
just as a body breaks, necessarily, with any notion

of *entirety*

(its disturbance)

*

With the notion of entirety broken, who then are we as individuals? How is it possible to inhabit a human body? Lani Maestro's art calls forth such exact, and inexact, reverberations. We are all histories stopped in time. At every moment we have to *establish* ourselves: not *re*-establish, but establish anew.

> "IS THERE A LOSS THAT CANNOT BE THOUGHT, CANNOT BE OWNED OR GRIEVED, WHICH FORMS THE CONDITION OF POSSIBILITY FOR THE SUBJECT?"
> ‖ Judith Butler, *The Psychic Life* (24)

Is this loss, the one Butler hints at, the loss Maestro enacts for and in us, through the visible, the tactile, the aural, the olfactory (the smell of bamboo), one that offers (as she has often insisted) a way to "heal"? Is the act of healing the act that constitutes the self?

"To inhabit a human body"—what impossible phraseology! It doubles the initial question. It implies, strangely, that a thing or force distinguishable from "a human body" can traverse, enter, and perhaps stop in it. What would this force or thing, this invisible subject, be? And what is this it, its it-ness, where the traversal coalesces? It's absurd to separate the two; they are not an equation. What will inhabit the body if not the body already there, already in and of itself, reversing Lyotard's libidinal band? To speak of the body inhabiting the body opens the realm of the tautological (a philosophical space that, to paraphrase Wittgenstein, lacks sense, but is not nonsensical).[3]

What of sense, then? Is there a sense to the world that can be thought or envisioned outside dialectical boundaries? Does take account of that continual gesture of *establishing*? A movement that moves back upon itself (Nietzschean "will" echoes here), whose *movement*, to paraphrase Butler, *is* itself.

*

    inhabitation
    inhabit
     habit
      ab hit
      a bit
    inhalation
    inhale
     ela
     elation
      late eon
     elect ion
     elect ron
       iron
       ironic   (absence)

*

To approach Maestro's work is to ask: what does it mean to inhabit a space? Perhaps a space becomes one *when* you (the subject body — but now we are back to that problem of embodiment, that turns on itself) inhabit it. As if our body is not primarily in space, but of it (Blanchot echoes here). *"The work has already taken place." "The work began as a response to light."* [4] As if a space is a relationality, not an object, a relationality or an occurrence. Maestro puts the weight on time, and in turn on time's variable effect on weight: a wall, a sound, a person, a smell. To walk into a corridor and *smell earth*, for example.[5]

"The work began as a response to light."

*

What if Earth (a place) were in fact a circumstance? An insistence or event. A disturbance. As a gallery is. Even as I am writing this (1 March 1998, 11:41 AM EST), the event of Maestro's installation has not occurred, and the artwork has scarcely coalesced, has only ghostly relationalities and a leaning-forward into the work of hands, which is, in a sense, the real "work." What if inhabitation, or habitation-of-a-space, were *event*?

*

    inhabitation
     habitation
      habitate
      habitable
in habit
   habit
    habeas corpus
     corporeal
     corpic
     orphic
      oceanic
      ocean   (speech) (pore) (real)

*

Maestro also makes me think of the relationship of light and the human body, of light too as a gesture worked in the present. How Lani Maestro's juxtaposition of seemingly unrelated elements — sea, sound, light — may be seen as gesture, evoking the cicatrice that draws the past in and through the present. The cicatrice that is memory's possibility. Memory's cricket. Gnarl. Embodied. The rolled bedsheet.[6] Where death is a fold hinged with and through rebirth. Is it a question of making the rebirth clean? Or of recognition, of recognizing the self among disparate, invocable elements? If recognition is possible, why has any gesture to be repeated?

*

Why has any gesture to be repeated?

*

how to establish that "difference" in "space" that is "identity"?
that fold?
silence.

how to say "smoke" or "water"
are markers of the artist/viewer's relationship with light

"establishment"

& how to make the spectacle (an operation always, not a thing or object)
enact the "everyday gesture"

of sweeping (perhaps)
the motion of a woman's hand, on a broom, in space
absolutely tactile & sonorous

& the relationship this might open with the viewer
having to be *of* the space wherein this sound
becomes "intention"

how to address issues of power's immediacy, phosphorescent
in all gesture, in space
as well as circumstance?
silence.

the fold in this space
the scintillate embodiment

oceanic: dive

*

inhabitation

apt	verse
hapt	version
haptic	
rapt	
gap	
ga'	

> "THE VISIBLE BURSTS OUT BETWEEN TWO PROPOSITIONS, AND AN UTTERANCE BURSTS OUT BETWEEN TWO THINGS. INTENTIONALITY GIVES WAY TO A WHOLE THEATRE..."
> ❚ Deleuze on Foucault, *Negotiations* (107)

*

(   )
(   )
(trēma   )
(   )
(   )

THREE NOTES ON LANI MAESTRO'S *CRADLE*

Lani Maestro
Cradle (1996)[1]

1

Tension in the strings — each string an alphabetic letter — its tension (is readerly).

Also its *shape* is its *angle*.

Angle and tension (reader, readability) make it alphabetic.
Also for what it reveals in its spaces, and not in the lines themselves.

These letters are arguing, but are also mute.

There are stringed instruments that can make sounds in wood, leaves, bone.

Cradle is a stringed instrument.

Its lines contrast with its planes — because it marks off space with planes. These marked spaces lie beneath the alphabet.

This is a description of discourse that is working for me.

2

One tent has any one relation to
any other tent, and to all tents.

The tension in the body has an alphabetic
pull toward space.

This relationship of tension/tents is also a
performance.

The tents themselves are words that
the reader must perform by watching
them (they do not perform).

Waiting and watching are
semantic performances;
they accept the inauguration

of a pull toward space,
which includes the soma
as constitutive of meaning

and meaning's refutation.

The wires or
strings invite sunlight and are
a script for air.

(It is a design for breathing.)

3

The fabric tents mark off breathing spaces. In some, there is only a single breath; it doesn't yet occupy all the space marked out for it.

The spaces (cubes) are breathing spaces for souls (heat).

The souls are clicks we can't hear because they are not linear but dimensional.

So there are planes, cubes, breaths, clicks all within the discursive field.

What is in a discursive field can be said to make it up.

All discursive fields include the reader, who performs not just in front of them, but in them.

In *Cradle* we play the reader.

The reader is a performance complicit with a tension in the body.

Cradle makes up my discursive field.[2]

A PAN OF QUAIL

▌ Some people who otherwise eat meat and fowl won't eat quail, even farmed ones. There's something about their smallness, perhaps, or the association with song. When birds might sing instead of quacking or cackling, we want to preserve the fragility of their song, of all song, because only then is our own song preserved in its fragility.

But there is a way of cooking that is not really an attack on these small birds, but a way of participating with them in the fragility of another act related to song, that of eating.

A funny thing to say, I guess. Mostly we westerners forget that eating's fragile too. Humans don't always eat, or get enough to eat.

I tend to think of eating quail as something close to gift, in the ancient way that a gift economy regulates our relations in the world, making us possible as subjects. When I bring home a packet of quail, I usually get frozen ones missing parts due to the machines, six in a package, and thaw them on the kitchen counter to the left of the stove. Later I take them out of the package and split them with a sharp knife and wash them, then put them on paper towels and wash my hands.

What's needed is the top of a stove, and a covered pan. It could be a fire or hearth. It's a way of cooking that's very old. I just put my quail in the pan glazed with oil and brown them gently. Then pour in about 60 ml of red wine and lift the stuck bits from the bottom of the pan with the spoon, shift the quail around a bit, sprinkle a huge amount of sweet pimentón — paprika from Spain — over it all, and cover to let them cook very slowly. Sometimes I add thyme, which I dry myself every year so it's always pungent in aroma and is leaves, not powder.

In another pan in a bit of olive oil, I gently soften a couple of chopped cloves of garlic, an onion minced finely, and some chopped red and green pepper. At this point, I can start to smell what it will all be like, later. When these are softened, I add a cup and a half of rice, or sometimes 2 cups, and stir it all up, coating and heating the rice. Then add 2.5 to 3.5 cups of warm stock. Into the middle goes the quail and stock from the other pan, with the addition of 200 ml or so of frozen peas. And some thyme. Maybe. And more pimentón. Cover and cook it til the rice has absorbed all the liquid, opening the pan if there's too much to let it evaporate, or if there's not enough, I just add in a bit more water. When it's done I shut off the heat and let it sit awhile, then bring the pan to the table.

You have to eat quail with your fingers; it can't be avoided; so you all end up with quail and rice on your fingers and lips. You use up paper towels. You talk to your friends; the food makes you all warmer. There's a pitch or register to the conversation. If it's right it should give you the feeling of being out in the field in fall, late fall. With all the sounds in the grasses.

Most of those grasses are obliterated by the weather now.

The rain washes over the oiled membrane of the coat you are wearing. It is the last rain of the year, not the soft incessant rain of Santiago de Compostela as the Berenguela so solemnly tolls the hour, but the rain of the province of Alberta in Canada outside the city of Red Deer, a rain blown almost horizontal, whitening, sticking to the cheeks and to the sides of the dry grasses, in that one moment when it is about to turn to snow.

THE FIRST SNOW OF THE SEASON IS A TIME OF GREAT PEACE AND, IN IT, WE GREET THE COMING OF LONG WINTER DARKNESS. THIS SNOW AND PLATE OF QUAIL ARE FOR MY MOTHER, M.I.M.

MORNINGS ON WINNETT:
TRUST MEDITATIONS

"TO AVOW"

1
We need to travel
Some see this as consent

some as antithesis

What making is   can be seen in cycles
                             or not

"it's amorous" counts for something here.

2
To resist itself a street is normal
strangeness. Do we hearten only
to endure? Later on, her situation
became "one" with toponymy.

Or toponymy's brave function
    toponymy

Topography has its signs for age,
synonyms for use of
water
water's use of *corpo* to
create forms (what we see)

(visible)

3

Composition has, then, several stages —
some of these involve commas
some hot lights
yesterday I wore King Lear's make-up
for practice
It was fresh on me
"oh my doubters" I cried out

making that mistake again, audibly

The "I" is a construct, surely, here.

4

Why are creeks in this vein difficult
choice's engine
To avow

5

And then I realized
any word written down could be biography
the next word would betray or wound it

"perhaps"

for there is always "perhaps not"
which makes — you must admit –
"perhaps" beautiful

that there could be a "not" and it
could enter

A grey sky in morning holds up
an indication yet of "some" harbours

she agrees
to harbour

Complex fractions can commit
or sway
reason's septicemia

these membranes separate
along a mesial plane
are "in fact" micronic gestures

There is not much else. (*A sentence at
the end of a letter from Guatemala,
1899.*)

"We too are affected every moment by oil's
plunge."

6

Topography a lure for surface features
this too poetry's mechanism in a
— girl — life
a language we have spaced or cowed,
not invalided
Failing to alight
Socketed, as teeth

To agree on obsolete terms, hand's
wench, my L plunder
who would hear to breast anew

also fed or nurtured

It is steadily to evolve
making life's increase inevitable

We who have stood by life
Where we worked at times   across intention
or across intention's foment

For sure this look doth proceed ontology
This she enjoyed
Our version in the ripe narratives

Birth to altitudes

7
To read one word "après un autre" *is*
location

or a difficulty in location

So how are we in space?

Whole trees of birch
        black spruce
        poplar
        willow
looking for these a life entire

to express gladness
(real trees)
where such is possible

my solace to reinscribe
and not to concur

No one will recognize this as a battle
feature
No one will walk up the small brown hill
and say

"I have altered the horizon"

They'll just walk up the brown hill
and say "it was a letdown"
on the other side, there was
"nothing"

which means they lacked the amplitude
to array catalysts for low-set
stimuli

Birch forests — it is not the first time
I have called on birches
The role of sign/parturition
Beavers knew them too for their fine wood
when they made the dams,
some trees died in that rich water,

beckons

palest thread of heron,
bird as category of evening light

bliss plumage

alors
------
tamén

* * *

L'autre comme transcendance,
droiture d'une alliance irrésiliable
Cette leçon

   marks us　　　　　　　solace's riven
　　　　　　　　　　　　　"　　　　"
　　　　　　　　　　　un deuil confus

which needs words' ligature

         harness

         to avoid harm's blesst mécanique
         a nosa dor

her blessed machine
         a whist's circumference
                stance

of no oubli　　　~ went ~

o you are so lovely
I throw my cloak down
to speak to you solely out of my chest
where the bone is
flat and still as a knife or pen

wanting what we did to be "beat of a bird's heart"
cataclysm of small field flowers

   orange　　　　d'alliance
   orage

                                         foray.

Last Notes

copious is not a wing of piety
or simulacra
or absence
or tear's harbour in my image
                            (naufrage)
basically alive
we woke up to "smell the coffee"

my mother
whose horse *King* had been cut away by her
from context
my mother knew when she did cut the photo
"this,"
and what the thread of context means:
an obligation
that often does not any more
astonish us

as does an opera in Berlin
that leafy street
the operatic circumstance we knew *ali*
threads of "to astonish"
Blaser does this daily
in a life where the skin permits and does
not inhibit
collects and does not endure
speaks of such circumstances

we write
knowingly   haunted
knowingly   amazed a fear

went forward into gladness
to be   such syllable we confect

do you love gladness
it is my fond syllable

I am awake now
singing the kettle's stream of air

chose or coisa
"take care" [1]

an exhorbitant body: citizenship, translation, subjectivity

POETS AMID THE MANAGEMENT GURUS

A FAD FOR BRINGING POETRY INTO BUSINESSES MISSES THE PARADOXES OF WORKING FOR LANGUAGE.

▌Last night, I dreamed I woke up as a poet in a huge corporation. I was there to release hidden creativity in the corporate types; a schedule full of beauty and truth lay before me. Idiot that I am, I'd read an article in *The Globe and Mail* right before bed ("Britain's Office Life Gets a Dose of Poetry," July 21, 1998), on poets being hired by British corporations to motivate people, to praise fish-and-chips or launch books at the zoo. So no wonder I was dreaming. It's all artifice, I shrugged.

And proceeded to my first workshop, where I tried to describe my current poetry to the corporate lawyers around the table. It's hi-toned obscurantist lesbo smut, I told them. I'm working on poetic form, on what the brain can understand emotionally from the poem as a whole (the macro level) even when in individual sentences (the micro level) semantic value is missing—there's no apparent sense. A lawyer leaned forward. "I've been drafting a contract just like that," he said. I could tell he was realizing the potential of poetry, so I went on. I talked about what it means to be part of a language community, yet a community whose values are set, altered, torqued all the time by commerce. "That's right!" yelped a vice-president who had poked his head in to bring me a fresh sonnet on his marriage. Or on his former marriage. Or for his mirror image.

In the next session I was to uplift secretaries, lathe operators, and desegregating engineers. Beyond the window, the world lies, I concluded, reading a lament for a friend who lost out to opportunistic infections before protease inhibitors enabled people to live with HIV. I wanted to explain how ambiguity in poetry could be intentional, how it can resonate, in this case, as if putting the twist to easy irony: Yes, the world lies outside the death room as possibility, and, yes, it lies. In a backward way, I was getting truth in.

"Ambiguity!" exclaimed a secretary. "So Monsieur Hautparleur is poetic when he writes, 'The meeting on Thursday the 15th,' when Thursday is the 16th and there are no Thursday the 15ths till past his retirement?!"

I tried to calm her. I continued to explain how poetry is not an expression of feelings, but an address to language itself, and out of language — working with how meaning is constructed contextually, between words and not in the words themselves. So for the hi-toned lesbo smut poems, I select from pages of sentences generated randomly by a computer program, then make some alterations. I change *he* to *she*, I told them, or *you* to *I*, and skew connectives and articles, while retaining the overall syntax and vocabulary permitted by the generator program.

One of the desegregators interrupted. She claimed the company newsletter read exactly like computer-generated sentences and it was a struggle to find meaning in it. Could I add some lesbo smut to that?

I wanted to, but had to rush off to help the company president rhyme a speech to the board. I suggested he use tercets, as in Dante's *Inferno*, so he could fit more circles of hell in. He called his piece "Ode to a Torpedo," and wouldn't listen that it wasn't an ode; he was the president, therefore it was an ode. I had to agree. He was the president, so it was an ode. "It's beautiful," I lied, thus sneaking beauty in.

At the poetry reading I gave to make creativity flower in the afternoon, I intoned a few lines of the smut: *Before exist caused play, the pound visualized her, and/ she gently drove until you had burst those skirts.*

Now they understood how poetic intensity works: no wonder management had grabbed onto poetry as the latest flavour-of-the-month distraction from some organizational horror they were plotting. Enough! Just as my acolytes made a blind rush to delete my poems off the Internet, Intranet, and Extranet, moving them to the Net Loss line, with one stanza left at the fax to nettle people, I woke up. Phew.

Joke is, I once was a poet in a large corporation. I started as a cook and left the echelons of senior management twenty years later. In some ways it was language and what I learned from poetic exploration that helped me to ascend the corporate ladder, working primarily in service design and customer relations, jobs that demanded an ability to understand how communication works and apply it to both structural and human possibility.

The corporation in turn affected my poetry; it was in many ways my first university. I learned there how noise, context, and culture affect meaning; I learned how people, locked into their own cultural habits and contexts, can't foresee the consequences of their communication unless they first listen to the ones they talk to. Listening then changes the context of the speaker, and alters what they were about to say. A new dynamic emerges, richer.

Listening is key. It is 80 percent of communication; only 20 percent is yap. Encouraging more talking, even creatively, won't do squat when there's not enough listening. Gradually, in the corporation, or in spite of it, I learned what poetry was for: not to tell stories or laud the chippie but to query, listen to language itself, let it pull me, allow it to resonate with all life's paradoxical splendour.

Which it can do only if it retains its difficulties. To paraphrase Spanish novelist Juan Goytisolo: "the writer's moral imperative is to return a new and distinct language to the literary-linguistic community to which we belong, a language richer than the one we inherited when we began."[1]

Still, every once in awhile, poets' organizations latch on to a corporate wave trumpeting creativity and scramble to make poetry, and poets, fit for consumption there.

But poetry is not about creativity or uplifting people but about risk, great risk, hurtling oneself at the boundaries of language, ears pressed to the borders of the structure and hearing its constraints, which also indicate openings. Operating at the edge of our belief about what language can do. Risking that you might not like or understand the result at first, or for years.

Maybe the real question is the other way around: how can the corporation be fit for poetry, when the corporate communicator's job is not to wrench open the circle of understanding but to close it? To find a path through noise, put the spin on things, make them acceptable? Results have to be understood; decisions have to connect to a definable future.

Great risks are taken in and outside of corporations (I know from experience) but not normally by communicators.

They are taken by rare people on fire with a vision of the possible that they enact out of personal, not corporate, values, acting out against the entropy that hardens all organizations and structures. And they don't need beauty and truth — they need higher-ups with ears to hear them, and the guts to trust and support them even when they don't yet understand.

Even when they do not yet understand. So there it is, then: there's the link with poetry.

Which is where I am now, head down, working. I work for language, which demands that I write toward what can't necessarily be deciphered or consumed by the marketplace yet. Because what we cannot decipher makes us who we are, and makes possible the struggle into the new. Illusion is the text. And poetry's book does, in the face of consumption, press its veto.

...*citizenship cannot remain without interiority, without the redoubtable constraint of an interiority and its figure...*
ll Jean-Luc Nancy (*Sense* 108)

PERSON, CITIZEN: SOME CUES FROM A POETIC PRACTICE

WHEREIN THE CITIZEN IS DREAMED AS *O Cidadán*

A CALL

Thoughts assail me now. A fear our went assailment. Assail. Where harsh argument stands in for doubt.

INTRODUCTION

Part of my need to speak publicly about poetic practice is that it's rarely a constituent of academic discourses, which deal mostly with cultural <u>products</u> and their formation, not directly with the <u>practice</u> of language. This practice comes, sometimes, from quite different motivations and tensions than one might think. In this age many are rethinking and reinscribing notions of citizenship — as in relationships between private and public, self and other — along with relations in and of civic space. Similarly, issues in the world, in my own country and in my previous work (which is a response to "the limits of that world") prompt me to write in a "civic" realm, and to want to speak of that writing as it occurs, as the speaking and response will influence the writing itself. Besides, I like these "worldly" reverberations! Product, here, is not what is interesting.

In fact, I often speak of my work from *a formative moment* which is, at the time of my speaking, scarcely textual; it is a work that participates in numerous multiply saturated moments involving many issues of thought and circumstance as yet unresolved, and that have not yet resulted in a "work." As such, my speaking is not a territorialization but a localization without territory. My thoughts here in no sense cover a field.

A POETIC PRACTICE: SOME *FRAIL* CONSTITUENTS

Le pays même émigre et transporte ses frontières.
❙ Jacques Derrida, speaking of Paul Celan (*Schibboleth* 52)

The poem or book never starts with something to "communicate," with an agenda, but with a sort of will that drives me to constellate possible, troubling figurations. Yet my work's effect is often called political, is said to deal with people in society, to be vastly critical or demanding of those societies, to examine what might be called "frail relations."

Here I will *say* frail relations; to break language itself back to its constitutive measure, having nothing but language, for, like Jorge Semprún, I feel myself language's citizen. My manner is to work as if striking a word with another word to examine the frailty of one *touch* against another, discovering which one fractures, what sound is emitted, and what this emission evokes or hurtles forward. I don't know why it is, but I belong to this, belong to a constitutive measure and not to a result, or place, though even a constitutive measure is a territory, *un terroir, unha terra.* (Discourse cannot avoid making it so.)

In this, too, the organism holding the words plays its role, for to strike word upon word gives a shock to the body, to the ropes of its nerves that carry pulses and that are the brain's extension throughout the corpus which, though personal, is also the corpus, or touches the corpus, of the world. The world is co-extensional with it. There are fruitful tensions here for a writer. As Wittgenstein says: "The limits of my language mean the limits of my world" (5.6). And Derrida argues that poetry works beyond this: "Le poème parle au-delà du savoir" (*Schibboleth* 63). Beyond the limits of my world. And beyond the limits of my language. A limit, a border, also has another face, one that can't be understood by dialecticizing it as outside.

What world are we in, then? How do we make our belonging visible? *The four fingers of air contiguous with the fingers of the hand.*

My writing process, from the start, is a constellative progression outward and sideways (at times in vain), not dialectical for dialectics disallows too many other types of determination (and here, to me, "determinations" are also "frail relations," not always determinate). Along with Donna Haraway, Judith Butler, and others working from feminist discursive practices, I believe that both terms of dichotomies construct each other, and that the body's boundaries are socially constituted — that bodies are, as Haraway says, communication practices, coding devices. I've always felt that we as bodies are constituted as selves through our friends and companions, which is why loss provokes such bodily disruptions, and this even in animals like geese and ducks, as we find out reading Konrad Lorenz.

The alterations in the potential for human thought push me further: in this age, we as bodies, as coding devices, also extend over virtual spaces. Which is to say that, with computers and digital processing, any locality, including a body, is extensible over and through what we know as the old boundaries of physical space. Bodies can also extend into new parts: the resewn hand of the Frenchman to the Australian; the English worker's right fingers kept alive by sewing them into the inside left forearm while the mangled right arm healed. On a more macro level of the same phenomena, economic globalization and digitization of currencies are obviating national boundaries, not completely, but as we once knew them (though the infinitely absorptive US empire is curiously and dangerously a sort of exception to this). People like Canadian poet and critic Roy Miki start to speak of "localities" rather than territories; I like his term. Still, we undeniably inhabit and are coded by national territories; we are not just persons, we also form peoples. I am a Canadian, and Canadian. I am a Quebecker, by residence and affinity, and Albertan (not an Albertan) by origin and affect. I am also of the two Galicias, one Atlantic, one close to the Black Sea; of the southwest of Ireland, and of French, not the country but the language, for that emigration traversed, and began, in Vienna. My writing, too, is necessarily a product of successive emigrations, of leaking borders. Not a product of the fragment (which can be thought only if you believe in the illusory whole), but of the *essai*, the essay.

My poetic work is largely seen in mainstream English Canada as difficult and strange. It is both product and effect of a particular North American minority culture, that of Quebec. There, I am partly invisible for I write in a minority—but still hegemonic—language, English, though I work and communicate in French (but I work in French *because I know English*: I am a translator; my Englishness is in a language only, not a culture). As a product of the nineteenth- and twentieth-century waves of European emigration toward a new world, I am among those for whom nation and place are restless notions, moving, diasporic, virtual, troubling. We have been, and we come back. We are here, and not here. We bear, always, elsewheres. People find us because of these elsewheres. Above all, we make elsewheres for and within ourselves — undoing the our-ness of any belonging.

In the place where I live, Quebec, consideration of such notions of nation and belonging is part of the everyday social fabric. I live where there is always a civic rending, because nothing clear can be rendered. I choose to be somewhere, but I hardly can fix where this somewhere is. There is, as Lyotard might say, a clash between phrase regimes. In my head, I hear Wittgensteinian laughter, as if *the limits of my phrase regime are the limits of my world.*

So far this cascade has brought me not to answers but to doubt as a human mechanism that is not an opposite but a correlate of belief, a word hinged deeply with notions of the citizen, for what is the polis hinged on but belief? It brings me to the thought that to deal with the concept of the citizen is perhaps to articulate what I call "an interstice of harm." For to be near another is to risk harm: physical proximity increases the risk of harm. As persons, or as peoples, then, are we perhaps always already repositories of harm? Also integral to my search is a droll query that echoes a kind of queer laughter: *What if O Cidadán were a girl?*

MY WORKING PRACTICE: *les enjeux d'*O CIDADÁN

I want to address the idea or coalescence of senses of "civic space" and what it is for the individual to address or traverse this space
When are we not traversing the space
(for what makes us "individual" is having a relation of movement between us or our multiplicities, which produces civic space)

Noise in public space and the boundaries of signals
"Testing signals across the boundary of the person"
Signal to noise ratio

An idea of writing as a "productive capacity"
Not *random* but capable of movement in space and time
Moving because capable
Capable because moving
This strokes out "causality" or makes it an axis only, thus invisible
This a libidinal band or möbius

Engaging or thus disengaging that space or time
Creating a space of dis-en-gorge-ment

This too I would want to say is historical

What if O Cidadán were a girl?
Yes, responsibility, ardour, and grief are assemblages of the person
Assemblages or shimmers, *coalects*
But responsibility also assembles the person outward
Coalesces "the person" in social space
Toward the other, which as Lévinas says (as novelist Robert Majzels cited to me before I read him myself), precedes the person, for an other is necessary for the person to *be*
Where can the other, others, and self be in space
What is the space of the citizen

How can this be articulated in poetry's space, *pace* or *page* or *send*
Not disengaging from history but producing it in a different way

Wanting to return to a smoother lyric surface, yet unable
The lyric surface disturbed by word structures/strictures
I end up more with molecular surfaces: a sound, a particular combination of letters

Aa Bb Ce

A WORKING PRACTICE: ITS ANTECEDENTS

Whereas *Search Procedures* investigated what it is for a human being to be a person, *The Frame of a Book (A Frame of the Book)* explores the constitution of human responsibility: act and consequence, judgment and circumstance, ardour and grief, the mechanisms of all these forces and how they operate in the person, their sensory aggregate. Working the word as material, subject to abrasion, erasure; using non-narrative elements or lines to create a "scene" or "scenes" that are not revelatory, but that work/examine the figural not as representation but as designation of being's "frail relations," of the failure of designation itself. The failure of poetic tension as well, creating unworkable tensions, with insertion or arrival of what seems extraneous matter, disturbing cortical responsiveness by letting in cold elements of narration disconnected logically but which the brain can absorb in simultaneity, each element gashing or abrading the other, opening silence as a gesture, a silence that also opens language's possible gestures.

For me "the permeability of boundaries in the actual personal body" is a fact: much of selfness comes from contextualization with or through the other; the play between autonomy and other. And this permeability means that, for example, libidinal investments exceed what we call sex, so that sex and sexuality also exceed what we call sex, opening up a fraught admissibility that also beckons to be explored, and that also is textual.

And sex brings me to face responsibility, this force that helps to conjure a self exactly where its two avenues (that of *autonomy*, standing before the self, and that of *the other*, standing before those who precede one) play through and against each other.[1] In the face of this interplay, a reified notion of the body doesn't work, can't be maintained, and is already in transformation.

Where diverse forces of being are linked by proximity and permeability, not logic; where the receiver can alter the message; where knowing itself is no longer data in one's head—persons are locational and recombinatory devices, "search procedures." *Which is also a possible definition of poetry.* For me, everything in writing proceeds from a notion of responsibility that bears both personal and civic dimensions: it is the only way to confront the impossibility of poetry, to face the word *Auschwitz* and the contradictions that word gives rise to, for it does not belong to me, this word, and thus, it must needs belong to me. In any case, it shouts at me.

A WORKING PRACTICE: *O CIDADÁN* SO FAR

And Lyn quoted Shklovsky:
"the role of art is to kill pessimism."[2]

O Cidadán puzzles out in poetry some trajectories of what it is for a person (a human being-in-society) to be a citizen (standing not just in societal relation to the Other but in historical relation) in an age where virtual connections alter notions of physical place, and underlie as well a globalization of culture and economy. The old structures of the state as administration and normalization, woven in and through with notions of collectivity or belonging, are perhaps in the process of altering their reach and meaning. This process and alteration bring me to face notions of civil society and public life, two linked or overlapping areas that are ever more commercialized (more present and marked, with the new markings becoming convention in turn) and eroded (vanished) in our age.

I find continental Europe an extremely interesting example of a changing relationship to *citoyenneté*, as if "coming together" may not necessarily entail loss of localized identity, and these localizations may even be based on something that national states erase, have erased. From this, one starts to see that the notion of national state is problematic; when pressed or subjected to pressure, especially (for some reason) internal pressure, it breaks down into a "racial" issue, as in the former Yugoslavia; as in the treatment of Roma people everywhere, even in North America; as in many states such as Somalia and Rwanda that are colonially constructed. Elements of so-called historical entitlement enter into the picture. And historical and national entitlement (a notion warped and split by colonialisms) always seems to mean some people have to die or be denied full citizenship in the polity, denied use of their language, because of their origins. Faced with this, what use are "origins"?

What does the notion of territory mean, especially when we are virtually connected with other people, and territory or community itself can become virtual? Of course, vast numbers are not virtually connected, and although this is outside the scope of O *Cidadán*, these people haunt it, are its inverse, and also make it more urgent. What does emigration mean (too many things to enumerate here)?

What could it mean to be citizen when the state no longer

has absolute economic sovereignty, and cannot function either as a racial entity invoking "nation" (though it might try — we have some difficulty in Quebec over this, a difficulty that is useful and should not be underestimated, because the struggle out of it can engender the new idea or constellation or effect), in a world where even the cell's borders are porosities, and where, as Derrida says (talking of Paul Celan): "Le pays même émigre et transporte ses frontières" (*Schibboleth* 52).

The view of the citizen that emerges from this work is, then, minoritarian and problematized. In O *Cidadán*, the cidadán is a woman and lesbian, and not necessarily, or not only, "a cidadá," grammatically marked as female. And this citizen — who is all of us, because men too have to accept reversal of their gender markings — is not marginalized, for the poems beckon somewhere beyond the dialectic of centre/ margin, displacing that problematic formulation. They urge toward possibilities beyond reified notions of the body, for the bodily delineation of the individual also exists in *public* space, and our conceptions of this body and its extensionality affect the conceptions we are able to have of public life, and of the citizen, and thus of history. Yet when the body's boundaries are questioned, a view of the citizen as belonging perhaps becomes untenable, too passive a relation. My searches point, rather, toward the citizen as enactment.

What seems clear: notions in language that deviate from the hopes of deductive logic help formulate our universe. Contemporary philosophical notions are changing the way we view bodies, systems, and relationships, just as technologies are altering the way we can view spaces and place. New technologies, though they homogenize and americanize culture to some extent, also allow smaller entities to thrive because physical locality is temporarily, or temporally,

reconstituted.³ Languages and cultures, such as Galician/
Galego culture and language (to take an example that is
local to me), become accessible to more people and are not
necessarily tied to one physical territory: the whole notion of
diaspora is renewed as a different kind of formulation. When
space and the notion of boundaries are changing so rapidly,
they can't help but affect, reverberate, and reconstitute not
only the body's boundaries and those of the polis, of civic life,
but also those of that other space: the surface of the page.
They thus renew the ways we can possibly see the page and
its bookness, its use, its praxis, its in/af/finities.

Though we often forget it, there is nothing inhuman or
post-human in these changes: the brain is eminently equipped
to absorb and work with difference, with incompletion,
and with what are, at times, extremely disturbed semantic
valences, suppressing a little longer the firing of the analytical
frontal cortex, so as to elicit different semantic orders.⁴

To push these boundaries is, I believe, to take up a civic
responsibility, but also not to censor myself or accept old
notions of the self and body, or of language, in personal
relationships or in society. It is not a process of resistance,
of an "antiæsthetic," but one of productive openings toward
an *elsewhere*, beyond a dialectical norm — an *anti-anæsthetic*.⁵
Readings of Donna Haraway, Judith Butler, Elspeth Probyn,
Gilles Deleuze, Jean-François Lyotard, and Jean-Luc Nancy,
alongside Milton, St. Augustine, Kant, Spinoza, and
more contemporary writers who lived in problematic and
exiled relationship to their language communities such
as Paul Celan, Jorge Semprún, Franz Kafka, and Ludwig
Wittgenstein, along with Canadians such as Roy Miki,
Ashok Mathur, Hiromi Goto, Lisa Robertson, Norma Cole,
and Robert Majzels, and Americans such as Myung Mi Kim,

among others, serve as touchstones and reminders, and often as interlocutors, as the work proceeds.

O *Cidadán* examines notions of who we can be in community, and what a citizen can be, for perhaps a citizen, like a poet, is one who works through and against received forms. As Jean-Luc Nancy says, "The resistance to the unacceptable ought to proceed from another sense" (*The Sense of the World* 24). As I have worked toward that sense, the words of Spanish novelist Juan Goytisolo, from his memoirs, echo as companions: *La única moral del escritor, frente a la que no cabe recurso alguno, será devolver a la comunidad literario-lingüística a la que pertenece una escritura nueva y personal, distinta en todo caso de la que existía y recibió de ella en el momento de emprender su tarea* (*En los reinos* 112).

THE PUBLIC RELATION: REDEFINING CITIZENSHIP BY POETIC MEANS

I

My reflections here on the nature of citizenship, on its future, stem from thinking given me through poetry, most specifically through the three years I spent writing O *Cidadán*. It's a book whose title pulls a word from a minority, and perhaps "minor" language, into English. "Cidadán" is Galician. Yet when it crosses the border into Canadian English, we do recognize the word — particularly when we hear it — as a correlate of citizen. It is *other*, unknowable, nearly unlocatable, but also already part of us.

This "cidadán," this word, breathes against English words in the poems. In some way, it alters our perception of them, their sounds, senses, resonances. Loosens the hold of the usual, the expected. Has a gestural effect on the words near it, on what they can speak and on how the words *hear*. For words do *hear* the words beside them, and around them.

I won't detail the contents of the book here. Suffice it to say it is a philosophical, civic, troubled text that uses

English as a "minor" language (in the Deleuzian sense) invaded or traversed in many ways, most visibly by other tongues — Castilian, Galician, Latin, Portuguese, French.[1] A language made strange unto itself, it echoes the very origin of English as a texture of incursions, invasions, settlings that first coalesced out of a need for trade over borders in the north of England — not specifically a globalization but a blurring of edges, performed locally, by people at those edges. In writing O *Cidadán*, the movement of a single word, *cidadán*, disturbed the very form of poetry. It created gestures, complications, ruptures in the text, unnerved poetry, dissimulated philosophy, perpetuated filiations and unthreadings that led me to think — and listen to — the nation and the citizen in a different way.

All of which is meant to indicate *at the start* that my suppositions, my findings, were not arrived at through analytic means. Thereby, I have no proof of what I am about to relate. Yet this unleashes possibilities, kinds of rigour impossible in analysis alone. For analysis, in its desire for constancy, can fail to notice and read the movement of paradox.

II

If I had to sum up my findings, I would say that citizenship is a mode of enactment, not belonging. It is a way of comporting oneself locally. It is a public relation. It is sited, but not rooted in soil or in soil's versions, and its terms remain open to the possibility of movement beyond the "already constituted," remain open to *constitution* itself as an open act, an act of *co-situating*.

As Jean-Luc Nancy says: "the public relation — citizenship — constitutes the political as *sense to come*" (*Sense* 91–92). Thus it is not a fixed sense dependent on a past, a duty to an origin. Citizenship's meaning doesn't accrue through origins or essences. In fact, at times it can set a person outside localized familial relations constructed on site alone, or on a fixed promulgation of some past siting/citing as an identity for the future. Nancy continues: "consequently, [it is] also a sense unsubsumable under the signification of a 'State,' unless such state implies a multiplicity and plurivocality of relations" (92). Citizenship is something relational.

Therefore, citizenship is a comportment, not a status. A status is fixed; citizenship is movement. But it is not a heroic movement. Citizenship, funnily, is more like *reading*. Both are motions or acts that occur individually, yes, but within a density and proliferation of language use. Both citizenship and reading, like weak-signal communication, rise scarcely above the noise floor produced by the system itself and do not disjoin from that system. Rather, they enact a porosity, a differential — and different — relation of desire as it touches reality. I think people are compelled to reading by desire, by desires not fed by reality. As Fernando Pessoa put it: "Literature, like all forms of art, is the admission that life in itself is not enough" (*Fragments* 53; my translation).

Citizenship's acts, I think, have to do with a similar insufficiency and thus with a porosity, with the seeping of a desire that will not be constrained in its relation to the real. Desire? The real? Am I losing myself in abstractions? To introduce a phrase from Fernando Vallespín: an ailing nationalism can be cured only through the force of abstraction. And as Jean-François Malherbe wrote in Montréal's *Le Devoir* on Saturday, September 15, 2001: "Face à la violence, penser est toujours un devoir." *In the face of violence, thinking remains an obligation.*

III

To be a citizen in my sense, I realize, is to occupy a forbidden and problematic position. After all, the very porosity of such a citizen can have its dark side. *Une frontière comme telle ne peut distinguer entre le mal et le bien.* Additionally, to address the citizen as I do, as a woman invoking herself as O *Cidadán*, is to inaugurate a movement of and in a subjectivity, which belies an unregulated interior as well as a public exterior.[2] And aren't subjectivities reckless by nature? That "she" calls herself "cidadán" opens a *fenda* or breach in the hidden structure of the social world. But the breach, like any *fenda*, can be occupied only for a moment. Still, once we've crossed a border, we can't expect the border to remain the same. It is marked by our passage.

Movement across a border, then. All this talk about movement. But a nation, as commonly understood, is not about moving but about a collective *here*, in a *place*. What about "here"? How can a version of citizenship as enactment help identity — national identity — stay stabilized in a *place*, a *territory*?

Let's stop a moment.

What does territory mean — soil's sovereignty? Doesn't our capacity for delocalized being — computer transfer and relations, internet, satellite positioning, laser-treated retinas, off-site manipulations, robotics, prosthetics, networks — deafen static notions of soil, just as it deafens any reified notion of body? Doesn't "national identity" risk returning us to notions of a closed familial structure of origins, a basis for identity that mimics (in the end) the construct required to assure/secure stability for paternity?

With many others, I see contemporary nation-states as products of ruling elites in the nineteenth and twentieth centuries, carved out of once-imperial domains to suit the economic imperatives of these ruling elites. The nation-state, then, is a consequence of elitism and colonialism. As Benedict Anderson says, they are also a consequence of a changing conception of time, wherein the perceived movement of time itself came to rest in the present, no longer governed by a sovereign past projecting a future end of time. One paradigm of this end of time is the Christian notion of *parousia*; the close of the nineteenth century marked the withering of what I think is a religious view of time's fundament. Time was no longer seen constantly as messianic, erasing the present.

Of course, remnants of this religious view do persist today. Religious and patriotic groupings in many countries still try to return to the ancient concept of time as a past that "*omen*isces" a future, where an *infinite* is proclaimed as justice in one form or another, or is proclaimed as salvation. As a thousand-year Reich. Eternal Spain. Or as "democracy" that necessitates a "war on evil" while eliding "for the time being" the poverty of the southern hemisphere and the increasing economic inequalities everywhere.

Originary thinking—war on evil, eternal Name-your-Country, infinite justice—brings us closer, I think, to fascisms. It removes others from our conception of ourselves, flattens the paradox of the citizen as movement, and the troubled and transgressive relation of this citizen to borders.

IV

Happily, the citizen one finds through poetry exists without the infinite, at least insofar as a concept of the infinite means *omen*iscing time. Poetry's citizen is the finite standing in its stead, extended outward and made possible only by the face-to-face gaze and encounter with the other. Not incorporative or denying or tolerating but an encounter that one might say exists in the frankness of an *écoute* (and here I use the French word in English for it is a listening but a listening "made strange" in some way), situated purely in a present, and thus is finite in the sense that it is ever "just occurring now."

The citizen is the one, in this view, who makes a border exist by inviting someone's crossing, while leaving the very terms of the encounter open to an *écoute*.

As an *écoute*, citizenship requires language. The citizen's encounter is in some way linguistic. Yet this encounter, this language, is not rooted in an origin or in an incorporative gesture but imbued with the movement of what I have called, in O *Cidadán*, the "not-yet." A kind of open predication. As in what Hélène Cixous calls, talking of Clarice Lispector, an "aproximação," wherein touch and meeting do not appropriate or domesticate but co-occur in the space of an encounter.[3] A zone overlap.

What, then, does this do for national territory, for the concept of a citizen as being rooted in a place, with a subject-relation to place?

It is as if site or country itself were performative or gestural, having more to do with languages than with soil (though languages can name a soil, at least *de façon provisoire*).

To nurture languages is to create localization not in soil but in events, for it is, strangely, events that *enact* localities. No site can pre-exist some event's *act*. And acts are relational, permeable. The *becoming-space* of a language or gesture, its localization, necessarily occurs in relation to *autrui*, to other as a radical and plural outside. I, facing you, whom I do not know, admit that *you* have some prior claim on me, one that precedes and enables the creation of my *self*. (Yes, this echoes Emmanuel Lévinas.)

And one of us can never be subsumed in the other, colonized, explained. Our relationship is gestural. Genuflectual. Proximal. The paradox of the construction of the self (which is, as Judith Butler says, performative) is a microcosm of the paradox of the construction of nation, of *nacionalidade*. That *écoute*. A place where porosities are possible, yet enacted locally. For it is in enactment that local becomes apparent and can be built on, opened, spaced.

V

How to reconcile this citizen with the problem, as Robert Majzels says, of "geographically defined nations that are oppressed, colonized, under imperialist domination, who have had recourse to national discourse in resistance to a/the foreign aggressor"?[4]

In fact, this *cidadán*, this *écoute*, this breaching, respects the right of self-determination (the right to determine the borders of one's government); it just adds to this the paradox (perhaps) that a nation's being demands leaky borders and cannot be based on purities. In the past, yes, nationalisms have often found fuel in purity and origins, but the problem with origins is that they lead to fascisms, damages, exclusions. In this era in which states are being subsumed by movements of capital beyond local control, we need new ways of defining and settling localities and nations, or the remote machinations of capital will be what regulate our public relation. And these new ways must accept and welcome the movement of peoples. Our very subjectivity requires this.

The old nationalisms of peoples may be still associated with hope and identity but, unless they are open, they risk too easily becoming monolithic echoes of the very supranational essences constructed by central states which they wish to contraindicate and defer. Better to have a nationalism that is locally based, and that bears upon languages, gestures, and events, yet admits the outsider to the soil and listens: one that says, as did the revered Galician nationalist Castelao in 1937, for example, talking about the black Cuban servant who emigrated to Galicia: *aquel negro era galego* (19). "Welcoming the other to the native, so well-loved soil," says Lévinas through Derrida, "may just be the test of being human" (*Adieu* 134; my translation).

This welcome, this nationalism, for me, operates in the field of "aproximação," of the "not-yet."

In Quebec now, where the national project in its traditional formulation has been largely *fracassé* for various reasons, there were glad indications of such openings in the 2001 report on the state of the French language, the *états-généraux*, which called for a Quebec citizenship (regardless of the fact that we are still bound in a state called Canada), a citizenship that acknowledges shared place and those gestures particular to a siting, gestures which create the site. Also, the report states, "English, the Amerindian languages, and Inuktitut must each have their place in the life and life-space of Quebec since they are essential components of Quebeckers' cultural and linguistic heritage."[5] Here, for the first time, there was an opening (not without its dangers) to a language once staved off, necessarily, as hegemonic and colonizing, yet now an acknowledged part of our gestures. Our encompassing. And our *écoute*. English, in this reading, was not a constitutional obligation and not a hegemonic manoeuvre, but part of a siting of a plural, French, *quebequidade*.

At the same time in Quebec, unfortunately, evidence still emerges from time to time of a hard nationalism of origins that views the exertion of the rights of others — any space of open encounter — as a collective privation.[6] It falls into a Hobbesian trap, believing that the collective individuality of a people merely suffers the presence of others, who can but impinge on the collective. This won't work to bring about independence and self-determination, because it won't let anyone move across the borders. And with no movement, as we have seen, there is no "here."

Creo eu que, nun movemento paradoxal, exceder as fronteiras, atravesar fronteiras sen as eclipsar, as fronteiras dos países e as dos idiomas (e as das mentes) é urxente para defender as culturas locais. Si é paradoxal, pero (eu creo) cómpre os paradoxos no noso tempo. Creo que sen a poesía non podemos pensar nestes movementos paradoxais. A análise e a lóxica déixannos moi lonxe do paradoxo. Suavizar os paradoxos é, en fin, cegarse.[7]

As Galician novelist Manuel Rivas's character Dr. Daniel Da Barca says in O lapis do carpinteiro, "O unico bo que teñen as fronteiras son os pasos clandestinos… As fronteiras de verdade son aquelas que manteñen aos pobres apartados do pastel" (13). In my translation: *The only good thing about borders is the clandestine passages… The real borders are those that hold the poor back from [sharing in] the pie.*

THE EX*H*ORBITANT BODY: TRANSLATION AS PERFORMANCE

A practice of reading is always embodied. A translation always translates a reading practice enacted on a text, not simply "an original text." And reading practices are codifications/decodifications that are historically and culturally determined. Given all this, a work, in the course of translation, provokes inscription of the reader/translator's embodiment (as a site of cultural production but also of resistances — to normative sexual definitions, to contemporary notions of urban life, etc.) into the translated text, whether or not this is acknowledged.

*G*iven Fernando Pessoa with his heteronyms and their exorbitant subjectivity, it is not strange that the translator/reader Erin Mouré, facing Alberto Caeiro's *O Guardador de Rebanhos*, was compelled to become Eirin Moure, a performative and ex*h*orbitant body announcing a textual inscription she calls a trans*e*lation.

What we love best in poetry comes simply from sound. And sound is critical in translation. *Alba/alma. Sol/soa.* How to make these sonal connectivities in English? Nancy Huston says that "l'écoute d'une étrangère (est) attentive plus qu'un natif aux frottements et aux coïncidences sonores. (Dans le titre de ma nouvelle 'Histoire en amibe,' entendez-vous 'Histoire en abîme'?)" (*Nord perdu* 45).

Frottements et coïncidences sonores — poetry plays exactly on these echoes, and they are the source of the tensions and tensilities in the poem.[1] Some of these sound effects are deeply rooted in the origin of the language and are not translatable or even ever translated, but are often, too often, erased in translation. Conventional translation has, it seems, as its primary (and mostly unspoken) goal, to fulfill "fluent" criteria that make the work sit comfortably in its new language, that is, without provoking disturbances in, or revealing the rough edges of, the target language.[2] The goal is not necessarily to render the work itself — for there is no "work itself," only a set of signs and a conjunction of reading practices — but to make it appear smoothly in English. Yet out of sheer contrariness, attempts to translate from foreign languages often uncover aspects of the target language that are *strange* or hesitant in capacity; this unveiling is, *bien sûr*, one of the great beauties of translating. Erasing it is a practice I disagree with.

To translate poetry, especially poetry that deals with exorbitant language effects in its own tongue, requires other translation strategies. Because the creation of such strategies is not favoured currently, poetry that can't be handled through fluent translation techniques is very rarely translated. This gives readers of poetry in English a pretty weird view of world poetry, and provides disproportionate support to one kind of poetry in our own language too: usually that poetry centred on a settled "I" that speaks the poem.[3] But there *are* other poetries, and translational approaches can be created to bring them to readers of English. Given the general translation context (so few books translated into English, and only those easy to translate), these works are harder to find, and the approaches are sometimes not even identified as translation practices.[4] For example, I've been accused with *Sheep's Vigil* of having created a "false translation."

Yet even the accusation describes the work as a translation. It is obliged to, even if it does not willingly believe it is a translation. Talk about begging the question!

Let's look further at sounds and *frottements*; they necessarily occur through a body, for the body is sound's instrument. It is the voice's instrument, in particular. The voice is felt in and mediated by the body, which is not yet an "I" (nor is it ever solely an "I," a speaking Ego) and is not an isolated organism. It is a Deleuzian body without organs, perhaps, or an organ that hallucinates its body, perhaps.

Because it involves the body, it is clear to me that translation, and particularly translation of poetry, is a performative gesture, a performance. It is a set of performative gestures implicating the body, performance because the translator does not enact her body as her own but uses her body to perform "the author." Or what we, as audience, tend unthinkingly to believe is the author: when you read reviews of translated poetry, for example, it is often as if — to be cinematic about it — the nuances of the Joker in the movie *The Dark Knight* were described without mentioning Heath Ledger, or Mankiewicz's *Cleopatra* were discussed with nary a notice of Elizabeth Taylor.

PART 2: SUBJECTIVITY

Fernando Pessoa, who created multiple characters called heteronyms who wrote poetry, is not, as some have claimed, a precursor of postmodern fragmentation of identity: Pessoa *loved* identity positions.[5] His particularity was that he didn't make a primary and irrevocable association between a single identity structure and *self*. With his heteronyms, Pessoa insisted on a plurality of the self, seeing the self as a mirror or performance of a plural universe. "Sê plural, como o universo!" (*Aforismos* 15)

Pessoa believed in excessive subjectivity, and his heteronyms invoked and provoked subjectivity's excess. These subjectivities could not be said to be "the self" in normative speech and, thus, occur or appear to occur outside the self. They are "the third body," the body as dis/resolving projectile: neither Pessoa, nor real characters separate from Pessoa, but something else. They echo Homi Bhabha's "hybrids"[6] and are always propulsive.

The fun part of translating Pessoa, and the origin of my strategy for translating his heteronym Alberto Caeiro, is that I realized, once I was aware that I was translating the work (for at first I was just playing), that *I* was one more of those propulsive bodies, outside Pessoa and yet "caused" by him, by his work, by Caeiro.

As a body, I am, of course, in and of a place; I am sited. "I," even if not "complete," physically exist *some*where. Or some *properties* of "I" "eu" do. Translating Pessoa's poetry had the effect of heightening my own corporeal sensations of sitedness in certain ways; one of these was to make evident my perceptual connection with my closest corporeal buddy, my cat Emma, who, unlike me, liked Toronto and all there was to see. Caeiro's language of direct perceptual habitation of space drew my attention to how Emma was seeing out the window.[7] She was drawn to the wild things in the environment: sticks, leaves, bits of garbage, birds, insects, other cats, small movements in and through not spaces, merely, but "volumes." Cats are architects, sculptors; they can integrate the dimensionality of space — volume — with time. They seem to use volumes as ways to organize space, instead of distances between objects. Elements like buildings, towers, stock exchanges, road networks, all so important to our human perception of environment, just don't exist on the cat's radar. They are screens, surfaces only; Emma didn't use them to map out where she lived. She used the sky and the way sky touches a leaf, for example, a leaf that moves over the ground, connecting it to the sky which was not empty space but a fullness.

    Through Pessoa and Emma, I began to inhabit Toronto differently, to be in accord with it as creeks, trees, scrub, air, sounds, and movements. My own corporeal sitedness inflected my translation of Caeiro/Pessoa, and is visible in the English version. Rural Toronto appears there instead of rural Portugal, and my sitedness let me as "I"-Ego become a Pessoan, or even Caeiroist (second-generation) heteronym, appearing in the work itself. It is as if what Pessoa had projected into Alberto Caeiro had then provoked an excessive subjectivity, an Eirin, an excessive habitation, in and of me.

    This process, of course, made my translation "false" to some, while it is still irrevocably a translation. It doesn't adhere to a fluent notion of translation, but to an exorbitance. Exorbit happenstance. Exstance. Extantiation. A performative gesture altering space, altering the original, and altering my own voice and capacity in English. All of which is, I think, the best that translation can do.

SUBJECTIVITIES: AN APPROACH THROUGH CLARICE AND FERNANDO

IN MEMORY OF "THE LITTLE SMALL"

I SOME FIRST NOTIONS: THINKING SUBJECTIVITY

Work is a tendency toward *gesture*. Work here being not "finished product" but the verb of work. I say "verb" rather than "act." I could also say: *Work multiplies gestures.*[1]

Linking "work" and "gesture" is one way I can start to speak about both translation and subjectivities — the positioning of an être as subject both in — and of — a writer's *work* (verb). Although an être is a subject partly because of interpellation from outside its own structure, interpellation is also work, a work, *work as verb*. Witness Judith Butler: "The act [hailing someone] 'works' in part because of the citational dimension of the speech act, the historicity of convention that exceeds and enables the moment of its enunciation" (*Psychic Life of Power* 33). Perhaps it is this historicity that gives us an emotional response to being interpellated, which can make our interpellation rise up in memory as if it had emanated from *inside*. (I hear Lyotard here as well: reversals of outside and inside are libidinal turns.)

Perhaps, in thinking subjectivity as involving the verb of *work*, we can look further, at how work's gestures leave open a space of approach, a spacing, neither outside nor inside the organism. We can look at how his idea of "approach," which I've taken from Hélène Cixous' writing on Brazilian writer Clarice Lispector, or *aproximação*, might work: to approach something is to give it room and listen. It is not to define or *superar* a boundary.[2] *Approach* versus *encroach* or *reproach* (so many echoes here).

This idea of approach can apply as well to Fernando Pessoa's multiplications of identity, and thus fuel an alternate conception and notion of subjectivity: as approach.

Further, approach has a relation with both space and time, a relation that is elongated. It is as if the pull and orbit of bodies were altered, and as if this alteration of pull and orbit moved, simultaneously or concomitantly, both historicity and citation from their old settled rigging. Perhaps. Cixous, speaking of Lispector, brings in ideas of receptivity and giving, of their libidinal workings or relation: "Clarice dá o(s) tempo(s). Ela é unha receptividade que se dá. Torna possível o dar-receber" (23).[3] Here, subjectivity also holds the notion of a receptiveness that gives. Not subjectivity as product, but as gesture. Multiplied. *Gues*ture. *Gif*ture. Listening and gift.

‖ FERNANDO PESSOA

I now let go Clarice's hand to take up Fernando's. Fernando Pessoa is known as Portugal's greatest modernist poet, but to me he is not simply modernist. He's more than that, which doesn't mean he is a postmodernist as such; he deals not with the fragmentation of identity and subject positioning, but with the amplification of identity, *grâce à la fébrilité de la constructivité du sujet* (febrility: again, that *guest*ure). He is allied not with the death of great narratives but with their reiteration, positing them "as such" against and upon one another, not deconstructing the narratives but excessively constructing them. It is not a post-postmodernism either but a lateral flow, one that lays bare the constructedness of identity but does not lament it. Instead, it uses this very constructedness to multiply and amplify the platforms on which identity is produced and on which it takes place. Thus engendering, yes, gestures — sutures, gusts, *ur*-gests, jests — between those platforms.

Pessoa, in short, does not reject stable identity or subjectivity but rather embraces it *excessively* in his heteronyms. He cannot rest with the wizened act of stabilizing a single subject position. His excess of foment and embrace crosses borders, situates the être firmly while re-situating it at the same time.[4] He does not create impediments or fractures or fragments, but interstices: multiple clarities that rub against one another, flow laterally to touch and alter, cross membranes, *se busculent*, resulting in a rubbed identity that has clarities and certainties in the middle but which also transverses/transfelicitates boundaries, sets up boundaries that seem firm then alter, shift.[5] Without necessarily blurring. This is subjectivity as a gestural practice, where movements across a plane shift the very edges of it and cross boundaries without necessarily, or always, touching them. And without (either) leaving boundaries behind.

Pessoa's structures and his positioning of his own heterogeneous work (movement), both in themselves and in their relation to societal structures, have not yet, to my mind, elicited adequate critical analysis. They have, however, prompted a book *pathologizing* Pessoa (as a paranoid schizophrenic) from society's viewpoint instead of — more usefully — pathologizing *society* from the viewpoint of Pessoa's own explorations.⁶ The latter trajectory would have pathologized the notion of the unitary subject instead of assuming it as originary. Why is it we-as-socius always seem to domesticate writers and artists (at times scientists too, yes Galileo), using our fixed assumptions to accuse their work of arrhythmia, while leaving society in a settled place? *O Caso Clínico de Fernando Pessoa* seems almost laughable except as a symptom of this anxiety syndrome so very active in contemporary society: the book assumes a prior notion of a stable subject position and does not admit that this base is first a convention, and that it might not even be the base from which Pessoa was working. Somehow, I think that an analysis of Pessoa in terms of gesture would be productive, for it would reveal how gesture can in fact be its own core, a *flow* and not — as first might seem — merely a dispersion. An erring or airing.

III   MEETING ALBERTO CAEIRO AND BECOMING *Eirin*

Translating the poems of Alberto Caeiro was my way of attempting a translational process that stays true to the multiplication of gestures that is *work* in Pessoa. Normative fluent translation was not my aim; there are already many excellent normative translations of the work. In positing or entering the multiple movements of subject spaces, my translation was able to absorb and project movement. It's the movement in Pessoa that called upon my listening; I wanted to transmit it in English because it exhilarates me.

In the process, I began to see myself "constructed" as Eirin, the old Galician version of my first name. A writer's *work*, as I said, multiplies gestures!

What could it mean that one of the gestures of my translating Pessoa/Caeiro acted to construct my name as Galician? Does this act not impinge upon space occupied by those who are Galician by birth? I argued in *O Cidadán* that even notions of birth and soil are conflations, are constructs, and that anything beyond the village — *aldea* — or valley is a construct (and that writers today start to return to notions of locality and the local, dismantling and circumventing the *nacionalismo do Estado* that stifles all). In my translation, though, I did not intend to impinge upon or occupy a space but to perturb one, in order to call all siting into question and make visible the gestures between sites. Perhaps here, as well, to perturb is also to love. The notion of constructing myself (hmmph! what self! dissolving here into impish laughter) as Galician in name allows me a point from which to precipitate myself forward. It is a disturbance, not a fixed identity, a kind of heteronym provoked by Pessoa.

There are examples in history of such wizardry: one does not *have* to be hailed for an interpellation to occur. Because the convention of hailing/interpellation exceeds individual subjects, one can "turn" and act *as if* interpellated. All without (curiously) entirely giving up the position one had prior to this "as if." As such, the mechanisms of subject construction can be used "independently" of "verification" to produce subjects! There's lots here still to explore, but to me it means there is perhaps a way in which I can occupy a Galician name, however temporarily. *Fingir* = *mudar*.[7] It is, I think, the kind of act that makes such a subject position, "Galician," ever more possible — for I believe that positions as citizen/nation/people are ultimately untenable if they cannot be entered from outside.

IV THE TRANSeLATION

While translating Pessoa's work as movement or gesture, I was also mulling over Roy Miki's writings on racialization and his descriptions of how contextualization produces race in ways that people then act inside of, or out of. Miki talks of how a certain racialized construct of persons, Canadian descendants of Japanese immigrants in Canada, can be Canadian/alien/citizen/correct/incorrect/redressed/multicultural, depending on context. Further, he points out that all these are fraught constructs emanating from "outside," for they exist in a power relation with a centre or state not directly acknowledged or exhibited. Finally, when the constructed persons aim to tip or refuse the power relation (like the Nissei group who, during the war, fought the authorities' definition of internment as valid procedure, and fought the way expulsion was given a public, white-washed reading as evacuation), they are punished harshly (in the Nissei case, with more severe camps).

If racialization can be seen as a construct of contiguity with an unspoken and legislative "outside," then perhaps I can be Galician (slipping) in transelating Pessoa. How so? The person I "insert" into my translating gesture is/can be seen as one that Pessoa's text itself constructs as a *supplement* to my (or any) gesture of attentiveness to his work. It's a double reversal, a Lyotardian libidinal band. And it brings me back to the idea of *aproximação* — approximation, approach — in Lispector. Approach is a gesture of reception of the text *as it is* but this *as it is* is always *affected*, that is, touched by *my* affect, my siting as translator, as well as my intellect. It produces or engenders, then, a proximal space, which cannot and should not be closed, ignored. Fluent translation would close or ignore it, but this is my very argument with fluent translation!

As Lawrence Venuti would say, it domesticates the text.

When Pessoa/Caeiro, who speaks the poems of O *Guardador*, emerges in *Sheep's Vigil* as a woman in early twenty-first-century Toronto — "we'll call her Eirin" — when he/she enters the grand metropolis of a Canadian state produced by colonizations, a metropolis at the centre of a process of urbanization of a rural nation, she is a woman who still has a child's sense of the rumpled wildness of the world. Each Pessoa line provokes an Eirin line, and sometimes the Eirin line provokes a further line, an ex*h*orbitance of gesture, a multiplication of Pessoan *effect*, and *affect*. As a translator, I just let the process of excess operate, freely but with attention:

> Aquela senhora tem um piano
> Que é agradável mas não é o correr dos rios
> Nem o murmúrio que as árvores fazem...
>
> Para que é preciso ter um piano?
> O melhor é ter ouvidos
> E amar a Natureza.   (2001, 40)
> --
> Some woman out there has a piano
> It's pleasant but can't match the current of rivers
> Can't beat the murmurs composed by the trees
>
> Why would anyone have a piano?
> What if you want to play a show tune no one likes?
> If you have ears at all
> you can go outside instead and lie in the lawn,
> the dirty grey cat will come to visit
> and be scared of you,
> and you can go to the manhole cover and hear the creek run.
> (41)[8]

V PARA DESPEDIRME [9]

Since I translated Caeiro, time has gone by so quickly. My cat Emma, who was with me as I translated and worked in Toronto (it was she, really, *a miña mestra*, my master), is dead. As for me, sometimes I wake up thrown violently backward into the year 2000. I am in Toronto again, where I worked on my transelation. Rain lashes against a cedar, its branches lash against a single window pane on Winnett Avenue. The cat is running up the stairs and is streaked with sunlight. Other times I am on a Portuguese *outeiro* or hill in Ribatejo, home of Caeiro, home of José Saramago too. My birthdate is April 16 or 17. Alberto or Erin: both words contain my nickname: *Er*. Alberto is almost Alberta, where I was born.

Sheep's Vigil is not a simple book after all but a confrontation through translatory methods (always acknowledged as tools, not as communicative structures: as transelations or translucinations in my practice) with subjectivities and the possibility of subject positions.[10] I translate a man into a woman. A century into another. Urban and rural are conflated.

Creeks are carried in buckets on women's heads.

Subjectivity is a notion that does not hold water.

Just as creeks themselves are passages. What is a creek? When you see it today, you are already seeing different water than I saw this morning... just as the rain that falls is never the same rain.[11]

FIDELITY WAS NEVER
MY AIM (BUT FELICITY)

▌ Although I earn my living as a commercial translator, my experience of translating Fernando Pessoa is different and can't be separated from my experience as a poet.[1] Writing poetry is its closest correlate — not the process of reproducing one text in another language. Like the act of writing poetry, translating Pessoa involves a process of listening to text or world and responding to it with words, unafraid of contradiction or paradox, unafraid of the incommensurate. Fluency be damned! On the other hand, commercial translation is always fluent. While its aim is to secure a reproduction, it is also focused on securing a voice that *appears at home* in the target culture, one that *appears to emanate from* the target culture with no taint of foreignness. In a curious turn, the faithful translation is as much about dissembling as it is about fidelity. These considerations aside, however, my principal reaction to language is as a poet — to make language leap, to cherish the sounds of words — and my first reasons for opening my life to new languages have always been to read poetry in the original: *García Lorca, Pessoa, the cantigas.*

When I opened up a bilingual (Portuguese/US English) edition of *O Guardador de Rebanhos* in Toronto at the end of the cold February of 2000, I didn't intend to translate it.[2] I was already familiar with many of the poems in American and British translations, but I had never read the whole sequence.[3] Yet when I opened the book, what startled and elated me was the Portuguese. I'd only expected to view the original language as markings, as *traits*, but because of my studies of Galician, I could read it.[4] It was a sudden, unexpected gift. Felicity! To suddenly know a language!

I read on in Portuguese, and read a book that I'd not known before. In English it was old-fashioned, even a bit stilted; in Portuguese it was wry, funny, the language simple but slightly bent, slightly country-bumpkin gone uptown. Caeiro was giving us his philosophy, but he was also having fun, dissimulating, and goading his fellow poets, de Campos and Reis. Wow!

The first lines I translated were from the middle of poem XIX, for after reading the book, I'd open it randomly to enjoy the pieces again, and on opening to poem XIX I felt compelled to make English words just to deepen the pleasure in my reading. I read:

> Lembra-me a voz da criada velha
> Contando-me contos de fadas. (56)

In my Canadian English correlate, this burst out with a tone of one resisting both her own upbringing and the strange and incalcitrant city in which I was living. What made me laugh as I wrote was that it contained a word that couldn't possibly be Pessoa's. Already my translation was preposterous, excessive:

> Sometimes I think of all the babysitters
> who told me lies. (57)

Those babysitters were followed by a further excess, an admonishment of such babysitters, in a line with no equivalent in the Pessoa text but playing off the word "fadas":[5]

> As if they knew fate!

This first outburst gave me a guiding principle: to make a leap where Pessoa couldn't have leapt, in order to articulate better what he was saying. I worked within a framework of my own readerly response that pulled into the translation not just the semantic level of the Caeiro text but also the chance or hazardous appearance of words provoked in me by the sound of Portuguese.[6] This totality (if one can say that) was what I translated. After pondering my first outburst further, I noted two more guiding principles. First, the idiom in the target language had to be resolutely Canadian but also a little old-fashioned, a little quaint from a twenty-first-century perspective (as Caeiro's Portuguese, it is said, was a little curious and simple as well). Second, the excessive or exorbitant gesture was permitted.

After I'd translated five poems or so, chosen at random, working slowly so as not to lose my readerly relationship with the lines, I realized that Pessoa had entered Toronto.[7] I read the poems over the phone to my girlfriend in England who laughed and said, *That's not Pessoa, that's you.* Of course, I objected. I'm a translator; I transmit the texts of others!

Yet her words made me realize quickly that Pessoa (his words, my only access to Pessoa) was having an effect on me that *altered me* as an addressee (a reader) and as an actor-upon-a-text (a translator). Pessoa's multiplication of consciousnesses in his creation of heteronyms, his exorbitant subjectivity as I have called it, and Alberto Caeiro's phenomenalism of presence and touchability, entered me.

I could not remain who I was, Erin, and continue. Long before my coming to the text, the author — Alberto Caeiro — was already false, a representation. He was already an Eirin. Now I had to answer to the Pessoan propulsion of the Caeiroist text, and not just to the text, and this altered "me." Mine was a performative, gestural experience, expanding — for my own pleasure at first, and as an extension of the act of reading — the circle of ordinary translatory effects to embody a Pessoan subjectivity as multiply sited, declamatory, proximal, refractive.

Still in Toronto, I realized I had to translate the whole book quickly, before I left for my home in Montreal and lost my particular and replete loneliness, my readerly elation: the siting that had driven the first pages of my translation. So I saw no one, buckled down, and worked as Erin's Eirin to bear Pessoa's rural Caeiro into Toronto, into its suburbs of the 1950s built over creeks and ravines, an undulated landscape that buried all water underground, to be heard only in manholes, deep under:

> I realized Pessoa had entered Toronto, living a pastoral life in Toronto's not-quite-vanished original topographies. In me, there appeared my master. Finally I could feel joy. I found Taddle Creek in Wychwood Park. Then I found the creek that crosses Winnett Avenue just below where I lived. After I found the creeks, I lived alongside them.
>
> And Alberto Caeiro came with me.
>
> ... I translated Pessoa by responding to him as a person. I, a person, and Pessoa, a person. For in Portuguese, *pessoa* is person. I just read the Pessoan

poem line, then wrote my line, or read a few lines,
then wrote mine. It was abrupt, direct, total.

At the same time, I couldn't write too many at
once. It set my heart murmur going. Besides, I
was afraid of responding to the context of what
I'd already done, and I wanted to respond only
to the Pessoa lines, using the context of my own
corporeal position in the world of mid-town
Toronto north of Vaughan Road. In just over a
week I'd translated some 30 of the 49 poems, in
a sort of ecstasy. It was a form of prayer I lit each
day, a vigil candle. (Pessoa, *Sheep's Vigil* VIII)

My translation was a way of bringing Pessoa into a Canadian
arena, into a present still tinged with an archaic past: the
1950s and the alteration of a still largely rural Canadian
society into an urban one. I just needed to find the current
of the river, the Canadian phrase equivalent to the *gestural*
value of the Pessoan phrase. Transmitting the exact meaning
would have distorted the joy and movement I found in Pessoa,
which were essential to the pleasure of reading. I wanted to
build a structure with the same weight and weight's relation
as the Pessoan text. I was also responding to Pessoa's gestures,
his sensitivity to how *la subjection débordent les frontières de
la personne* (I have to overflow the borders of English, into
French) as individually constituted. Translating was a gesture
of excess *person*, of what exceeds the person. Perhaps language
itself is always a gesture of excess, for language's vibrations
exceed boundaries. I worked as though there was no border
between "myself" and Pessoa, as if limits were smudged by
excessive movement, exorbitant tracing, as if translation were
the performance of an exhorbitant body.

In places, this expansiveness was obliged to exceed all semantic sense; the person is truly *fervente*,[8] as in the last line in the long poem numbered V, where

> E ando com ele a toda a hora (18)

became, unbeckoned, a translation of Pessoa's God (ele) into my own:

> And go with God, on Winnett or Vaughan
> Road, or down Winona to No Frills, where
> Garrison Creek is, heading southward to
> the Lake and America and the ocean and
> the Lakehead and the whales and Gibraltar
> and my heartbeat, fraying, and the high
> towers of Chicago, and the road southeast to
> Albany, the graveyards where the workers lay
> and Coaticook where I taught once, and my
> heartbeat, fraying, and the emigrants from
> Poland, and *I love you*, and Niagara Falls. (19)

Fidelity in the sense of reproduction was never my aim. I had the urge to be resolutely true to the gesture and movement of the Pessoan text, to the humour in it, and to Caeiro's philosophy. The use of fluent tactics to reproduce the text in English wouldn't have helped me; they would have created an archaic-sounding result — bland, remote, not-present.

But what justifies an exorbitant translation in the face of the fact that there are already normal translations of Caeiro and that more are possible? Is *Sheep's Vigil* really translation?

While every written work seems unique and settled, and thus a fit object for translation, texts continue to shift as their cultural context shifts. And shift it does —!! — just ask successive generations of readers.[9] Place, time. Ah. And this alters and augments a given work's translational possibilities, which are always already multiple, even in English, which is not one language, but several closely related ones. Given this, my Caeiro is constructed as translation (printed with bilingual facing pages, etc.) while acknowledging its difference in the word "transelation."

Nevertheless it is a translation, for it has the structure of the prior text and could not have been created without it. The prior text was its impetus but did not impede it or offer it a closed door; rather, this prior text accelerated, encouraged the translatory work, even to the point of altering its translator. And such shifts (amazing!) are among translation's openings, even if they are seldom lauded, or even acknowledged.

TRANSLATION AS ABSENCE, BOOKENDED AS GIFT

▌ It so rarely happens that languages other than French and English are present in public life in Canada; thus one of the pleasures in publishing *Sheep's Vigil by a Fervent Person* was seeing a Canadian book include Portuguese. It was a pleasure only slightly diminished by the fact that Pessoa's name was originally left off the cover and title page by the Canadian publisher.[1] Public culture can be mind-boggling at times! This absence leads me to ponder translation and translation practices in Canada.

    I might start by saying that talk of a Canadian context for a translation, for reception of a literary text from a foreign language, is not common here, and the work of translating foreign literatures — other than Quebec or Canadian French into Canadian English, or vice versa — scarcely exists publicly in Canada. When translation does occur, particularly in English, the resulting works are rarely published inside the country, or are published precariously, with no funding assistance from arts councils. Even more rarely are they inscribed publicly as a translation practice.

Because of this, the translator is not a natural person to us, is not one of us — is occluded or must emigrate, is not entitled to funding. As if to translate foreigners is unCanadian. And perhaps it is, for the translator calls into question our purest, most originary beliefs (which we would call non-beliefs, for we don't even know we have them) about our own language and expression in that language, and about ourselves as citizen-members of a state. Were the state to support translation from other languages, we Canadians might end up confronted with some hard questions about who we are.

A state! There's the crux of it. In the Canadian state, to accept translation from languages other than French and English would put our founding myths at risk of foundering in some way. In our arts councils, funding limitations for translation don't exist for the sake of the promotion of Canadian literature,[2] but to maintain a certain figuration of the state, of Canadian nationhood or, in Quebec, of Quebec nationhood.[3] This figuration in English Canada is structured on the veneer (very attractive, at that, but building a structure on a veneer doesn't ensure stability) of conviviality and equality between French and English (which aren't at all equal), and thus other languages need to be shut out as less, as non-Canadian.

But there are still those of us who, unCanadian and unQuebecois, move between more languages than the nationally accepted ones. Knowing another language, and a third language after that, has altered us, and continues to alter us. As Nancy Huston says in her collection of articles from *Le Monde*, *Nord perdu*, "L'acquisition d'une deuxième langue annule le caractère 'naturel' de la langue d'origine — et à partir de là, plus rien n'est donné d'office, ni dans une ni dans l'autre; plus rien ne vous appartient d'origine, de droit et d'évidence" (43). In my translation: "The acquisition of a second language nullifies the 'natural' aspect of the original language — and from then on nothing comes as a matter of course any more, not in one language or the other; nothing belongs to you originally, legitimately, or without further ado." Precisely because of this effect, translation enriches, challenges, and finally alters possibilities in the target language. Writers who read in foreign languages and try translations — and there are many — do bring this influence indirectly into our English language, but when the work is not published locally or supported, the influence on the language is minimal. In other countries, translation into one's own language is considered essential for survival of local idioms and culture. Our Canadian idiom — and there once was one that I grew up with, that was recognizably Canadian — is deprived of this nourishment, thus weakening its possibilities.

This is partly a structural problem. Our state cultural agenda has long tried to define Canadians as different from US Americans, ignoring the rest of the world except insofar as it can be incorporated and domesticated as state multiculturalism, which is itself a way of occluding Quebec nationalism and of demarcating "otherness" merely so as to contain it, thus reinforcing, not so surprisingly, an overwhelmingly white, anglo and bourgeois state. Our structures of literary funding, appreciation, and value reflect this agenda. The Governor General's Awards, Canada's highest literary accolade, which generously applaud "every" type of literary production, have no category where the translation of a foreign work by a Canadian translator would fit. It's work not deemed worthy of recognition as a production.[4] Further, the work of foreign writers translated into English is not generally "received" as English usage by university English departments but considered purely to belong to the foreign literature, squelching the translator's sitedness entirely.

But, as I've said, translations are also reading practices, thus culturally and historically embodied, and embodied here in Canada. Bringing foreign works and sensibilities into one's own language is a source of nourishment for one's own words and for one's own nation yet because the work we receive in Canada from world literatures and languages is mediated so overwhelmingly by US and British reading practices, choices, lexicons, approaches, and values, Canadians largely forego this nourishment. This process denies us an important source of growth for a particularly Canadian English usage, a growth that would be heterogeneous, unlike the homogeneous growth of economic globalization.[5]

With that long prelude, I return to that small book of mine and Alberto Caeiro's, *Sheep's Vigil by a Fervent Person*. This book represents three things that are important to me. First, the book is a surprise and a gift, for Pessoa helped me to see Toronto, a city I couldn't see at first in 2000, when I was writer-in-residence at the University of Toronto. I was bewildered and unhappy there until, through my readings of Fernando Pessoa, I found a submerged culture of creeks and water in the city, a topography and way of being that I recognized and which I did inhabit, in the end, with great joy.

Second, it's that rare thing: a translation of a foreign writer by a Canadian, published in Canada. The physical book at first elided that it was a translation, which just inscribed the pathology I described earlier: an indigenous practice of translation from foreign literatures doesn't exist, so it can't exist. Even when it does exist, it still doesn't exist. So the first edition of the book was printed without Pessoa's name on it; it fell off. In the face of my protests, the publisher corrected their lapse by stamping Pessoa's name onto the title page, and putting the full title of the book on a bookmark. The book cover, please note, was too small for the whole title to fit, but it fit later on a bookmark![6] Such is the power of thought to structure reality.

For the book is definitely inscribed in the framework of translation practice. It's Alberto Caeiro through and through. It's just not part of the translation practice most common in English that claims to "represent" the author, while eliding the translator and the translator's sitedness. *Sheep's Vigil* leaves the translator visible to the reader. In doing so, it respects the original's archaic, simple, inelegant (the elegance of inelegance) use of language, respects the philosophy and wry tone of Alberto Caeiro, and iterates Caeiro's concerns. The exorbitance of the translation is visible even to the reader who does not understand Portuguese, and translation as exorbitance echoes Pessoa's own exorbitant subjectivity. My translational exorbitance does nothing more than echo the "crease" in subjectivity that translation always enacts.

So the first two of my three important things are *gift, translation*.

The third is *water*. The book is a history of water, for Toronto — where the translation takes place — is a city of water, built on running water. It buries water but water continues to define the city. And where there's water flowing, and bits of scrub poplar, *bidueiro*, ravine, and creek-beds, there are cats. Yes, cats! They know where water is and aren't fooled by surfaces. They're the flocks, the *rebanhos*, of Toronto. This book is a miniature Toronto, and returns me to the notion of gift, for it is my gift: giving Toronto back to Toronto.

It's in this way, as gift, absence made visible when bookended as a gift, that translation can surprise, and locate us. Locate us as foreigners to what it translates, necessary foreigners, and — at the same time — as inhabitants of our own language, our own place, and our own opened possibilities for literature.

stakes, poetry, today

The future is exactly that which exceeds representation.
‖ Jean-Luc Nancy, *La création du monde*

STAKES, POETRY, TODAY

Make a box with a hole, inside which is the outline of the speech. By looking through the hole, you are in the position of "Fred." By looking in from one corner, you can see all six sides of the box. It is a stage. This talk is constructed as such a stage. Our bodies are its amplification and stand at a spot where public and speaker are easily confounded.

1 DIMINISHING THE LYRIC I

Fred. And the variants of Fred: Federico, Frédérique, Freddy and the Dreamers, Phrâ, Râ, Frodo.

I'd feel remiss if I didn't open with the word "Fred"; it's a word that will often hang in the balance, or be part of the suspense, suspension, and even suspicion during this gathering in which we are all about to collaborate.

It's a word, that "Fred," which hangs just above and with the three words I am going to address now: *stakes — poetry — today.*

2 FAKING IT

What are the stakes for (of, in) poetry today? That's my question. For poetry always bears (as if on a string) stakes: outside itself, inside itself, as well as the stakes "present to itself."

3 RACING THROUGH POETICS

The stakes *outside* poetry, of course, are language, or rather, languages, for poetry can only take place in languages.[1] (Not just in one language.) It occurs in what we have heard.[2] It is (of) a multiplicity of hearings, not tautologies, but heterologies, and heterodoxies.

Its stakes *inside* itself are poetry wrestling with its own history, in its own idiom, and with the possible located there (which possible is, generally or as a rule, not available to us): they are the hinge (pli, seam) wrested from that wrestling, that history, and that idiom.[3]

Poetry's stakes of *presence to itself* have to do with the impossibility of settled and unitary presence.[4] They have to do with *autre/autrui*, self and other/s, with the body (this body=[sign]) as prop, as instrument of the voice, as evincing; and they have to do with narration, which is another way of saying "the body," inasmuch as the body is an organism continuous over time because of language's unfolding, narrative's repeated neural guise.

This third set of stakes, of presence to itself—to oneself and, thus necessarily, to a self outside the self that is not one's self—is vital, and it is here, perhaps, that we can situate race—racial—racing (but without an antiphonal *e*, even without *my* e,[5] for the opposite of racing, of course, is *e-racing*, which is also *effacing*, unfacing, refusing the other's face). For this "presence" does not *want* (or call upon, or desire) that binary of self and other, English and French, of white and First Nations but, again, beckons to a heterology, to a heterological moment, *a momentiño* that is "just about to occur" and that can't be predicted, predictated, predicated, but that is *dichten*. Poetry demands this heterology, and demands it *of society*. Elsewhere, in O Cidadán, I called it the "not-yet."

It—this presence and this *momentiño*—is in suspension; like that word "Fred" it is a bridge or *ponte*. It is, perhaps, a *ponte das poldras*, which is triply a bridge of young mares, of fillies, filiations; a stepping-stone bridge, and a place: you may have to get your feet wet.[6]

4 ENGENDERING PRACTICES

So we have three sets of stakes. A taxonomic gesture (i.e., one of many). I now want to return to one phrase embedded in this taxonomy, that may perhaps bring about its unravelling. Or its engendering (as those young mares are gendered). The phrase is this:

Poetry—and this, before we ever define it as poetry, so I use the "p" word in suspension, in suspense, as a "thought held above"—occurs in what we have heard. Before we ever write it. Poetry is heard; it is the heard thing.

Even when we look at concrete poetry, we make as if to hear it. For what is written down is also heard. *A marking can be heard.* (And — a side note — what would this hearing be to someone deaf? It would be gesture/motion. So I don't mean "hearing" as reduced merely to the physical sense, but the larger sense of hearing that is part of every sense.)

What's important to note is that this "hearing," all this hearing, passes alongside (outside) "understanding." For, as beings, we always "hear" more than we understand. We would not be viable as beings were this not the case. We would be merely organisms.

Can you imagine if we heard only what we understood?

- You might say we would then live in a nearly silent world.
- But I wonder in such a case: would there even be a "we" to experience this near-silence?
- The "we," the "I," that can think of such silence already hears.
- It already knows what "understanding" is.

So there is a relation between hearing and understanding that is at no time resolvable in the sense of being finished. And poetry — this suspected, suspect word — this word thought held in suspension and suspicion — falls on the side of hearing (rather than understanding).

I sometimes draw this as a fraction:

$$\frac{< \text{what is heard} >}{> \text{what is understood} <}$$

or as an equation:

$$\frac{\text{hearing}}{\text{understanding}} > 1$$

5 BIOTEXT

Heard and falling. Thus, embodied.

The person, the *being*, who must deal with these three stakes, all at once, daily, and with this hearing, is embodied. As we all are. As I am. Before you now. For we can imagine poets only as embodied. We imagine Homer, for example, as similarly embodied to us. To Fred Wah, Homer looks like Fred Wah.

It is true that we might imagine some writers as animals. For example, is Kafka's cockroach not our image of Kafka? Or perhaps it's that we imagine some animals as writers: Kafka's cockroach, for example.

Clarice Lispector, the *brasileira* whose first language was Ukrainian, however, eats the cockroach. Or she puts it into her mouth, *cando menos*. Thus, embodied.

In my *O Cidadán*, which is really a document about what thinking might be possible (fleeting access) with and in poetry, a document that inserts such thinking into poetry in a bid to open poetry by ruining it (apparently), I came to talk about poetry's place as facing the "not yet."

The "not yet" is *aproximação* — which does not simply mean in English "not quite accurate, approximate, a guess." It can mean this, but its larger meaning is that of becoming proximate, going close to something, moving into proximity. There is both citizen and poetry here. There is a relation between self and community that exposes the self, or leaves the self exposed. It is not fuzzy thinking, or the slippage of meaning, or the invalidity of meaning. It's not a huge mush. In Jean-Luc Nancy's words, the singular does not vanish (or proximity would not be possible); rather, the "final multiplicity bears with it the irreducibility of singularities" (*La création* 71).

Lacanians — to detour a bit — say we seek the *objet a*, the object lost long before desiring comes into play. The impossible object (which is not even an object, an *a*). I think that, yes, we *are* formed out of its existence, but it's important to note that the impossible or lost *a* is not embedded in a past or prior moment; it is an impossible object that accompanies us as a future. It is akin to what Galician writer Manuel Rivas calls an ecology, akin to what he defines as a *saudade do futuro*, literally — or most closely rather than literally, and problematically — a *nostalgia for the future*, but not really our English "nostalgia" which is too stuck in the past. *Saudade*, more closely, is hope-memory-longing-projection. Such *saudade* has an object, but an object that already doesn't exist, that has never existed, yet we carry it with us. Maybe it *is* us. Our irreducible singularity.

Fred Wah said in an interview with Lola Tostevin that he doesn't like the word *nostalgia*. I think he would be better with the word *saudade*.

And I like to think of the *objet a* as the *objet ah*, or *huá* — which I've been told is the Mandarin word for the Cantonese Wah. The *objet huá*: noise; clamour. The sign *huá* is also a part of the words "mutiny," "in an uproar," "uproarious laughter," and part of a phrase that means "to try to please the public with claptrap." Not to mention that other *huá* which means "magnificent, splendid"; "prosperous; flourishing"; "grizzled," "grey," "your," and "China."

The suspension of that sign for "poetry," which we also know now as "Fred," seems to include all these senses of Húa and Wah, and thus is embodied. A biotext.

In Galician the senses are *os sentidos*, which can refer to the senses (physical), or direction, or meaning. I like this heterogeneity; it points to a hybridity that opens.

6 HYBRIDITY

I want to open a hybrid space for you, one that originally took place in another language than the one in which I am writing. I said I'd be back to Jean-Luc Nancy, and now I'd like to explore a small heterological "raisonnement" or set of thoughts in Nancy, from two essays in his 2002 volume *La Création du monde, ou la mondialisation*, partly to share with you my pleasure in his text and to share my curiosity, and partly as a kind of underpinning, *ostinato*, to the stage on which I will leave us standing.

Even if you do not know French, it will not be difficult to *hear* the thoughts (without "understanding" them, which is not the issue) that follow, these thoughts about poetry *surtout*, if, above us, we hold as an example — in suspension of course — what we hear and understand of the work of Fred Wah. If we might realize, as in "make real," Fred Wah's work as one embodiment ... of our suspicion ... *suspended!*

Il est à tous égards non seulement raisonnable, mais exigé par la vigueur et la rigueur de la pensée, de se refuser aux représentations : l'avenir est précisément ce qui excède la représentation. (53)	"It is in any case not only within reason but also essential to the vigour and rigour of thought that we refuse respresentations: the future is precisely that which exceeds representation."
Bien évidemment, ni le sens comme direction, ni le sens comme teneur ne sont donnés. Ils sont chaque fois à inventer : autant dire à créer, c'est-a-dire faire surgir du rien ... (57–58)	"Very clearly, neither sense as direction, nor sense as content, are given. They are each time to be invented: or one might say to be created, which is to say to bring forth from nothing."
Cela ne signifie absolument pas que n'importe quoi fasse sens n'importe comment : cela, précisément, est la version capitaliste du sans-raison ... La mondialité est la forme des formes qui demande elle-même à être crée, c'est-à-dire non seulement produite en l'absence de tout donné, mais tenue infiniment au-delà de tout donné possible : en un sens, donc, jamais déposable dans une représentation.(58–59)	"This absolutely does not mean that any old thing makes sense in any old way: this, precisely, is the capitalist version of the 'without reason' ... Worldliness is the form of forms that itself demands to be created, which is to say not only produced in the absence of any given, but held infinitely beyond any possible given: in a sense, then, that can never rest in a representation."

In Nancy, the word *sens* brims: it is sense-direction-meaning-content. *Sens,* says Nancy, is never containable in a representation. Yet this does not mean "everything goes," for that is the commercial version of "sans raison," of the breakdown in representation's value. (It's not "the breakdown of sense," but the "breakdown of one rigid vision of sense.") Nancy links *sens* to "value" and brings us to our task today:

Notre tâche aujourd'hui n'est rien de moins que la tâche de créer une forme ou une symbolisation du monde.... C'est la tâche extrêmement concrète et déterminée—une tâche qui ne peut qu'être une lutte—de poser à chaque geste, à chaque conduite, à chaque habitus et à chaque ethos la question : comment engages-tu le monde ? Comment renvoies-tu à une jouissance du monde en tant que tel, et non à l'appropriation d'une quantité d'équivalence ? Comment donnes-tu forme à une différence de valeurs qui ne soit pas différence de richesse en équivalent général, mais cette différence des singuliers en quoi seulement consistent le passage d'un sens en général et la mise en jeu de ce qu'on appelle un monde ? (60)

Cependant ... la lutte est d'emblée et définitivement l'affaire d'égalité concrète et de justice effective. (60)

Here part of the sens is sound: the sound of French. Many of the words I cite exist in English and do not need translation, just hearing. Were I to translate all Nancy's text here without the hesitancies of the voice—for on May 16, 2003 when I spoke this text my translation was extemporaneous—I'd be engaged in an appropriation that elides the "becoming proximate." The appropriation of a quantity of equivalence. So here I'll just suggest that in bringing into being what might be a world—in other words, everything that is in "stakes, poetry, today"—sounds and words would come into play from another language to which the reader must gain access using their own wits. I will, though, translate the last bit of the text on the left:

"All this said, the struggle is above all and definitely the business of concrete equality and effective justice."[7]

A page or two later, Nancy speaks of art's work as involving a "labour that does not submit to the finality of mastery (domination, utility, appropriation), but exceeds all submission to an end." And he continues:

C'est ici l'art qui indique l'enjeu : le travail de l'art est toujours aussi un sens à l'œuvre au-delà de l'œuvre, aussi bien qu'une œuvre œuvrant et ouvrant au-delà de tout sens donné ou à donner. (63)

Here Nancy speaks of "stakes, art, today": in French the similarity of the words "work," "artwork," and "opening" (œuvre, œuvrant, ouvrant) is key to the movement of an argument that surges beyond all sense.

Nancy speaks as well of how we might decide what would be a world worthy of the name "world":

> la décision sur ce qui vaut d'être visé — par exemple, « un monde », un monde « digne de ce nom » — ne peut pas être un choix entre des possibles, mais seulement et chaque fois une décision pour ce qui n'est ni réel ni possible : pour ce que n'est en aucune façon donné d'avance, mais qui fait l'irruption du nouveau. (67)

He invokes Lyotard to indicate that it is not enough to substitute plurality for unicity, because monological thought, as such a substitution, just risks perpetuating the same old structure of thought. "The final multiplicity bears with it the irreducibility of singularities" means that singularities are still present and we can't abolish them. Singularity and multiplicity exist in another sort of relationship (which is still to be defined, always: the not-yet).

My final quotation in this movement in thought I have pulled from Nancy is, like the other quotations, taken out of Nancy's context and placed into ours:

… comment rendre justice, non pas seulement au tout de l'existence, mais à toutes les existences, prises ensemble mais distinctement et discontinûment, non pas comme l'ensemble de leurs distinctions, différences et différends — justement pas ainsi —, mais comme ces distinctions ensemble, co-existantes ou comparaissantes, tenues ensembles multiples. (72)	The idea of the "comparaissant," the "co-appearing," enthralls me here. The co-existent, all the existents, "held multiply together."
	Which ends what I have to say about stakes, poetry, today.

ENDNOTE: WRITING IN COMMUNITY

Now that I have created a small six-sided stage for us, I would like to end by emphasizing that *hearing* (perhaps, at times *seeking to understand* in the sense of seeking to work) is always a frayed, fraying process.

The part of this process that occurs alongside understanding, where hearing leaks openly, is always the most interesting. It's a process of folding, or suspense. A process of suspicion and suspicious behaviour, of suspect behaviour (not of circumspect behaviour, though perhaps of circumsuspect behaviour). It does not have an end, an edge; it finds leakages in borders. The already-understood does not make an organism possible, as a being. This is the beauty, both of the process and of being. This is how the work both contains sadness and is, in the present — it so happens — sadness's remedy.

▪ Communauté. Ce que communauté veut dire: nous, assemblés ici sous le signe de Fred et de Pauline, où ce "Fred" et cette "Pauline" ne sont pas des signes qui *tout couvrent*, mais des signes qui *surtout ouvrent*, des signes qui ne *couvrent de tout* et qui *œuvres-tu?* Et des signes… qui dessinent et qui, en dessinant, designent.

▪ "Fred" et "Pauline" sont nos noms aussi. Non pas le nom singulier Fred, ou Pauline, qui demeurent dans leurs singularités Fred Wah et Pauline Butling, mais ceci : nous sommes, ou nous incarnons, ici présent, comme communauté, l'invitation qu'incarnent, à son tour, ce Fred et cette Pauline. Comme des *êtres* cette fois, *comme un être*, et signe de l'être, et ceci, à la lettre, *à commettre*.

▪ Il s'agit, finalement, d'une invitation, qui contient "vit" donc vie et vits, *life and balls*, et qui veut dire aussi que Fred ne nous remplace pas à son événement, mais il, ou son nom, indique pour nous un avènement, auquel nous sommes convoqués.

I would like to conclude with a few words from the artist Lani Maestro, taken from a recent interview: "If one wants to insist on origin, I truly feel that this is where I come from — the country of making art."[8]

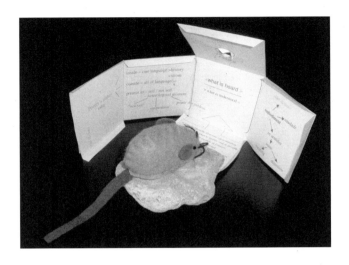

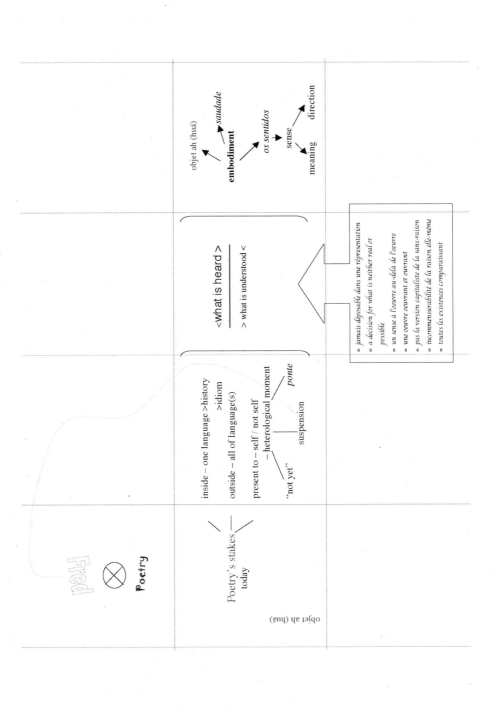

*RE-*ÇITING THE CITIZEN BODY

Circulating is the first ethical act of a counterimperial ontology.
Hardt and Negri, Empire (363)

The decision on what is worth aiming for —for example, "a world," a world "worthy of this name"— can't be a choice between possibles, but only and each time a decision for what is neither real nor possible: for what is in no way given in advance, but which irrupts as the new, the unforeseen/unpredicted."
Nancy, La création du monde (67; my translation)

The system of beauty —our little gamine— is about to crash.
Moure, O Cidadán (110)

En fin de compte, ma patrie n'est pas la langue, ni la française ni l'espagnole, ma patrie c'est le langage.
Semprún, Mal et modernité (102)

A perturbance of locale might be, perhaps, first, a disturbance of the body.... (belief's construct opens here)...
Moure, O Cidadán (121)

Ç

In our era of transnational *agonías* constructed politically and socially as metacrises of economy or war, where are *we*, each of us, as citizens? What of our citizen-body, the real physical body, named and not faceless, different and particular, the body that migrates across borders, bearing languages and experiences across these borders, thus shifting all lines into elsewheres not yet mapped or marked?

For people have always done this. Citizens have always made decisions, *ethical* decisions, to open and/or cross borders without regard to their impermeability.

How can our physical body, so often a bearer of the cicatrices of nation's harrowing, perturb and displace/ disgrace fixed national definitions?[1] And why might this be of any relevance to writing poetry now?

If nation stems neither from ethnicity nor terrain (which both risk closure) but from a collective imaginary, how and where do *our* imaginations site, and cite, us? In what ways are we absorbing languages, comportments, bearings? Who are we when we cross "the border"? Who are we when we see someone else cross? How does what is left out of official declarations of the national imaginary, its residue, which resides in a no-place which is still *somewhere*, feed our unofficial national imaginary? How can poetry work with and through these questions?

As fronteiras tamén admiten pasaxes.[2] I want to insist too that there are situations in which the multiplication of borders does not cut space up, but enlarges it. It increases the possibility of reverberations, which are riches. O *Cidadán* argues for a notion of frontier or border as a line that admits filtrations, that leaks, a notion of borders as not rigid, not sealed, not marking strict limits of outside and inside when dealing with identity. *O Cidadán* argues, in effect, that identity finds its stability in the fluidity of limits, in the "not yet." This "not yet" is a *saudade* — a memory-to-come — that constitutes us as subjects, subjectivities. The globalization or "making world" in which I see potential riches is one that admits and strengthens these kinds of subjectivities, strengthens localities and pluralities — a plurality of localities — neither based nor congealed in myths of origin but which can admit such myths as proper to, belonging to all.

Ç

Take my own locale, Quebec, in the city of Montreal, where I've been writing for twenty-five years. Here I work daily in the common language, French, while I write in the language of my place of birth and first education, English, and also in my adopted language (in which this essay was originally written — the version here is a translation), Galician. Galician hardly exists at all where I live, but does exist because I speak it, and because it is dispersed throughout the entire world, marked by passages, emigrations, searches, losses, hopes, arrivals, sojourns, cries, silences, interments.

To write in Quebec in English is to feel one's English opened up, split, and in constant motion. It is in no way a natural language but one that must be recreated every moment. In daily life, of course, French predominates as the common, civic language and Montreal is also a place where a minority culture exists that expresses itself in English and chooses to define itself as minoritized (in fact it exists in a English-speaking continent, in a sea of English). But there is also a culture that rubs up against the borders of many cultures, that is not only of the historic French/English binary. This culture does not thrive in a vacuum, but in the midst of francophone culture itself.

I am of this third culture. Of the culture of borders that leak. It is not a rare culture; neither is it one that clamours, perhaps because it is not "one." Yes, English is my mother tongue, but in me it is also a faulty tongue, has wobbles and errors, because I don't speak it enough, and because the English of Montreal is beautifully infiltrated by the French language. It is the philosophy in French, along with French theatre, feminisms, everyday politics, and ways of seeing that are most closely mine. On top of this, I exist in Galician: a language that, as Galician writer Manuel Rivas said once to me, belongs to those who love it.

Mais ce frottement des langues, des sens, des tournures d'expression, est possible seulement à partir d'un quotidien riche qui se passe en français, cette langue qui appartient à tous et à toutes, et qui nous facilite et nous ouvre la vie de tous les jours. Ce fait transforme, peu à peu (ce qui veut dire: beaucoup!) la rélation que l'on peut tenir avec sa langue maternelle quand cette langue est autre que le français. Dans mon cas, la rélation avec l'anglais.

English itself is thereby changed, subject to leakage, to beautiful pressures. This process is one that my work in poetry makes evident in many ways, I think, and it is an effect, irrevocably, of living where I do, in the beautiful and replete languages I live in.

ç

The only good of borders, says Manuel Rivas in the voice of one of his characters, *is their clandestine passages.*[3] There are borders of language, of class, of north and south, of Canada and the United States, Anglo America and Spanish/

Portuguese America, of race and ethnicity, of accent and history, of crossed oceans, recrossed, of civic posture and bearing, and these borders are traversable and traversed by us and others all the time. Where are these idioms taking us? Where might they take us? Does it matter? If these are not useful questions for poetry, which questions should we be asking? These are the questions of the third culture, the citizen-body that is constantly re-çited, recited, and re-sited.

I long to address these questions in community, with others who wish to nourish and provoke their own practice of poetry or prose (or visual practice that includes words) or investigation to create seepages, *cépages*, pages: circulating writings that would risk a "not yet" of citizen being, a possibility or *aproximação* that calls upon us in and through our differences (our each-ness), as inhabitants of Montreal or of several cities, of a city block or neighbourhood, of a field or shore, a raft or boat, an ocean, which is to say a crossing too of bodies, enacting a hybrid in-between space not acknowledged or, even, flatly refused by official national considerations.

The stakes here, I think, are crucial in poetry as in nations: we must act and find ways of thinking that make new ways of acting toward each other possible, so that the word "hope" does not disappear from our vocabularies. As it has, wrote Edward Said in *El País* in 2002 in a phrase still apt in 2009, from that of the Palestinians.[4]

ONE RED SHOE
NARRATIVE AS A PRACTICE OF POSSIBILITY

1 STARTING POINT: THE BODY

My thinking on narrative has developed through my writing practice, a practice in language, in poetry, but also in space — the two-dimensional space of the page, and the three-dimensional space that is not solely "the book" but is also *pages*. In a book, two pages are always open beside each other, with the gutter between them, and thus are no longer simply two-dimensional spaces. For me, the page is not just a support on which words are typed, it's the background or *fond* and is part of the work itself. That each page has a recto and a verso, and is bound with other such pages to make the book, means that the reader's body is part of the book, is the book's prosthesis. For the reader must open the book. If this were not so, then there would be no difference between a book of pages, and a book painted on a block of wood.

Over the years, because it involves space and spaces, words and spacings, my work may seem to have turned its back on narrative. We are trained to think of narrative as being related to the action of characters over time but my work seems to ask, rather: what does it mean to exist, to communicate, to love alongside each other? What part does a social framework play? What are the limits of "the person," of grace, of honesty, of speech? How do we situate our selves as entities, organs in the civis, in *civil* society? These forces that link us, that make us persons and not simply organisms, compel and hold me.

Yet I think that the relation between *these forces* and the body, any one body — the body writing these words for you to read, for example — is necessarily narrative. And this relation stands, necessarily, in a world where the borders of individual identity are more and more blurred, refractory. The skin is not even a container for a serum body; we leak so variously. We leave remnants of DNA everywhere, remnants that are part of our individuality. Other questions arise. What does it mean for our bodies when we work with a computer, and no longer see our interlocutors? What do avatars mean and why does emotion accrue there, too? Are these distances from the human really distances? Or is distance an inevitable effect of bodily incarnation, part of that incarnation or corporeality, and thus a fact of any text as well? Are corporeal distances knitted together by some kind of narration? Does narration make us tenable as organisms in the face of incredible leakages, of prosthetic and avataric reaches?

2 NARRATIVE PRESENCE

Our brains map perceptual and autonomous nervous information in sheets of neurons that lie against each other in the cortex. These layered and overlapping neuronal maps have been well studied in the case of sight. To see what we *see*, we use dynamic brain processes and structures for movement, for edge, for colour, for shape, sound, etc., but nowhere in the brain is a picture assembled. What I see out in front of me is not mirrored exactly "like this" anywhere in the brain. Rather, it's an active process, not a representation; a process, not an image; a narration, not a sequence of stills. No wonder we can say we are shimmers, coalescences, coalitional, relational: we have several kinds of inner narration going on constantly in the brain.

In the brain, what we might call a fragment—edge, colour, curve, speed—turns out to be one of many overlapping mappings associated with no assembled whole. Once this becomes apparent, the word "fragment" ceases to bear the same weight, for "fragment" requires an idealized whole to make sense as a word. One might say that the common use of the word "fragment" reflects nostalgia for the possibility of wholeness. This wholeness is social, not biological, and is idealized. Once we know this about wholeness, or don't accept that illusory "whole" or fit into it, our fragment becomes something else. What was a fragment may prove to be entire, *sufficient* to open us up to another space, an altered coalition of conditions.

Oliver Sacks, the American neurologist, wrote at length about patients who suffered brain lesions that marred their functional constructs of identity. In *The Man Who Mistook His Wife for His Hat*, he describes how people with brain damage compensate in order to keep themselves intact as individuals existing in a continuous present (as much as is possible). Sacks points to the importance of narrative:

> We have, each of us, a life-story, an inner narrative—whose continuity, whose sense, *is* our lives. It might be said that each of us constructs and lives a "narrative," and

> that this narrative *is* us, our identities ... Each of us *is* a singular narrative, which is constructed, continually, unconsciously, by, through, and in us—through our perceptions, our feelings, our thoughts, our actions; and, not least, our discourse, our spoken narrations ... To be ourselves we must *have* ourselves—possess, if need be re-possess, our life-stories. We must "recollect" ourselves, recollect the inner drama, the narrative, of ourselves. A human *needs* such a narrative, a continuous inner narrative, to maintain his/her identity, his/her self. (105)

He goes on to say that normally this narrative is quiet and interior, and is continuous: it just breaks out and up in strange ways when people suffer damage (from strokes, etc.) to their cerebral cortexes, and their organisms try extraordinary means to patch the breach.

In other descriptions, Sacks writes of those with amnesia as having "lost their inner melodies and scenes. Both alike testify to the essentially 'melodic' and 'scenic' nature of inner life, the 'Proustian' nature of memory and mind" (140). So, in Sacks, we have a picture of a narrative as "melody" and "scene." Later in the book, talking about a young woman, he writes, "Rebecca made clear, by concrete illustrations, by her own self, the two wholly different, wholly separate, forms of thought and mind, 'paradigmatic' and 'narrative.' And though equally natural and native to the expanding human mind, the narrative comes first, has spiritual priority" (174). Sacks's work shows quite readily that narrative is the way the body maintains its own identity over time.

Narrative is also the way we identify what's outside us, now and over time. To return to sight as an example, the fact that the brain processes all the elements of the sight of a chair separately means there is no picture of "this chair" in the brain. But this is very useful, for if there were such a picture, we wouldn't be able to recognize "this chair" when its position is altered, let alone recognize a different chair. What we have in our minds instead of pictures of chairs is the ability to generalize about chairs, to recognize a chair. In other words, we all, in this culture, have an inner narrative of "chair" that lets us recognize a chair we have seen from another angle; it tells us what "chairness" is (and "chairness" itself is narrative, and not fixed; it is a relation, and not what "this chair" is). This "chairness" is very Wittgensteinian; it is largely grounded in use-value. Can we sit on it? In some circumstances, a car fender or a windowsill can be a chair. When we need to, when we are tired, for example, or in an unfamiliar environment, we recognize the qualities of a chair in many things.

We tend to link, generalizing from prior experience and knowledge, creating music and scene. We are active in the production of music and scene, even when we are reading a book, reading an artwork. Meaning arises from linkages, from functional constructs in the moment they are functioning, and not from set or fixed structures. There is no picture of a chair in the head. There is a narrative of chair.

As Gertrude Stein, the famed American novelist, playwright, and lecturer, said: narrative is any one thing after another. Narrative's shimmer is not necessarily an order of events based on an outside paradigm, though it is an ordering: it is rhythms, echoes, beats, and silences as well. It takes into account what is left out of standard paradigmatic orders. It patches breaches and makes its own links. That's why narrative elements — scenes — can be developed in so many different ways.

An example from my own work is the poem "Morphine, or the Cutting Stone" in *Search Procedures* (21). We as readers link the elements that repeat — rain, mud, cows, and cowboys in yellow rain slickers that are as bright as flowers — as our brains can't help trying to make narrative. There is the figure of the woman, very crabby, who is dying and worrying about her purse. The speaker in the poem, who can't stop this person dying and who sleeps badly (as one does when someone close is ill), steps out of the house to chop wood in the night, and feels wonder. The situation demanded a kind of narrative that made the turmoil of waking apparent in order to make the tumult of dying apparent, the tumult of impending grief. The reader has to undergo the turmoil too, not just read a report about it.

Another poem in *Search Procedures*, "Tales of the Sumerians (Auburn, NY)" (87), focuses on what it calls the "syncope of narration," meaning what narration necessarily fails to include. In this case it's the woman's story in a history of emigrations of men. But there is always and everywhere a syncope in narration. Narrative, in making links, also creates exclusions.

3 THE RED SPADES

Part of what poetry reaches to include is those exclusions, which I call "red spades." Among the sense-data that reach us are bits that the mind in its narration tends to reject or discount because they don't fit with what we already know, with the functional constructs in which we are already "trained" to operate. But part of the job of poetry, and art, I figure, is to reach past what we already know.

There is a good example of this discounting and rejection, and of the way it often occurs on a level *below* conscious perception: it operates *before* we *know* it. The example comes from a film I saw many years ago that cited American science historian and philosopher Thomas Kuhn on paradigms, those structures of thought that can actually prevent us from seeing situations and patterns differently.[1] The film animates a scene from Kuhn's book: a game is played on-screen with the viewer's perceptions to show how paradigms can actually alter sense data to fit our old knowledge, to leave undisturbed the paradigm we already know. It is a card game in which ordinary playing cards are displayed on screen, and we are asked to note anything strange that we perceive as the cards are revealed. At first, when the cards are turned at high speed, we perceive nothing out of the ordinary, just a continuous whoosh of black and red. Yes, we are seeing a deck of cards, alright. As the card-turning is repeated at slower speed, we see more details in the whoosh and, curiously, a few small gaps between cards once in awhile. After several more repetitions, each conducted more slowly, we begin to identify the values of the cards, and in what was the gap we see a whoosh: a card that is blurred. Yet the film makes clear that the cards are each presented for the same length of time! Finally, the cards are presented one at a time, and the gap card, the blur card, turns out to be a red spade. The game shows us how we perceive only what our already-created categories will allow; other data that does not coincide with our paradigm for playing cards is rejected. At first, we do not even perceive it was there; it is so effectively eliminated. But something IS there; the red spades turn out to have been there all the time.

The role of poetry in all this is to enter that syncope in narration, because it doesn't have to follow already-created categories. In challenging the way the brain works to put things together, a poem can use narrative order to create effects as rich and paradoxical as life itself. It can reach for the red spades and not exclude them from the narrative; it can create non-paradigmatic narratives. These different uses of narration and order then open up sense perception differently, past what our already-created categories will allow; a richer world becomes possible. Richer subjectivities become possible.

4 THE CITIZEN

Even if O *Cidadán* could be considered too dense and philosophical to be narrative, it employs narrative elements and flashes, narrative links and leaps. For all its philosophy, it cannot avoid (nor does it desire to avoid) engagement with narrative.

In "Document 13 (porous to capital)," we find an argument for our emergence as subjects as being a turn in language, as being approximate, belying the possibility of strict identity. The text enacts this philosophy in its own structures.

> To persist
> somatic coalesce does imbue a fetter
> wherein "I am" reiteration's frank motel
>
> which is a fold or distal not proximal
> ...>
> that thing drawn 'cross us like
> a scar or want   is "us"
> ...>
>
>   to iterate is to endure
>   "us" only visible as the frame delects
>   (37)

On the preceding page, "Eighth Catalogue of the *in jure* of Harms" ends explicitly by linking "one's own merging subject" (which could be emerging, but is curtailed as it emerges, thus the word itself is curtailed) to narrative:

> a flow of text through citation's multiples
> went particulars
> an ancestral soil "tant aimé"
>
> We are glad of these
> "gate holograms"
> cartography of the mesial plane
>
> whereupon the fold or equity
> a diversion
> of perimeters   vast enjure
>
> Sedition's faint trace
> an "abrigar"   fr. harm's way
>
> a touch who doubts and wanders
> That one's own merging subject is itself a torpor
> inadmissable to citizenship
>
> grammar we had called in
> our last match lit the sky for narrative
> (38)

Here a fold is equated with equity, and both fold and equity are called a diversion of perimeters, that is, an alteration of borders. A fold—just fold a piece of paper, and you will see this—prevents strict delimitation of boundaries. Sedition (treason) is an "abrigar" which is Spanish for "to shelter": this suggests that shelter from harm's way might be treasonous. Here, too, a merging subject, that is, strict identity, is torpor, a slowing that is inadmissible to citizenship. So we call upon grammar to define that merging subject: "our last match lit the sky for narrative." A lit match can be adulation, or it can be the utter end of light, as it is the last match. But what kind of match can light up the sky?

These lines about narrative take us back to a point earlier in the book, to the lines "grammar we had called in/like a bet on narrative" (10). And what kind of bet is a bet on narrative? The poem that follows this bet, "Second Catalogue of the Substitution of Harms*" (11), seems simply to defeat narrative: it presents words in the form of fractions, destroying our possibility of reading according to usual methods. In the fractions, harms sit oppressively in the top half of the fractions, and world, forms, kids, mayors, pain are all sited below. The substitution: is it working?

Narrative, presence, and language come up repeatedly in O Cidadán.[2] There is an insistence throughout the book on the need to work across boundaries, not to naturalize them, but to create and support new tensilities in language, in material. The book urges creation — continuously — of folds in narration as critical to understanding ourselves as citizens, as subjects.

5 THE RED SHOE

A signal poem in the earlier *A Frame of the Book* struggles with the whole notion of description, a term very linked to notions of narrative. The poem, "14 Descriptions of Trees" (10), takes up a very narrative element: a small red shoe. When there is even one red shoe, there is already narrative. A shoe holds a body; we know this. And one shoe is a crisis. Further, a red shoe is probably a dress shoe, not an ordinary shoe. And a small shoe likely belongs to a child or a woman.

All these elements are part of our paradigm of shoes. As such, using the words "one red shoe" together is enough to trigger the brain's narrative capacities, the narrative engine that links us as beings to our environment and to others and that makes us who we are. "One red shoe" is a small building block of narrative.

In the last section of the poem, entitled "CODA (replaces 8–14)," the poem gives up on its promise of fourteen descriptions, and claims to have finished telling the story.

> I have told you the story of a small red shoe
> Most of the time it is irreplaceable
>
> A far journey is ours, is ours
>
> That much is clear from the terrible story
>
> It is the saga of a small red shoe
> the journey itself is unmistakable
>
> Most of the time it is a word that shatters all   (14)

Most of the time, it *is* a word that shatters all: language makes, and breaks, us. This coda to the poem "14 Descriptions of Trees" is, curiously, on page 14 of the book; the end of description (on page 14) — or perhaps it is the impossibility of description — does not signal the end of the book. Something, descriptive or not, is still possible.

6 A LAST BET ON NARRATIVE

Here I will place a few of my last bets on narrative, by invoking some names of writers whose movements in narrative have had an impact on my own poetry of late:

Clarice Lispector
Gertrude Stein

Christa Wolf
Thomas Bernhardt
Nicole Brossard
José Saramago

I'd like to make one more little jump (a "jum p"). Some say that the goal of art is to resist tyranny. Some say, as Viktor Shklovsky did, that the purpose of art is to destroy pessimism. I say it's both.

CO-TRANSLATING "NICOLE BROSSARD": THREE-WAY SPECTACLE OR SPECTRE DE TROIS?

▌ In habitual parlance about literary works in translation, the translator is the ghost in the machine, and the one who wrote them in the first language is the person we call the Author. But this Author, in fact, enacts nothing in the translation. The ghost does it all. There are great similarities, of course, between the work of the first writer and the writing of the spectre, but these similarities are visible to us only if we speak both languages. For without two, there is no visibility, no movement ... and no misfortune! Translation is usually directed at the monolingual reader, which is any reader who does not understand the source language and must rely entirely on the language of the ghost.

When Robert Majzels and I enact the later poetry of Nicole Brossard in English, we do it on a stage on which we also create "Nicole Brossard."[1] For, as Verena Andermatt Conley says of her translation of Hélène Cixous, "the author emerges from the movement of translation" (39).

It is an outrageous statement, for it implies there is no author before there is translation. But rest easy, because there is always and ever translation: we say someone is "author" either by reading their words and "author-izing" them as author — which is already a kind of translation — or by hearing about them in the culture where such author-ization is conferred by others even before we read, which is another layer of translation.

In fact, the author you read in a translated text is created by the translators, and how clearly you understand that this author is a creation of the translation depends on how much you accept, or not, the notion of transparent transference between languages. The more readily you accept the notion that writing can be transferred between languages transparently, the less you will believe that the translators created the author.

It's funny that the readers most likely to accept a notion of transparent transference between languages are those who have just one language, and who thus must translate everything under very difficult circumstances: without any language of origin. To have a language of origin you need a language of arrival; without at least two languages, neither exists. There is just, ever, language.

In such cases, there is just, ever, one culture so absorbed in its structures that any one individual speaker cannot question and challenge many of its assumptions.

2

Syntax is normally used as a device to constrict meaning, singularize it, pare away extraneous possibilities of interpretation by settling meaning into determinate structures. In Brossard's work, syntax is quite the opposite of this, for she makes syntax and semantic possibility do *all* their work at any given moment. And what is this work, this *all*, of which syntax is capable?

- to be so flexible, finally, that it is double jointed, bending across line-breaks to read one thing on one side, another on the following line, and a third reading across the line break

- to allow us readers to decide, on the spot, about meaning, but also to lead otherwheres, to pull the structure sideways even as it uses structure

- to build up and release energy, cause pulses, motions in the work

Nicole Brossard enacts, and we trans-spectres must enact in English, a *syntaxualité* that multiples sense possibilities as well. Often Brossard's preposition "de" is *both* of and from. Her use or not of the definite article "le/la" before a noun provides additional weight, or doesn't. The register or level of language is also difficult to maintain at times in creating the translation because the most common "equivalents" for French words are in a different register in English, and can't be used without breaking the poem's construct of sound and sensibility.

Speaking of sound, a word must often be changed for a correlate so as to maintain the sound movement in the Brossard poem — as in the line "nuque nuées d'oiseaux" which appears in English (27) not as "nape swarm of birds" but as "nape nests of birds" to maintain the "n" sounds.

An even more potent example of the play of sounds in Brossard's work is her paralleling of French and English sounds in lines 2 and 5 in this excerpt:

> un goût d'univers et de naissance au bord des lèvres
> des élans si forts qu'on s'y brise)
> le cœur
> les soirs d'été le long des côtes du Maine
> (*sea breeze*
>
> (*Cahier* 77)

We translated these lines using the same sounds but reversing them, as:

> a taste for universe and birth grazing the lips
> fervours so strong we're mere debris)
> the heart
> summer evenings along the coasts of Maine
> (*brise de mer*
>
> (*Notebook* 66)

Again, we sought a correlate; "mere debris" is less a semantic equivalent of "on s'y brise"— literally "we break up there"— than it is the aurally recognizable consequence, after the fact, of "on s'y brise." It is an ideal translation.

At times we are able to destabilize a meaning only in context, as in Brossard's line "l'oubli de l'eau" which—apart from being a marvellous construct of sounds—could be the water forgetting or someone else's forgetting of water. We translated this line as "water's forgetting" (26) and though our line seems to point in one direction only where the Brossard line points in two, our next line in English destabilizes any certainty, for "water's forgetting" could link, or not, with the line that precedes it, or the one that follows it:

> then the world spreads out
> digital and rewind
> light crosses over
> water's forgetting
> the fluidity of selves:
> *récapitulons*

The word *forgetting* here could be verb or noun; the line-break makes the syntax wobble and opens up the kind of possibilities that a translation of Brossard needs to maintain.

There is an additional level of work. On the macro level, Nicole Brossard's poems generally stake out a foreground (where there is a disturbance of the syntax and the surface relations of words) and a background (where there is flow). We have to translate not once but twice, simultaneously: spatializing both foreground and background, balancing disturbance and flow so that their relationship in the translation matches the one in the original. The sense of the poems as a whole emerges on the micro level across the line breaks, and on the macro level between this foreground/background. The movement of sense arises from the rhythm of the piece as a whole, and to transmit this movement of dilation and contraction, continuity and reversal, is fidelity.

It is clear, then, that the task of translation can't just involve finding equivalencies for words. In a given context, *nuée* is not necessarily *swarm*. The gaps between languages are in fact unbridgeable; there is no equivalency, and thus no technician can find the solutions. If translating directly, word for word, à la Babelfish, will help us read an instruction to locate the exit from a burning building, in Brossard's work we are ever in that building, and we can't get out. And, yes, it's burning.

At the moment of translation, there is a synapse between languages. The uncrossable gap that is to be crossed. It is the *momentiño* of what I call "perturbed serenity," and this moment must be opened and maintained open, held open — for it allows the pulse of the work to be transmitted neurally to the translator, in the substrates of consciousness really, and this then allows us to leap. I feel that I absorb and generate this sensation of perturbed serenity in my chest, in my solar plexus. It is a site of pleasure and of difference, which is to say, differentiation, which is to say: creation. In holding the moment of perturbed serenity open, we destabilize any notion of equivalency and maintain, as long as possible, an absolute undecidability. And thus freedom: anything could happen. One is most faithful to the work, the first work (the original) and the work in process (the translation), when engaging this freedom.

3

The voice Robert and I give Brossard is, curiously, a voice she doesn't have. It's my voice and Robert's, and thus neither of our voices as an individual. It is an *espace*-spatialization, already "spectacle" for there are two bodies and the voice is outside these bodies, about to be conjoined to another body. It is thus an alternating vibration in space that breaks space itself. It is an extraspatialization, an excess of spatialization, and it takes place in another tongue, in another way, at a new moment of foment.

The moment of undecidability between "nape," "neck," or "scruff" for *nuque*, for example, depends on an interaction between our two bodies, between our responses to the text, at the very moment of translation. This moment has nothing to do with Brossard except that it involves our projection of Brossard. It is, thus, spectacle.

It is Brossard, the "author," who is *spectre* in the end, whose spectrality we fill with our own bodies in order to bring her work into being in an English that both disturbs or distresses "our" English, while at the same time opening it. The point of utter/unuttered undecidability — the synapse of translation — is the point of an intensification. In the end, it confounds the split between translation and creation. Which is which?

4

Who writes? Who is the author? Who is conniving here? Who is copying? Who is creating?

The funny part is that the author-ization of any piece I write, or translate-write, or write-translate, occurs not in me, or in a me-Author, but in a social scene outside all bodies. My translations of Pessoa — which kept that *momentiño* of perturbed serenity open in order to be faithful — were, funnily enough, authorized as my work alone at first by the publisher. My work with Majzels is authorized, of course, as Nicole Brossard's voice in poetry. But my work translating Chus Pato from Galician is authorized, by Pato, as the work of Moure! Because Pato cannot read it, it can't be her work, or so she once claimed. She acknowledges a relation with the work that is spectacle — we often read together on a stage from the poems — and she does see it is a projection of "Chus Pato" into the Anglo-Saxon world, but she does not claim authority for the voice or words, even when she plays the role of the Author.

In the very process of translation, as well, the different insistence or clamour of a Pessoa text is not the clamour of another Pessoa text is not the clamour of a Brossard text is not the clamour of a Chus Pato, and the density of an Andrés Ajens poem in Chilean Spanish is not the density of a Christophe Tarkos in French or the illicit movement between languages of Wilson Bueno's *portunhol*.

Suffice to say that translation's field is far more ample than it is normally seen to be in Canada. In this country, where the split between translation and creation is a deep trench over which much anxiety is expended — *ce pays* needs this anxiety or the trench will heal over quite naturally and, as such, it is a constitutive trench — my work is often seen to fall on either side of the split: translation, or creation. And where neither of the two fit, or both, the work is pushed off the edge of the abyss toward one side or another: thus the Pessoa becomes creation (the publisher leaves off the name of the author) or becomes excessive or bad translation (some reviews). My renderings, through my own body, of the poems that imitate the Galician-Portuguese medieval repertoire, which are the root of my book, O Cadoiro, are received by some as bad translation. Or not as translation. Most beautifully, a critic who understood the text in a tongue-in-cheek and utterly lively way, called them "a pseudo-plagiarist's pastiche."[2]

And it is so, for the poems of O Cadoiro are a stuttered frank homage to the medieval Galician-Portuguese lyric verse, and some of them move very close to translation. Some of these texts, sewn and in colour, would be considered stumbling howlers if offered as translations, but, as texts, they are wrought and anguished and beautiful. They hold further texts, as well, in which I translate, in this case, some words of Jacques Derrida. I do so, curiously and most faithfully, by leaving them in French. The process enacted upon them was conceptual: I fragmented small combinations of words from Mal d'Archive, recombined them, and compressed them in space so that their rhythm is highlighted. These texts-within-texts are a translation though they do not leave their language, for my hand is visible in the work, and it is spatialized in an English-language poem.

O Resplandor, more recently written, takes another tack, for here I am not even myself when I inscribe words, and the language of the "original" is unknown to me, and unknown to the translator, Elisa Sampedrín.[3] Yet her work is true to the original Romanian in so many other ways, all rhythmic and haunting. So much of meaning, in poetry particularly, does not pass through the dictionary! And translation brings such surprises, to those open to listening to what the work itself demands, to those open to seeing all the possible things that can happen in one's own language in the clamour of "foreign" voices.[4] Letting yourself be foreigned by language as you work: this is the key.

And — to close the circle I have opened — this is why we, Robert Majzels and I, created our Nicole Brossard in English, in response to the sounds, echoes, and shimmers that we found in her poetry. We then gave our Brossard to our friend Nicole, so she could embody the words in English and carry them into the book and world, where you can read her joyous disturbance of words, not as ours, but as hers.

CROSSING BORDERS WITH A GALICIAN BOOK OF POETRY: TRANSLATING A REALIST POET[1]

▌ Though I am a translator, I always affirm that translation is impossible. This appears to be, but is not, an unsustainable situation. It is, rather, creative.

Always between two languages there is a river to cross. A river has *orelas* — banks — just as a body has *orellas* — ears. The river too is a body that listens. Made, like our body, of water.

And between two languages as different as English and Galician (or other Romance languages), there are *ríos* — rivers — or perhaps *rías* — wide inlets — or even a sea to traverse. There is no linear relationship between languages. Going from one language to another is not a simple passage. To translate, we have to touch this body, pass through the body. Through the *orel(l)as*.

To affirm the impossibility of translation is not to deny that there is translation. In effect, there is lots of translation. It just takes place within that impossibility.

Why affirm an impossibility? Is it not true that the words

in one language have equivalents in others? Is there not a whole industry of dictionaries that lives off this fact? An entire Europe that lives off this fact?

Of course, words have equivalents, though no equivalencies fixed in space and time. For each word in a language is affected, touched, perturbed, wounded, split by the culture in which it is used, by history, and affected as well by the words in proximity, and by voices as well, by bodies, by ears. There are equivalents, yes, but each equivalent is fed by approximations, proximities, usages, ravages, splits, absences.

Afectos. Affects.
Infectos. Foulness.
Intactos e tactos. Intactness and touches. *Tácticas.* Tactics. *E rupturas.* And ruptures.

Because of this, translation for me is not a task in which we seek equivalents for words, in which we try to tame the source language by making something readily recognizable in the target language.[2] Something accommodating. My tactic is to listen to the *text of departure*, and let the text speak.

When we do listen without preconceptions to the original text, the *text of origin*, it always indicates tactics for its translation. What interests me are the perturbations that can result in the *language of arrival*: for me, translation has to perturb the complacency of my language. It is this that attracts me about translation, that a text in a language unknown to readers in English can perturb and alter English, the comfortable language we inhabit as if it were natural. I don't believe in the naturalness of one language in the face of others, but I have confidence in what my body tells me, my ears, when I read.

A MIÑA HISTORIA

I began as a poet in English, simply because I grew up in an English-speaking region of Canada. I learned in English at school. My parents spoke to each other in English. I know the literature of this language. It is, I affirm, my language. I love it. But never in my life have I thought of English as a natural language. To me, the most natural language was always silence. Colours. Flowers. Silence.

When I learned English as a child, I started to use it in thought and in writing at virtually the same time. Much later, when I learned French, thinking started in me in French and French started to infiltrate my work. In a single language, I felt almost not present, non-existent. And when I learned a little Castilian, what we call Spanish, words in this language started to appear in my poems. I never saw the sense in writing in only one language. When my body expresses itself in more languages, why present a thought in only one? Why shut down the forces that are at work in the poems? Why restrict thought's possibilities in the poem, sound's possibilities?

And when I learned Galician! In my mind, thoughts arrived in Galician, in Canada where I never hear it spoken. I started not only to translate from Galician into English, but to write in Galician. To be embodied in Galician.

Through Galician, I discovered in 2000 in Toronto, Canada, that I could read in Portuguese. I could read Alberto Caeiro, one of Fernando Pessoa's heteronym poets! Startlingly — to me — I received the work of Caeiro in Portuguese differently than I had in English, and my reading opened new paths to me for understanding Caeiro, paths that were previously inaccessible. I had to translate his humour, his vitality, into English. The meaning of words, those equivalents, was less important for me; what was important was to transmit the levity and the wit of Caeiro, his droll tongue-in-cheekiness or *retranca*. I had to listen to Caeiro, and not to the rules controlling what is and is not translation. I had to listen to Caeiro and translate his affection, his fondness for the world, and translate this through my own body. We can't listen to a text without having feelings, without being affected by the text. As I have said before, a translation always translates a reading practice enacted on a text, not simply "an original text."

Like Borges, I don't believe in a general theory of translation, applicable in all cases, but in a strategy for each case. There are academics and poets who say that my Caeiro is an interpretation, an adaptation. I insist that it is a translation. I am not afraid of revealing a split or break in our notion of what translation is.

This split or break, I think, is the body. The translator's body. It is the culture that exists inside and around a body. A culture not fixed or stable, that can never be fixed, frozen — that fluctuates, that is always co-incident.

This relation of co-incidence is absolutely reconcilable with my usual language, English, which from its earliest days was a language formed from infiltrations, influences, confluences, splits, intuitions. It is not a language calibrated from an official centre. There is no Royal Academy of English. There is no excluded thinking in English. (On the other hand, that's why it's the ideal language for the growth of capitalism, because capitalism evolves by absorbing differences, resistances. It consumes what is foreign to it. It too is a language without central control and this greatly helps this consumption-nutrition. Just read Lyotard's *Économie libidinale*.)

Infiltracións, filiacións.

What interests me in Galician, one of the things that interests me, is that Galician too has many infiltrations, which are called dialectal variants. The language supports variants, multiplicities. Bodies. And can at the same time contain resistances without absorbing them. It's something special, and for me is a language of possibility and openings.

ENCONTRANDO CHUS PATO

On March 20, 2001, I was in Andel bookstore in Vigo with my friend (and first Galician teacher), writer and translator María Reimóndez, buying dictionaries and simple books to help me learn more Galician. After paying and before turning to leave, I saw on the counter a large book with an incredible knobbly cover, bright orange, bearing the inscription: *m-Talá*, and below that, the words *Chus Pato*.

I had no idea what it was, or what those three words meant. But I could tell it was a special artifact. It was a book that refused the standards of book marketing, that made itself into a stunning object, that gave you no image of what you would find inside, that absolutely refused to interpret the book for you in advance.

I picked up the book and opened it.

My story ends here. All the story of the *before* and *prior* ends right here.

For from this point onward, it's no longer a story. The prior and before are annulled, and a new anterior, interior, posterior, exterior, polyterior are opened. An entire life changed right then: mine. There are books that produce a before and an after in a culture. One of those books in Galician literary culture is Chus Pato's *m-Talá*. For me, too, life really has a before and an after, because of this book.

In March of 2001, I could hardly read what I had before me, but the forms were visible to me, and the torrents of words, in which I could make out phrases such as "o infinito de linguaxe" and "o meu corazón segue un ritmo veloz tal astro," amid Pato's dense and winding texts, her jammed verb tenses, her signs saying "this is a personal poem, keep your nose out of it," and her helter-skelter syntactical leaps amid the forms of newspaper articles, dialogues, and theatres. I was immediately rivetted.

This is amazing poetry, I said to María, and I told her: *I want to translate this book.* María really exclaimed now: *You can't translate that book! Your Galician isn't good enough! Vou aprender,* I said. I'm going to learn. *E logo vou traducir este libro.* And then I'm going to translate this book. *It's impossible to translate,* María said. *I can tell*, I said. *That's why I want to translate it.* We both bought copies.

I carried it with me everywhere, this book *m-Talá*: I underlined in it, highlighted in it, read it aloud, wrote notes in it. I googled things in it. I was in the heat of Babylon, on the steppes in the cold, listening to a radio show in Galicia, in the belly of the whale with Jonas, in the river with Ophelia.

Later, in the summer of 2001, I headed back to Galicia, to Santiago de Compostela to learn to speak Galician properly, and Nicole Brossard gave me a list of people she'd met the year before in Galicia at a PEN International conference. Trouble was, she didn't give me any contact information. Except for one: on her list was Chus Pato's email address. I had the email address of the woman who wrote the book that was so important to me! I wrote her, in a few stumbling palabriñas de galego, and in French as well in case she couldn't understand my few bits of Galician.

She wrote back, saying: Never mind French, write me in
Galician. And who are you? And yes, let's meet.

Thus I met Chus Pato that summer in Compostela on
the ancient Praza de Mazarelos. She arrived in the Cafetería
Candilejas, where we had arranged to coincide, bearing a pile
of Galician poetry books to lend me. I gulped (impossible!)
and took them, and that summer I learned Galician poetry
along with Galician. No wonder I say I went to Chus Pato
University! And all because of the orange cover of a book,
beside a cash register.

Two or three years later, I'd at last translated *m-Talá*.
And was friends with Chus Pato, nunha desas amizades que
durarán unha vida enteira.[3] When she finished *Charenton*
in 2004, Pato showed me the manuscript, and I started to
translate it that summer, before the book even came out in
Galicia. Curiously, I translated it not in Canada but in the
UK, in Macclesfield, Cheshire. Talk about crossing borders
with a Galician book of poetry! In 2007 *Charenton* was
published in the UK, distributed in the US, and co-published
in Canada, and *m-Talá* followed in 2009.

UNHA POESÍA INCOMESTÍBEL

I return to a sentence I speak frequently, for it bears
repeating: A translation always translates a reading practice
enacted on a text, not simply an original text. It is a set of
performative gestures implicating the body. And reading
practices are not just embodied but are determined by
ideology, culture, and history. They are codifications and
decodifications. As is the case with everyone, my reading is
determined by my history and culture: I am a writer from
Quebec who speaks fluently a dominant and globalized
language, English, which crosses borders easily and is

nourished by exception rather than the law, yet I live in a culture with a huge literature in a smaller language, French, which thrives in the sea of this English. As such, I read other cultures differently than would an anglo-Canadian elsewhere, let alone an English speaker elsewhere.

    I understand that meaning, signification in any one language is already largely contextual, occurs as coincidence, in every sense of that word — *co-incidence* — co-occurrence. The letter is autonomous but only prior to signification; at the moment of signification, it is co-extensive with something else. When meanings are required to pass between two cultures, there may be coincidences of meaning, but words do not coincide. *Je* in French is translated as *I*, but *je* and *I* are not equals. I is the centre of attention, je is my me speaking in a crowd of others about something; the weight of the phrase is on the *something*, not on that pillar-like word "I".

    The contexts of languages can be bridged at times only in a gestural way, that constantly abridges itself, annuls itself, can complete itself only in annulling itself, in a complex gesture of avowal and disavowal. For this reason, I often insist that translation, and particularly translation of poetry, is a performative gesture, a performance. Further, some of the effects of a given poetry are deeply rooted in the origin of the language and are not "translatable" or even ever "translated," but are often, all too often, erased in translation.

    I wanted a poetry that refused erasure. That clamoured. *Quería, e quero, unha poesía incomestíbel. Non consumidora. Que nos deixa pensar.* I wanted, and want, a poetry that could not be simply ingested. Not a consumer poetry. I wanted a poetry that lets us think.

TRADUCINDO UNHA POETA REALISTA

My recent experience with Pessoa helped me a lot when I saw the poetry of Chus Pato for the first time. I already harboured the idea of a productive multiplicity, of an "I" that is not limited in a single name, a single propulsion.

As Galician critic María Xesús Nogueira wrote of Pato's poetry in *Charenton*, it is a torrent, abrasive at times yet remarkable in its fluidity, and this, I'll add, even when Pato is ignoring rhythms, dissecting poetry itself, dissecting a country, interrupting herself to slap tremendously opinionated statements on the table, or leaving the reader abruptly to go out carousing until morning in a bar.[4] In *Charenton*, Pato again employs multiple forms: she uses the language of pamphlets, political speeches, lists; she twists Peter Weiss's *Marat/Sade* so that it has Galician characters, uses lyric lines that are baroque in their excesses, is sly, sincere, tears apart absolutely what it is to be not just a poet but a speaker of language, and this in a world that is an asylum: a Charenton. She flies forward at top speed through epochs and eras, accelerates us backwards in history, jumps in and across on herself, is not herself, is Sara-nat, is Jivi Noor, is not Jivi Noor but the Mathematical Muse who has grabbed control of the writing stick. Pato describes events and dreams so that they collide in a jumble, then untangle and spread. She is on a raft, in a bar, the circulation of the blood carries her onward, she is back in time, it is the 1970s, she is passing a Canadian lake on a train, then she leaps sideways. She switches verb tenses seemingly at random, is blatant, postures, is sincere again, erupts in a clamour of grammatical impossibilities, claims to be lazy, invites a multiplicity of characters to speak in the text, particularly women, historical and, well, I want to say "imagined" but really they are not imagined, they exist fully: Maximiliana, Mariana, Ruth, Liberdade Aguirre, Ingeborg Bachmann.

Reading *Charenton*, we get a wild and dense and particular sense of what Galicia is as a country, or not as a country, for it is, rather, an ancient and venerable and brave nation, a nation riven by fascism, by clientelism, by opportunism and usurpations, scarred by a transition to democracy in which the former usurpers became the new usurpers and continued as before by imposing huge silences. Yet Galicia is maintained stubbornly by literature, by the literary, by the ancestors whom Pato lists, by the recent present she assumes in speaking, and by her sense of what it is to be a woman in such a place, a woman raised under fascism but whose project is absolute freedom for the space of the poem and the signifier. Charenton is Galicia. Galicia is you, is me, trying to live in a locale under globalized capitalism, trying to pick up our fractured history and NOT make it whole, absolutely refusing to make it whole, but get it back, tear it away from the usurpers, and run with it.

Chus Pato is, in short, to use her words, a realist poet.

Where others are content to dream, Pato enacts. Where others construct transparencies in order to conceal commotions, she reports exactly everything. I think of her when I read Agamben (*Le temps qui reste* 115) for Pato creates in her work an "operative" time that is not linear. She lives at the Kilometre 0 of poetry, Lalín, a place where every absurdity of language, power, history, politics, and economics is condensed and acts upon the person, resident, or visitor. She was born just south of Lalín, in Ourense, the Roman city of auras of gold (ouro) and water (auga), the place where the Romans stopped because of the hotsprings of As Burgas, their water steaming at sixty-seven degrees Celsius.

It must have been the water. That's all I can say. What made Chus Pato? It must have been something in the water. I call Ourense the capital of poetry.

What attracts me to a text as a translator is something in the language, something in its insistence, and when I read a text that enters me and in my body insists without stopping, I have to translate it. Chus Pato's writing insists. It insists in such a way that it changes my English, changes my mouth, my mind when I read this poetry that rejects lyric (though it's a ploy because this is impossible, or is an operative contradiction, for it is also possible) to press forward in history, to confound every time and place, because her place, Galicia, Ourense, in its interior, in its sea, already holds all times, all places. Its bars are planets. Its streets are galaxies. Other literatures enter into her poetry too, and women of literature, like Ophelia, along with Lear, and Kafka. They are Galicians, in the poems of Chus Pato.

This is why I can bring into my English, into Canadian English, an English doubly colonized — by having been a British colony, and by existing in the shadow of the USA — the Galician space of Pato, realist poet.

IMPOSIBILIDADES

Yet María Reimóndez was right. The poetry of Pato is impossible to translate. It is within this impossibility that I found the freedom to work. Pato's impossibility does not come from the fact that the poetry is so rooted in Galicia; it comes from the language itself, from the way Pato uses Galician. Her poems don't "represent" "meaning" in Galician; why would I try to make them do so in English? Her poetry is impossible even in Galician!

Yet because Chus draws on tropes and references that

participate in world literature, like the theatre of Peter Weiss in *Charenton*, his *Marat/Sade*, her poetry is easily graspable by an audience outside Galicia. The land of the insane asylum, which is Galicia, could easily be Canada, America, or England as well.

What of the clamour of all the references to Galicia and Galician history that do not echo easily elsewhere in the world? On pages 82 and 83 of *Charenton*, when we read Pato's list of the names of her poetic antecedents and ancestors in Galicia, we are already steeped in the book, and this gives the reader all the context needed. By now, the reader already has his or her own Galicia, born in the reading of the book. When we come to the list, we know that it is one of writers, even if we can't identify many of them, and that it is necessary to translate this list into one's own list of writers. We have to admit that we too are inheritors, possess a literary inheritance that is ours alone. That's why I didn't replace Pato's names with names English speakers would recognize.

Even if the English-speaking reader is estranged from such a list in a way a Galician reader wouldn't be, the estrangement is part of confronting the text, drinking it in. And language, the language itself, penetrates the body of such a reader, leaves its trace in the body. There are no empty bodies when we read Pato. There cannot be.

The history of Galicia as a nation is more difficult to deal with. Who in Canada remembers much of the history of Spain? Of its civil war? Of those who had to flee? Those who were forced to emigrate to save their lives? Almost no one remembers this in the countries where I translate. We don't think much about Spain, or about Galicia. The history of Galicia is one of those things that somehow must penetrate the bodies of Pato's readers, not the mind. Thus I did not provide footnotes.

What penetrates, one thing that penetrates, is that every place must be seized fully and viscerally in order to transcend it, or to see how place transcends any fixed site. Pato's work helps us do that, to physically and viscerally inhabit not just the place of Galicia but our own place: *your* place, *mine*.

Charenton is not so specifically Galician after all: if we look at the structure of the book as a whole, surprisingly, the most Galician of references don't occur until three quarters of the way through the book, around page 75. In the first quarter of the book, up to page 25, we are in a place built over bombarded cities; we are in a forest that grows over one such city; we are in the dream of the trees. For the next twenty-five or thirty pages, we are in a barrage of poems thinking out facets of reading and writing, of representation and enactment. From about page 57 to 74, we follow women in their native place, which we inhabit alongside them, so that when we reach the pages that most strongly implicate the nation of Galicia, we are plunged into Weiss's *Marat/Sade* played in the asylum at Charenton, reenacted with monstrous Galician characters and peppered with Galician references from Ferrín poems to Cunqueiro poems. We may not recognize either of these latter names, but clearly it is a section of politics and legacy. The poems are absolutely strange, yet not strange, to us. The text is avowal, and disavowal. The bridge is built by making us leap, and we do leap! Chus Pato's poetry changes our English, changes our relationship with poetry, with language. It amplifies our relationship with mystery, the mystery of being and being incorporated in time and history. Pato's poetry opens my own literature. And it changes my mouth. It makes of me a Canadian who is different than I was before picking up the book, and I translate to share this.

INCOMODIDADE E RESISTENCIA

It is ridiculous to divide anything — a notion, an argument — into two categories. It's false from the start. But I am going to do it. There are two types of poetry. That of comfort (consolation), and that of discomfiting (perturbation or restiveness). The poetry of Chus Pato discomfits the reader and, within Galician culture, it discomfits both those people whom society accommodates and those whom society always tries to marginalize. Either of these groups can accept or reject the discomfiting that Pato offers. Even if they accept it, they can let it open paths to them of other possibilities of seeing and being, or they can simply try to recuperate the poetry, explain it away, use it to reinforce their pre-existing feelings.

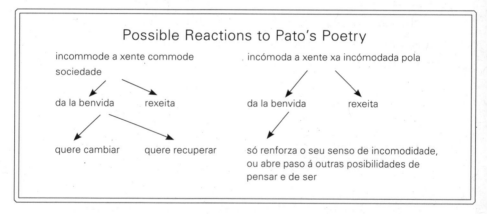

And in Canada, what reaction does Pato's poetry provoke? I think she perturbs readers and poets with her avatars, her multiple beings, and with her clamourous and racing use of histories, for we don't learn much history in North America. On the other hand, although we read *Charenton* in a hegemonic culture with much larger numbers of people, it seems, reading Pato, that we are also Galicians!

Further, Pato's poetry has sister poetry in Canada (mine, for example). The history of Spain and of Galicia vanishes (references to it are not caught by residents of my country), alas, but the qualities of language and the formal challenges to poetry are recognizable. Her literary references — Kafka, Lear, de Sade/Weiss, de Lautréamont — are recognizable as we too are part of Western European culture.

Why translate a Chus Pato and not another poet? My answer is that I want to perturb my language, my relationship with language, because I am also a creator of poetry, not only a translator. I seek a relationship with a language, with languages, that changes the mouth, and alters possibilities in social space. It thrills me to make this poetry come alive outside its native land — a poetry that is great in scope, crucial — and see it grow, in the words of others, both readers and poets. In the poetry of Chus Pato, we are actors, *auctores*, and not merely consumers. We have bodies and language. We are. In a world that wants to obliterate our differences in the name of money, of capital, of exchanges of goods, Pato makes operative an exchange of words that lets us discover who we are more powerfully, and who we can be in a future we can make ours. This book helps us be and defy, and resist and *be*.

*Le sujet... est la possibilité que la langue ne soit pas,
n'ait pas lieu – ou, mieux, qu'elle n'ait lieu qu'à travers
sa possibilité – de ne pas être, sa contingence.*
▋ Giorgio Agamben, *Ce qui reste d'Auschwitz* (158)

SHAGGY MAMMAL
INTERVENÇÃO[1]

▋ These days I've been thinking a lot in Galician about the notion of site or place as provisional theatre. Thinking about and in spacings, placings, stagings, and how to think and be in such spacings — a thinking always in language and always spatial, physical, as well, because we are sited, incorporated beings. The purpose of this thinking is to learn how to be able to act and enact (and this is an emergency, how to emerge) in the world in a way other than that which hegemonic politics today would construct for me. Since community and politics –the "what is around us" — act to construct us and condition us as individuals, we urgently need thinking that pushes the boundaries of spacings.

This brings me to notions of modifications, insertions, volumes, and placements, and the "essentiellement lacunaire," "que importe qui parle" (*L'archéologie* 89). The quoted words are Michel Foucault's. Along with Foucault, I see notions of author and novelty as ideological constructs destined to brake, limit, and constrain the proliferation of ideas, meanings, refractions, ruptures, and thresholds. "Novelty" and "innovation" are also regulatory devices, or can be seen as libidinal bands, that is, they also perform the opposite of what they claim. Not all "novelty" is new, and the ways in which it acts to *regulate* novel formations need to be examined.

To the "essentiellement lacunaire," with its echoes of contingency and the "ne pas être," I would add the notion of archive. Derrida has said, in his marvellous text *Mal d'archive:* "On associe l'archive avec la répétition et la répétition avec le passé. Mais c'est de l'avenir qu'il s'agit ici et de l'archive comme expérience irréductible de l'avenir" (109). The archive is *an irreducible experience of the future.* Archive is not memory and storehouse, says Derrida, but dispersion. Its site moves outward in diffuse ways, for if archive reaches us in any way, it will be only in the time to come. Of course, the "time to come" is always already coming and, thus, already arriving. It presses on us now, and *now.*

In a sense it was Fernando Pessoa and his O *Guardador de Rebanhos*, a book from the early twentieth century, that were my opening to archive, for Pessoa created his own archive in a steamer trunk that still, today, is being deciphered. When I translated the poems of O *Guardador* in early 2000, they prompted me to think as well of theatre and thus of place, and even of the site of writing — a *site* that is the *moment* of writing — as theatral. Here I don't use the word "theatrical" for it has the sense of excessive or staged or performed, but theatral, to mean "disposed to enactment," disposed to participate in a scene, with scene understood as being something constructed and not totally predictable. My translation activity also led me to ponder — and even laugh at — Pessoa's super-abundance of authors, of writers. Perhaps Pessoa's is the best response yet to the "que importe qui parle."

Once led to notions of theatre, community, and voice-personality as a staging or disposition-to-staging, I realized that perhaps, against the huge and destructive forces at work in the world, *esforzas pequenas, pequeniñas,* small forces or efforts, small but situated, could work better than bellowing one's resistance. I was reminded of the strategy that we used when I worked in Customer Relations in VIA Rail with customers who yelled at us on the phone. We'd talk in a low voice, and slowly. If the customer continued to bellow rapid-fire into the phone, we'd soften our voices further and speak more slowly. Sometimes we'd end up whispering, but eventually this tactic causes the indignant person to slow down and speak normally. My *esforzas pequenas* in poetry became Little Theatres. I wrote the book while translating Chus Pato's *m-Talá*, a book of poetry that embraces and concocts theatrical formations. In fact, the diminutive *teatriños* comes from her, to me.

Little Theatres also surged from the book that preceded it. O Cidadán was – in its very form — an argument against purity in which essay surges as a form proper to poetry, and one that promulgates lyric as a form or force that lives in poetry irrevocably. In its forms, O Cidadán enacts what it speaks of, to insist that the crossing of borders, that leakages in borders, is what makes entities (countries, persons, communities) possible. Leakages in writings are what make writing possible. Leakages in languages, idioms, make languages possible. Thus the *teatriño* in Galicia became the little theatre in Canada, and migrated later to America, across a border to a place where editors in a country in terrible need of little theatres first published some of the poems.

All these notions of community and spacing in writing, some of which came from Galician, return me to Foucault, and to his curious words from *L'archéologie du savoir*: "Plus d'un, comme moi sans doute, écrivent pour n'avoir plus de visage" (28). It is the statement par excellence of the theatral.

Is it visible here in English that I am accustomed to composing, writing and thinking in different languages? My relation with English is complicated, and anyone who speaks another language or languages will relate to what I say. For thinking, dreaming, living in other languages besides English makes English a kind of strange place to be. First, it means English is no longer a natural language. It is always hypothetical and, thus, at risk, for it does not, and cannot, contain everything.

To me, it is the most beautiful thing to put language into my mouth. It assuages what burns there. So I put French there, I put English there, I put Galician there. *I put Galician there!* As a practice of poetry that involves both writing and translating, mine is a practice of contingency and permeability, rather than representation, a practice in and of language as social space, as social spacings in which embodiment and speech both play a role. The body alters space, and language alters space, language(s) alter space. Alter our mouths. Alter each, and each other. In imprévisible ways. Language — especially learning another language — alters the mouth, the body, the body's borders. And thus alters the ears.

To deform a quote from that swell book of Derrida's, "Autant et plus qu'une chose du passé, avant elle, l'archive la langue devrait mettre en cause la venue de l'avenir" (*Mal d'archive* 56).[2] Because of this future, and its *venue* which is always coming, a question keeps nagging at me: what does it mean to *trobar* today? It is a question always current with us, whether we acknowledge it or not, when we set out to write or read or study poetry. And the accent we bring to our task — which is, in a sense, also part of our answer — is an affect that effects and affects the language we write in. In my case, the fact of thinking this question in Galician and in Portuguese, *et en français*, affects my English. And your English, if you read the result and if we both, all, write. And language thus affected is alive, and bears new possibility with it.

After *O Cidadán* and *Little Theatres*, I found myself increasingly intrigued by the construct of "lyric" voice. I was led to explore one of the founts of lyric in Western European poetry, the *trobadores* of the Iberian peninsula, who wrote in an era when writing poetry, *escribir poesía*, had a single word instead of two: *trobar*. In looking at the way their constructions worked both inside and outside the poems, and querying our record of them and what we have made or not made of that record, I found ways of seeing lyric that altered my own prior views. Theirs was an interesting time, for between 1100 and 1250 or so, a construct took form in their literature. Instead of the epic voice and the narrative where the speaker was outside the poem — an omniscient voice recounting history — there was the speaking voice of an individual recounting the poem, talking about "himself" or "herself" and his or her "feelings," and addressing another individual interlocutor. This voice was a construct. It was not "pure" and did not masquerade as "true." All kinds of things arose for me from this exploration, and still arise, provoking questions of subjectivity and how it is built, and of archive, of how documents have come to us, of how we tend to make these documents speak *us* and *our world*, excising all in the first document (which is never an original document) that does not fit what we believe.[3]

In doing this I feel a breath of such fresh air: I feel so unfashionable. Realizations of relatedness, and — if you think from the perspective of wholeness — of the "fracture" of the self, which result from poststructuralist and feminist exploration, have led many poets to reject lyric, as if it were just an expression of a united "feeling" or of the inner states of an "I" who is an unquestioned and centred subject. Invoking the lyric voice seems quite at odds with current views of the subject's plurivocality and multiplicity, its torqued nature, and at odds with thinking transcendence and its problematics. For perhaps the old problem of "the soul" rises here again, and most poets — who are secular and philosophically materialist — don't want to take it on.[4]

Yet lyric arose (perhaps again … there's Sappho of course) in our western languages at that medieval time as a breach in what was epic speech, though epic speech itself was already bending. This lyric spread across Iberia from France partly because of religious pilgrimages, partly because of the restlessness and abandon in society at large that set many people adrift (not all pilgrims were that religious), and partly because of wars, crusades, and their resulting displacements. It picked up local and popular culture references, rhythms, tendencies, songs, and references. Lyric was both fresh and weary. Its "I" was something resolutely constructed, not the "I" of romanticism: the lyric "I" was *theatral*. This intrigued and intrigues me. What was it all about in 1050, in 1200, in Galician and Portuguese? How has it been described for us and handed down to us? What was going on in the language then; what were the pulsations, the affects?

This led me to look concomitantly into the workings

of archive and of knowledge, those experiences of the future. In Foucault I found words that helped me:

> Une formation discursive [in this case, the cantigas] n'occupe pas tout le volume possible que lui ouvrent en droit les systèmes de formation de ses objets, de ses énonciations, de ses concepts; elle est essentiellement lacunaire, et ceci par le système de formation de ses choix stratégiques. De là le fait que reprise, placée et interprétée dans une nouvelle constellation, une formation discursive donnée peut faire apparaître des possibilités nouvelles... il s'agit d'une modification dans le principe d'exclusion et de possibilité des choix qui est due à l'insertion dans une nouvelle constellation discursive. (*L'archéologie* 89–90)[5]

I knew that my reading of the medieval lyric would cause that particular discursive formation to be "reprise, placée et interprétée dans une nouvelle constellation." Why? Simply because I have a body, *this* body; I am embodied "like this." I am a body, reading, and I live in another time. If, as Derrida noted, it is the archivist who produces archive — "l'archivation produit autant qu'elle enregistre l'événement" (*Mal d'archive* 34) — whatever physically happened to me when my body confronted these manuscripts would determine, not in fixity but in dispersion, what is produced. Poetry, yes, is produced, but the process also produces a bodily change in me.

Who said there was a burning in the mouth and what that burning was ... and how the mouth was changed and what the word was and if there was a word and the sound that the word made in the air, and the arms rising with this word.

Who burned in the mouth. *Quen queimaba pola boca.*

Whose charred mouth, charred word. Charnel. Carnal.

To learn a new language changes the mouth. *Cambia a boca.* We were hurt in this, we found ourselves in this, our speaking veered off, my speaking veered, whose speaking veered?

There were these and these broken material things.

Falo. Fáloo.

———

And poetry. The movement between the is and the not-is, between the not-is and the is-not, in this space which is huge and full of teeth and valleys, poetry is first made, poetry's first making, teeth and grass, dirt and fingers. And the mouth. That mouth that won't let us forget it ever.

Why do we have a mouth?

———

And yet, also, the cohabitation with what is always outside the self, for language is also forever outside the body, continues, goes on, the body falls, the body is *enfermo ou doente*, the body is enclosed/*encadeado*, the window is shut, the street noises are faint in the ears and the dreams are loud...

And language is in the body. For with the death of a single body, an entire language can die.

> And burning. And the memory of houses. Of leaves. Of cries. Not of a fixed or stable origin, but of every origin, and of crossing borders and boundaries, ears wide open.
>
> I am not sure. We are not sure. The I of us is not sure.

Here my essay veered off, but in its veering you can see perhaps a bit of my trajectory and difference in practice, in which multiple languages are at work and the "author" is underlined and set aside so as to wade into the proliferation of sense that otherwise — or always — risks being shut down, flattened, rejected as "red spades." If I could sum up my project in writing, I would do so with the words Stéphane Mallarmé wrote in his note to his poem "Un coup de dés," a note re-cited by Derrida as an epigraph in *Writing and Difference*, thus a note already archive, archived, *modified, inserted volumnal, placed* and, always, "essentiellement lacunaire":

> "Le tout sans nouveauté
> qu'un espacement
> de la lecture"   (v)

> Todos os discursos, qualquer que fosse o seu estatuto,
> a sua forma, o seu valor, e qualquer que fosse o tratamento
> que se lhes desse, desenrolar-se-iam no anonimato do murmúrio.
> ‖ Michel Foucault, Ditos e Escritos III (264)

O CADOIRO: THE CATARACT

▌ *O cadoiro* is, literally, *the place where falling is made.* In Galician, *cadoiro* is one word for waterfall. Cataract, perhaps. Thus, *the fall.* This to me is the place of poetry. For whoever writes poetry must be prepared, ever, to fall down.

And in 2004 I did fall. Having already fallen into Galician and then Portuguese, I had barely stood up again when I fell — or leapt — into one of the founts of lyric in Western Europe, the troubadour poetry of the medieval Galician-Portuguese songbooks, the *cancioneiros*. These songbooks hold what remains to us of the two hundred years of medieval Iberian poetry, all written in Galician-Portuguese, predecessor of both modern Portuguese and modern Galician. Influenced by Provençal verse of courtly love, the Iberian peninsular cantigas also bent and amplified that lineage, incorporating indigenous elements, such as evocations of the sea, or the tradition of women's song.

The troubadour verse speaks to us in the first-person singular, in a breach with the epic narrative mode and with ecclesiastical modes of praise. Gregorian chant and Arab love poetry preceded and infiltrated it, just as Provençal poetry was concurrent with it. Richard Zenith, attentive translator of these Iberian cantigas into English,[1] in his *An Unsung Literature* wrote: "The troubadour poetry that began in Provence and spread in all directions — northern France, Germany, Italy and Iberia — was one of the first expressions of the unrelenting individuality that was to shake the Church's foundations via heterodox reform movements and eventually lead to the Renaissance."[2] In this verse, the speaker's own subjectivity, own feelings, are the poetic "substance," yet these are quite consciously *constructed* by the poet, never "unmediated," always social, intended, and profane: directed toward another human, not to God. This human "turn" is at the very root of lyric, and the act of turning is a movement of incredible fragility and febrility — a turning away from God's love and its purported sufficiency toward a secular love that never purports sufficiency.

Three Iberian songbooks have come down to us. Together (for they are not entirely coincident), they hold three main types of poem: *de amor, de amigo, de escarnio e maldizer*. Courtly love; feminine longing for the absent lover; scorn and slander: such ripples in language. After years of dreaming "Erín, go to Lisbon to read the books," I went to live in Lisbon in early 2004 to read these *cancioneiros*.

It was as if the geeky Lee Meriwether had let go of her clipboard and entered The Time Tunnel.[3] Reading is already ever a wandering and in Lisboa, Olispoa, port of Odysseus, I entered the *cancioneiros*. The "fingerprints" of these books — their inscription, their orthography, their graphemes — took hold of me. How I loved the movements and jointings of the lines and letters that lay bare the cadence of voices and the attention/inattention of the copying hand. In the *cantigas de amigo* of the *Cancioneiro da Biblioteca Nacional*, and in the *cantigas de amor* of the *Cancioneiro de Ajuda*, I fell into such tapestries of word and sound, the "wallpaper"-repetitive sonorities of, yes, an unrequited love. Oh *cancioneiros*, oh ports of portu-cale, with the lilt of Celtic marking the vernacular of vanished Rome. *Camiñarmos polas palabras....*

The most extensive of these three songbooks, the *Cancioneiro da Biblioteca Nacional*, holds over sixteen hundred cantigas of all types. It was copied, or created, in the sixteenth century, three hundred and fifty years after the cantigas were first written and, curiously, not in Portugal or Galicia but in Italy, from an earlier copy or perhaps two copies on scrolls that were likely disintegrating at the time of transcription and which may have been contemporary with the troubadours. At the time of this copying, the first grammars of Portuguese were only just appearing; the written language was not yet as settled as our English is now.[4] As such, the cancioneiro's script follows the pace and expression of the troubadours' voices. In these songbooks, poetry works against itself as mythic quantity, as transcendence, as voice; here, writing itself scratches the lyric.

By closely studying the poems in a lithographed reproduction of a photographic facsimile of the sixteenth-century manuscript (the "original" was too fragile), itself copied from an "original" and vanished epigraph, and studying later transcriptions as well—critical/diplomatic but also modern anthologized versions, I hoped to respond with my own corporeal presence to questions that burned, and burn, for me:

What is a work of art?
What is an archive?
What does it mean to "trobar" today?

Reading the songbooks, I was very aware of reading a copy of a copy of a copy. With Derrida's *Mal d'archive* and Foucault's *Archéologie du savoir* echoing in me, I let the poems' so-called secondary effects absorb me—the many aspects of the poems eliminated by modernizing transcribers who diverge and alter them in their effort to make "content," "regularities of form," and the "author's intent" appear. I began to recognize that the idea of an "original" poem is ever-elusive; the original exceeds our grasp *always*.

I looked to discern, in my own way, the first copyist's (who was of course never first at all) markings, looked for the surfaces the copyists might have seen and then reproduced, and I examined how they made the forms before my eyes. The original script—simple, smudged, worn—is beautiful; in it, the words' physical presence is a veritable record of breath and rhythms of speech, of accent. In this script and in its forms on the page, I looked at what propelled lyric, what made it *palpable*. What could not be standardized, so was later dropped. What was called an error.

The poems awed me with the liquidity of their repetitive sonority, the levels of non-meaning, of plaint, of vibratory extension. This sonority breaks against the reader's own *langue de fond* as surprise and murmur, in that traverse or cut that a person schooled in one language experiences in reading another.

The cantigas opened other lyric doors to me, too. I discovered the medieval synchronic sense of time, a space where the solace of the Fichtean curve (with its rising action, conflict, climax, denouement) does not operate. As Portuguese scholar Stephen Reckert says: "we see here the typical medieval disinterest for chronological sequence, often substituted by a vision of events that was simultaneous and pictorial."[5] Narrative advances differently. The aspect of salvation and new life, introduced later into lyric by Dante in his *Vita Nuova*, is not yet present, and without the prospect of salvation — the resacralization of the profane — linearity does not function in the same overarching way.

The *cantigas de amor* especially and perversely drew me. They are the poems most influenced by Provençal verse, that is, by the conventions of courtly love, and express a kind of sexless longing where bodies never touched and names were never named: a sexual tension and withholding. These cantigas are so repetitive, so predictable, yet within a few set phrases and conceits, schemes of very regular rhyme and metre, they induce such *saudade*, longing, *soidade*, loneliness. Their sonority is their beauty; their repetition is their glamour. They embrace banality on banality's terrain and then exit it on some other field entirely. What emerges is an expression of great peace and longing and breath and orphic variability. Variability, yes, for mastery was often shown by deviations, by a simple twist, a break, by a line that didn't rhyme. These disruptions of expectation, these disjoints, marked delight, excellence.

The *cantigas de amigo* are much closer to what we today recognize as lyric — on the surface. Beneath it, there's a sexual mirage and gender usurpation that highlights the constructedness of the voice — for men write in the voices of women, borrowing from a long-standing local tradition of women's song that likely predated Roman occupation and is still present in Galicia today. These poems are not courtly but common and, in them, concrete images emerge for the first time. In response, I wrote plaints of my own, enacting, mixing and echoing, translating but two or three poems and enclosing them among those that are sheer invention, and attributing my own poems impulsively to whichever troubadour's name was most proximate in my notebooks.

The forms and plaints of the cantigas thus seeped into my work, unseating forms, compelling variegated sounds and capacities, irregularities. Now, I hope, the cantigas, rife with ambiguities and errors, can resonate for us, too, in Canada, in English. With the *cancioneiros* as *fond* from which to draw sounds and layerings of interpretation, transcription, my sole aim was to transpose a tone and delicacy, a splendor, a visual pleasure into my own poems. A wandering and turn.

The exchange from one language to another in the work occurs, above all, on the level of tropes, soundscapes. At the same time, my poems incorporate formal structures of archive (use archival numbering, and the names of troubadours, as part of what I wrote), the material substrate of the cantigas. Related texts and textures also enter the poems, pushing at or revealing aspects not of the original text but of my own transcription of the transcription in the photograph, printed on a printing press, of the transcription of the now-lost apograph we have never seen that we so confidently call the *original*. And subject to noise, to the noise of my own being and experience and language. They are, simply, poems.

In a reverse tide, understandably, the troubadours started to infiltrate my other reading. In Jacques Derrida's *Mal d'archive*, which I read wandering the steep streets of Lisbon in the February rain, I discovered an *archive ache* that his words do not anticipate, one which in *tone* approaches the Galician/Portuguese untranslatable word *saudade*. Derrida "sounds like" the medieval *cantigas de amor*. It is as if the cantigas also, secretly, bear something of the Hebraic.[6]

As I worked, I began to corrupt and invent Derridean lament into the text'ure of the paper, creating three-dimensional readings, volumes, and even performances, interactions with other people, with stone walls, with spaces and texts and voices. As if I could learn better how the poems could work on the page by disturbing what we know of page itself. What I give the reader of these poems is a synchronic band of libidinal space-time *where writing itself scratches the lyric and where the thread of speech itself is palpable, illumined.*

In *The End of the Poem*, Giorgio Agamben wrote:

> the troubadours want not to recall arguments consigned to a *topos* but instead to experience the very event of language as original *topos*... an absolute proximity of love, speech, and knowledge. The *razo*, which lies at the foundation of poetry and constitutes what the poets call its dictation (*dictamen*), is therefore neither a biographical nor a linguistic event. It is instead a zone of indifference, so to speak, between lived experience and what is poeticized, an "experience of speech" as an inexhaustible experience of love. *Amor* is the name given by the troubadours to this experience of the dwelling of speech in the beginning: and for them love is therefore the *razo de trobar* par excellence. (79)

Such was the place where I fell. It became "place" in the act of falling. A place where I could fall and keep falling. Where I wrote poems that were palimpsests, markings, and echoes bearing the shiver of the archive. Origin is always already lost here, lost again and again, and its very losing makes origin possible. And if this fallen trajectory of origin stabilizes at all, it is somewhere far ahead of it. At the time of reading. No wonder we trip and fall.

As Derrida urges: "The question of the archive is the question of the future, of the future itself, a question of a response, of a promise and a responsibility for tomorrow. If we wish to know what the archive is trying to tell us, we cannot know but in the time to come. Perhaps" (*Mal d'archive* 60; my translation).

Perhaps. Poetry is a remnant that moves toward a future people, says Chus Pato (my translation, paraphrased from her *Secesión*).

Is this the reason why I find myself, again, and ever, in the falling-down-place? The place poetry is made. The "not-yet." The very falling poses the question of the future. The Peninsular—Iberian or other—is not an island, but part of the Maine. In its turning from the certainties of God to a human insufficiency, it is a promise and a responsibility for tomorrow. *Mâine.* And this, "peu importe qui parle."

What I hope my poems open to readers, as they did to me, their first reader, is that a subjectivity, an I, an *eu*, in entering and being altered by words, fallen, befallen, enters the *saudade* of world. Enters Agamben's "whatever singularity." Enters Norma Cole's "body of expectation." Fred Wah's "music at the heart of thinking." Robin Blaser's "image nation." Or his "cry of Merlin." Fanny Howe's "full heart." Lisa Robertson's "stuttered accoutrements." Chus Pato's "infinite of language." Choral. *Nin sen chorar.*

STAGING VERNACULARS

ABOUTNESS
1

We are always about to speak. There is an abruptness in the body, about to speak. We are silent. We have nothing to say. Our hands form words. We lean forward or turn away. We are about to speak. Our mouths shut.

Speech troubles us. Speech troubles us in order to speak. We shake hands and move our hands. We enter speech. Our faces enter speech.

Speech enters us. There is a cæsura.

This cæsura troubles us. In the sense of: gives us trouble. Troubles the where of us.

vernacular_cæsura

2

We have access to the vernacular. *Cette frontière tenue qui sépare le grave du comique, le sublime du grotesque.* The mouth opens. The mouth takes in. When we speak, we speak the usual. We speak occasionally, to suit occasions. To the friend, we mention: "My tooth hurts." At the dentist, we could say, "My tooth hurts," but we could also say, "The long part of the tooth that is rooted in the bone below the gum line is giving me a feeling of pain that jags into my ear and throat." Both of them are the same vernacular. The addressee is different.

3

Is it because of this addressee, then, that this vernacular is a surface that can never be flattened out, that instead offers a ground that is stippled or bent? It *is* still flat but *is it?* We are always unfolding its aspects, or it is "to be unfolded." A potentiality, thus. Thus beautiful. It is in us. The mouth takes it in. The vernacular needs us in order to move. Corporeality, cadence. *Cadou.*

4

Your cadouri, I write to her this morning. *For which I thank you,* I write to her. The dawn comes. The roosters made dawn. I'll explain this later; it's in a vernacular, our vernacular. Split or chosen from a common tongue. Selected or indigenous. To us, indigenous speaks a heartsong here: *agasallos, cadouri.*

5

The vernacular is a folding of the common with the particular and, like every folding, is a staging because in folding, it takes up space. (In the sense of "occupies" but also in the sense of "taking up" a hobby, mathematics, or knitting.) Or it makes space possible. It has embodiment. It mimics the body. Then echoes it. Then mirrors it. As such, it is staged and as staged, it is also prosthetic. It is not "us." But it "obtains" us, and we engage it to obtain, or seize. Thus, prosthetic.

Here is a model of the prosthesis:

indigenous_proper

the vernacular is characterized by its ability to move with the user

Wittgenstein: "*The limits of my language* mean the limits of my world" (*Tractatus* 5.6).

The vernacular is enacted in the tension between the everyday and the distinctive, the common and the particular, and this tension, possibly, in some senses, constitutes "staging," and is the very stage on which a vernacular is enacted.

That this tension is productive. That the staging is temporary, always. That "native" is "exposure" here too. For as in Giorgio Agamben's elaboration of singularity in *The Coming Community*, the native is always that which is exposed to its own outside, which is ever "adjacent to." Otherwise, how would we identify it as native? How would native as singular be staged?

"*C'est à l'intérieur du trouble qui existe entre le parler et l'écrit,*" says French playwright Eugène Durif, "*que se site la notion même de théâtre, bien plus que dans le concept de personnages ou d'action*" (n.p.). This "trouble" interior to language (thus us) also has an interior wherein theatre is situated and, as such, it is also exposure.

6

All of this means that the native or *indigenous proper* may make possible a fraying. A passage through the trouble of the cæsura. But is there fraying, or is time just passing? Could these imbrications of time mean that "native" is absolutely not essence? The "casa americana," the American house, in Galiza of the late nineteenth century, built in Cuban style with Cuban flourishes by the returned emigrants, by "natives" come back, is now, in the twenty-first century, a variety of "Galician house."

What essence pervades here? None, but stagings. Tensionalities, which depend on context and are thus ever exposed. Like Derridean signatures, none of them guarantee the presence (ever) of the one who signed them, whose purported original presence gives rise to legal value.

A staging always undoes this knot. Opens the very cæsura…

7

The vernacular is tied deeply to notions of legal value. The mention of legal is thus no hazard here. The "vernal" of Rome's vernacular was, first, a legal distinction, the slave born in the master's house, thus never purchased, therefore both inside (absolutely housed) and outside (spacing, the law of consumption). Thus "versus" came to mean "native."

We must remember then that the vernacular is never purely constituted, that it takes place within a master's house, thus is always already inside mastery, a mastery that is not it but which contains it, so that the vernacular cannot be or conduct a fraying on its own. Nor is it "natural."

The vernacular takes place in the locale of its confinement, yet is exposed to its outside, or confinement itself would not be sayable. And we *are* about to speak. And even before we speak words, utter sounds,

> there is this possibility: someone else *will hear*.

8

What does the vernacular say then about borders or edges? About the hem or frill? What are the borders of its staging? If it is "in the locale of its confinement," where does the locale end? The lip of the proscenium? The fold, or seam? The flounce?

That the outside constitutes the inside, we know from Judith Butler. Locale ends because another locale abuts it. This abutment makes the vernacular visible. Thus border is threshold only. Permeable in its very nature. Permeability is, I guess, its nature. Sill or frill.

(Nature always has to be "guessed at." Nature moves too.)

And this abutment, this alongside, is the first *para-deigma*, as Giorgio Agamben wrote in *The Coming Community*, and is the root meaning of paradigm. To lie down the length of one against the length of the other: this is how the vernacular thresholds us.

9

The fold dissimulates. Alongside another fold. Raise its flap and it says something else. Raise its flap again. The vernacular is often a dissimulation for this is its structure. It can't help its folds. The fingers enter. I ask you a question. We unfold a response. The tips of the fingers can't quite touch, but appear to. This mimics the mouth. The vernacular is a septum. Its model is our prosthesis we use to foretell.

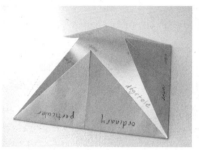

vernacular_boca

10

Who are we, then, as common people, in particular? Apparently the vernacular is our common voice. Yet, though common, we bear particulars. We move in time. Time moves around us. There is a displacement of air in the mouth. The wing rises. Occasionally, we find this pleasant. A vernacular binds us in a mastery, but we can move. We open our fingers. We select. We ask the other to select. We count letters. We select and code. We are told. We are answered.

11

I have struggled some time now to deploy a set theory for staging vernaculars:

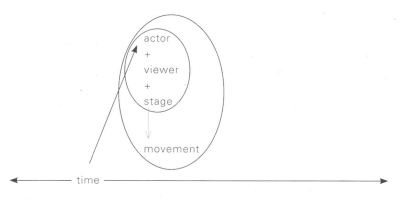

staging=>construct (thus an outside)=>exposure

The vernacular gives me reason to talk (again) about staging. It is the staging here that interests me most of all. Staging's body or incorporation. The body emerges as the site of tensions: an exposure outward, an unfolding, an absolute inwardness.

The viewer sees, or listens. The deaf and blind viewer feels the actor tread across the boards of the stage. This "felt" is "seeing."

The vernacular is, I think, ever a projection into a theatrical space, or into a space that (of course) is theatrical. In most of our envisioning, "vernacular" is a space projected as natural or local when it is in fact a construct, and this construct is blurred, has blurred edges or folds, has amplitude. Has light. Is prosthetic. And moves in time.

Today's vernaculars will be altered unrecognizably by time. Shakespeare wrote in a vernacular English that is riddled to us now. The medieval Galician-Portuguese cantigas of scorn and slander today bring puzzlements and need footnotes to explain the jokes. Where the listener is different, altered, then the joke is lost in time.

There is a time of languages, too, that makes some sayings untranslatable. Ah, I say to the dinner guests, this song (in Portuguese) is so beautiful. What is it saying, the diners ask? It is a folk song, I say: "My country is more beautiful for selling flowers." Then I say it doesn't make any sense in English. (But it is perhaps even more beautiful for being impenetrable, for laying clear the limits in our own tongue that can't speak this beauty. Time's separation has pulled vernaculars astray.)

indigenous_folded

12

Let us go to the dictionary, as if it could knit time together again.

ver.nac.u.lar

- the distinctive language of a profession, class, or group
- the common spoken language of the people in a particular country or region
- the architecture of a particular place or people
- the common name of a plant

=

- as opposed to official or formal language
- as opposed to the style used for large official or commercial buildings
- as opposed to writing

stag.ing

- the act, process, or style of presenting a play on a stage

- a temporary structure of supports and platforms used in building or working on something

- a technique to increase the velocity achieved by a spacecraft's launch vehicle by using multiple propulsive stages, each being jettisoned after use.

(Encarta World English Dictionary, © 1999 Microsoft Corporation)

13

Is "to stage" to fake or tamper? To speed up? I like the idea of rocket stages: "multiple propulsive stages, each being jettisoned after use." This is my way in poetry (perhaps).

14

Because two of my three tongues, Galician and French, are Romance languages, "derived from Latin's roaming," I will also speak here of the vernaculars of Latin, their spread across the south of Europe, where each of them is a staging or transition. Bearing time. Stemming not from official diction but from the idiom of soldiers, rough with use, mixed with the idioms of those already in the place, the conquered peoples, the administered. Thus every time it is the language of the common soldier (Latin) exposed to the particular (place, accent, settlement). Even where the lexicon of the settled language has vanished over time, its accent is still borne in the roaming vernacular that still enacts a transition, a movement in time.

For a vernacular bears an accent. It is common but it is particular (the accent of one valley is not the accent of another).

The vernacular is rooted in a place, but must exceed its border in order to persist in time.

15

But not in the way capital exceeds borders: so as to consume and ignite consumption, in order solely to make "fake" money for the few — fake, for they are not even spending it, they are "investing"; fake because it is not used to ensure well-being; it is not needed — and to instill its own vernacular into the common polity. For capitalism has its own vital language, common and particular: values, mission, customer.

The vernacular of which I speak will not refer to v., m., c. On these subjects, it has nothing to say.

The agency of capitalism's speech is not desired by the vernacular. Though, yes, v.'s speakers still almost everywhere wear c.'s clothes.

16

Does the vernacular desire? How does it desire? (The "what" of desire is always already lost or, if not lost, then receding.) Not agency but adjacency. An adjacency not *figée* or fixed in one language or time but moving across the border of its own touching with the other. The inward side of exposure.

There is a limit to my language that exceeds the limits of my world: one that is translatable if not representable.

17

The vernacular shimmers, I think, with Agamben's idea of the "absolutely unrepresentable community" (*Coming Community* 24,5). It is his definition of "ease" as adjacency rather than agency that compels me here, and moves us away from the border crossing that is typical of capital:

Against the hypocritical fiction of the unsubstitutability of the individual, which in our culture serves only to guarantee its universal representability, Badalona presents an unconditioned substitutability, without either representation or possible description — an absolutely unrepresentable community.

Ease is the proper name of this unrepresentable space. The term "ease" in fact designates, according to its etymology, the space adjacent (*ad-jacens, adjacent*), the empty place where each can move freely, in a semantic constellation where spatial proximity borders on opportune time and convenience borders on the correct relation. The Provençal poets (whose songs first introduce the term into Romance languages in the form aizi, aizimen) make ease a terminus technicus in their poetics, designating the very place of love. Or better, it designates not so much the place of love, but rather love as the experience of taking-place in a whatever singularity. In this sense, ease names perfectly that "free use of the proper" that, according to an expression of Friedrich Hölderlin's, is "the most difficult task." "*Mout mi semblatz de bel aizin.*" This is the greeting that, in Jaures Rudel's song, the lovers exchange when they meet." (*Coming Community* 24)

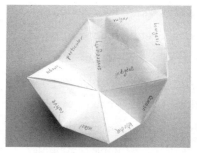
vernacular_sovereignty

The "taking-place in whatever singularity" is, to my mind, the staging of the vernacular par excellence. It is the local exposed to ease, to the "free use of the proper." This, yes, is *ethos*.

In this, Badalona could be, too, the name of the space of translation.¹

18

Translation borders language by lying down alongside, the full length of the body ex-posed. It is improper always. And necessary. Otherwise the arguments — yours and mine — are embodied solely in Northern and Western monoculture. (The Southern hemisphere is silenced, Africa is not heard, the boreal forest is vanishing, water trickles away.) For translation necessarily involves the ear of the listener.

Perhaps the vernacular also needs a theory of reception, of its reception. How else can we talk about nature, unless it is through reception?

We return to the addressee here. We move across time.

19

To think out the space (if space there is) between common and proper language is to think of movement, incessant, as site. This is the site of the present tense, thus the everyday, whose proper home is always the present.

The stage on which vernaculars are mounted (take place, ride) is portable, provisional. The stage for vernaculars *is* the world. Or not the world but "its" world. Thus its potential insularity. And its commonness. A vernacular needs only two to operate, to be "common": *agasallo, cadou*. And it needs adjacency — translation — to be exposed.

ABOUT TO SPEAK
20

In my own work in poetry, I often try to first think out a shape or physical presence, spatial, to advise me for each book. This is not a deliberate thinking but seems necessary to me so I do it. Or: the book comes to me as spatial entity. Or: language itself for me is already spatial.

In O *Cidadán*, this shape took the form of the fraction or score. Its stage was small enough to project a word's relation with another word as penetrative, interpenetrative, interresonant, but not hierarchical. As repetitive (for there were many fractions). As dispersed spatially in order to avoid emphasizing tonality (as sentences or verses do, as a matter of course). O *Cidadán* was drawn out in response to the emergence of these fractions, drawn out as a public space wherein the private (Georgette) and sexual (Georgette) are also political gestures, and occur in language's spacings.[2] The public space also includes an argument for proximity, and for the engagement that results when two bodies (or words) are proximate, placed into the same visual field without any logical or syntactic connectives. The sexual and prosthetic both make the citizen exist somatically, and this soma is visible as fold. Thus there are pages "between" the pages. We are marked, socially marked, by what is between the pages (and by our forgetting of history, which we do not yet see).

In *Little Theatres*, staging is addressed explicitly. The book asks what kind of stage we need in our times, and posits a simple surface where the smallest gesture reverberates in its smallness. The book allows a second language to enter English, not to fray English but to expose that it is always already frayed. Incomplete and exposed to a *cadou*, if we will just see it.

The "divinity" of the word (the divine on earth, or in it, not transcendent but not immanent either) is, in *Little Theatres*, removed from semantic significance by changing languages, from English to one that sounds, in English, like water. The penetration of the staging with another language, Galician, avoids monolingualism's blindness to space and time.

In *Little Theatres*, the word doesn't reveal; it reveals only what it says. It rustles or ripples. It rains into the road. We are wet, reading it. We step into and out of the river.

21

Could the vernacular be the absolutely non-divine? That which is not immanent but lacquered or scaled, that which is not transcendent, but rough in use? Why does it shine so, then? Why do we adore it, staging it again, restaging it? Why do we use it for our divinations?

"In the society of spectacle," says Giorgio Agamben, "in fact, the isolation of the Shekinah reaches its final phase, where language is not only constituted in an autonomous sphere, but also no longer even reveals anything—or better, it reveals the nothingness of all things" (*Coming Community* 81).[3]

22

In the vernacular, the fingers move to touch each other in a gesture but cannot; they are shrouded. They approach each other identically in these shrouds. Their touch is not touching. The vernacular is not a touch but an opening. For when the fingers move to touch, in the vernacular, nothing can be said, the folds are shut. It is when the fingers open that the vernacular is available for us. Touch, thus, is found paradoxically in opening and folding, unfolding. With the eye of the listener present, and the ear.

The "folded over": here there are words that rest on other words that we don't yet see or hear. This means movement is necessary. Utterance needs movement. And play.

indigenous_touch

23

When Giorgio Agamben writes "the image of the line is not gratuitous" I know he is talking about the vernacular.

> This is how we must read the theory of those medieval philosophers who held that the passage from potentiality to act, from common form to singularity, is not an event accomplished once and for all, but an infinite series of modal oscillations. The individuation of a singular existence is not a punctual fact, but a *linea generationais substantiæ* that varies in every direction according to a continual gradation of growth and remission, of appropriation and impropriation. (*Coming Community* 18–19)

His example, of course, is that of a line of writing: in the act of writing, the passage of the hand forms the commonality of letters, but the particularity of marks identifies the presence of the one who writes. The fold is breached (and the breach folded). Yet, as we know from Derrida contra Austin, this presence is no guarantee of singularity's presence; it is rather an absence, a deferral or chimæra.[4] The mouth opens here.

Next, and curiously, Agamben jumps from his image of the hand to the image of the face: "So too in a face, human nature continually passes into existence, and it is precisely this incessant emergence that constitutes its expressivity" (*Coming Community* 19).

This continual passage in expression marks the vernacular, unfolds it to us.

> The passage from potentiality to act, from language to the word, from the common to the proper, comes about every time as a shuttling in both directions along a line of sparkling alternation on which common nature and singularity, potentiality and act change roles and interpenetrate. (19)

Thus the vernacular (my vernacular) interpenetrates and changes roles. Agamben concludes by pointing to usage, which he calls ethos.

> The being that is engendered on this line is whatever being, and the manner in which it passes from the common to the proper and from the proper to the common is called usage — or rather, *ethos*. (19)

(It is a formulation for the beautiful, too.)

24

The line of this passage from potentiality to act is, at the same time, not a line for it is not singular but chamberal; it moves in spaces in which the listener waits. Even in the listener's absence, the listener's chair is always present, for the listener might arrive at any moment.

The listener looks into the vernacular and selects. The listener is already imbricated before "vernacular" and, as such, shimmers spatially. Is elected as she elects.

Thus: staged.

And is to stage the vernacular not to disturb it? To expose it to what is other than it, and this, without judgment or expectation, except "that it be exposed."

25

To say: the staging of the vernacular. Dada is not a vernacular. Surrealism is not. A vernacular refers to use, for that line from the common to the singular obliges use, passes through use, through the hand that is writing. The staging of the vernacular quells impulse by directing the motion of the vocable, of the letter.

It is this quelling that some would *like* to call the vernacular.

But it is not the vernacular. The staging itself is what quells, but only *if and where it does not expose.*

26

It is this ability to quell and/or expose, to draw the hooded fingertips together to touch in a touch that impedes touching, that allows — paradoxically — the movement's opposite: opening up, exposure.

Opening up the fold and unfolding it to the gaze or ear — this too is staging. The fingers open. Words are written on the palm of the hand, which is paper.

The palm of the hand touches a face.

The face faces outward. Facing. The face faces the who of facing. You are the who of facing that the face faces.

27

You are troubled by your face. You cannot see it. Your face thresholds you to world, and not its world. You are exposed.

28

But what is it to be exposed to language in the book? In *Little Theatres* there is such a staging, an exposure to a language some would call foreign, a willingness of the face to receive vocables of water, which is to say, vocables from which a semantic declination has been declined.

To let one's own body lie on the stage, then sit up. This is exposure to language. We can make a model for it, this exposure of body and word, tipped vertically and set outside:

vernacular_cerul

29

It is *her* portrait against the sky. Her — she who speaks only offstage, to stagehands. She speaks on buses and someone else hears. She was once on the subway in Toronto at Dupont station. She stood up in the Sala Quimeira in Lisbon. She stages little theatres across such boundaries because the infinitely small is her desire, and the stage is folded, not transparent, open to movement and the ear.

Elisa.

Later, after *Little Theatres*, which is full of her words, I found out Elisa Sampedrín had gone to Bucharest. In search of traces of the Canadian woman O. who had translated the Romanian poet Nichita Stănescu. E.S. arrived a year late. And started her own translations of the acclaimed Romanian poet, but without knowing his vernacular, his *limba română*. She translated by engaging the surface eruptions of his words.

As such, she, Elisa, *traductoare*, could produce only a physical or staged response to Stănescu's language, a line of writing that opened and did not shut.

Such a language begins immediately to be learned, to lodge or dislodge. The hands open.

Elisa herself, elsewhere (as yet unpublished) has talked of "unhanding herself." As if the vernacular's temporary staging were discarded. As if the rocket boost had occurred and the stage could be now jettisoned.

Whose vernacular do we bear, now, Elisa?

30

The vernacular itself stages this motion without jettisoning:

vernacular_degetele

31

Could it be that the vernacular, though characterized by a position of mastery, is not such a position itself? Can the common occur within a formation bound by mastery that then exceeds the common?

To avoid being engulfed in this common, must the vernacular itself shift constantly?

What is the relation to the multitude? Or of the multitude to the common, and to the particular?

What if we step outside the common to the commons?

Vernacular: for ordinary people. To step outside the master's house. But can we? A tension here (productive).

32

The other beauty, so closely related, that I love in Agamben is his notion of "improperty," which to me is our belonging always to the improper, free of "essence." This is, to Agamben — and now here — an ethos, a way of being in words and place.

"Perhaps the only way to understand this free *use of the self*, a way that does not, however, treat existence as a property, is to think of it as a *habitus*, an *ethos*" (*Coming Community* 28).

"The improperty, which we expose as our proper being, manner, which we *use*, engenders us. It is our second, happier nature" (28).

That improperty, rather than property, is happier: oh yes, I say. This provides a line of flight for the impossibility of any essence of vernacular. The job of poetry's staging: to ruffle ever, to revel, in this improperty, this impropriety, this imp.

33

The roosters pull the night away from the sky to release daybreak.
All it takes is two to make a vernacular. A speaker, a
listener. Movement transitive and transitory. Where time is
detained in small elements of lexicon. "They exchange roles
constantly." Condensation is my structure here.

> Where structure = exposure, there is incessantly
> a troubling. In the body. *In corpus meu.*
>
> that any modulation of the hands crosses both the
> particular and the common
>
> that any modulation of the hands changes the face
> as well
>
> that the face is a kind of palm
>
> the extending-outward of speech
>
> in the hands
>
> that the vernacular is constantly in motion and not fixed
>
> it does not fix identity but enacts an *era lure* or
> *éraflures*, abrasion-scratches, across a fluidity;
> it is a solidity that moves, variant and variable
>
> it is not mastered by any discourse, or the moment it is
> mastered, it turns away
>
> an attempt to fix it is to simulate an origin that does not
> exists, for origin itself moves …

vernacular_matei

THE POLITICS OF PRACTICE: ARTISTS AND INSTITUTIONS (MY ASSIGNED SUBJECT)[1]

a

I am "someone who writes and lives outside institutions," which for me are *dispositifs de control,* control mechanisms. Control over persons and, as such, over acceptable behaviours, but they also exercise a control over thought, from within their very structuration.

Notwithstanding this, these institutions are necessary; they provide a framework for many people. They are instruments for sharing, interacting, encountering, discovering, but they are risky as well, in that they exclude other regimes of thinking, and other sites of thinking. And they exclude the possible collapse or downfall of their own framework.

I believe in a multiplication of sites of thinking, and in the possibility of their downfall and reintegration in new forms: sites where institutions are not able to frame speech, nor act to regulate the spaces of inside and outside.

INTERRUPT:

Some itineraries of absence

1 = In community colleges there is a relationship between the faculty and students that is somewhat distinct and oriented in a different way from that in universities, with different objectives, and where it is possible to arrive at different and distinct conclusions. In university conferences, there is no one from these institutions.

2 = There is also a relationship between philosophy and cooking, a useful and strong relationship, that is left outside the site of discussion in universities. There is a relation between cooking and chemistry, and between chemistry and the eye, the functioning of the eye, and a relationship between what we eat and what we think. These mechanisms of thinking and discovery are not available to us in a university conference, because of the strict boundaries between university and universality, because, in short, of exclusions created by the institutions themselves, by the very functioning of their mechanism.

3 = (absent) (visual artists, visual workings of material, skies)

4 = (absent) (children, boys and girls, animals, cats, plants, skies)

X = Yet, if this essay were presented in a conference on cooking, I would insist here on a reading of Foucault.

b

Sometimes, institutions give me valued financial assistance and occasions to speak as well as providing interlocutors for interchanging, listening, bumping into, finding, thinking, realizing.[2] I am very thankful for this, and I often accept the invitations. I only wish to mention, and suggest, the ~~importance~~ of the porosity of their borders, borders that are too highly protected and left unanalyzed (and are nonetheless highly charged). The borders of the university as primary institution, as principal site of thought, must also be open to commotion, rebellion — *reflexión, rebulicio, rebelión* — (not belligerent but not angelic either — *non bélica pero non polo tanto anxélica*). I always suspect interlocutors who are not able to call the terrain they occupy into question.

→ URGENCY

c

For me, what is always fundamental is (the thread that links language to justice)...

SO? AND?

~~PROBLEMA ESTRUCTURAL~~

[In a sketch of a productive node of organisms and information, there would be no podium and no book.]

"if you do go there to speak, just make sure you know why you are really going"

- distribución de poderes
- porosidade
- rebulicio
- viricidal/virilidade

AFTER DREAMING a, b, c

The issue isn't only the porosity of borders, and talking about them. It is that I would be in contradiction to speak: how can I step inside the borders when I do not recognize their applicability? Recognition would imply an acceptance of the mechanism, and of how it establishes borders between inside and outside.

I don't work, in fact, in the *shadow* of institutions, nor *outside* them, nor *in the margins*, because I don't recognize this construction of the world, of my world.

I work in the midst of a life centred upon and grounded in art, which has nothing to do with CVs or job positions but with listening and with the exchange of ideas-thoughts-forms-sounds-visuals-gestures-colours. With the surfaces of colours and the textures of reasonings, not gelled in time even if I am tied to time's measure, to sites' locatability ... or not.

From time to time I enter those institutions for conferences and debates, and I make and maintain friendships there. Yet to me these events still have structural problems — yes, structural — that are in large part invisible to those who exist everyday in them and who have already given up something of a possible vision in order to hold a position, a contract, to be professors or doctors of thought, to be able to articulate the conclusions of their research in conferences. My own research is done in the moment; I am doing research even as I write these words. When I speak, when I listen, I do not bring forward conclusions already drawn, completed; I bring forward simply a body, a living instrument, cellular, nuclear, a female organism that acts and reacts and activates and reactivates with other beings, other women, other men. I am one vibration in a productive node that does not contain me, and that does not contain only me. For me this dual band of non-containment is at the root of the possibility of ethics.

To me, speech is possible only when the subject who speaks, the speaker, places herself in a situation in which she could be changed, altered, by the other, by the one to whom she is listening. This too is ethics. And it does not occur in the majority of university conferences, where neither the research nor the speaker can be changed, deformed, or reformed by the river, the thread, the net: *o río, o fio, a rede*. The light. A colour. A vibratory node. History. Ethics. Love.

Furthermore, and related: I exist in a world where cooking and philosophy occur together, where river and word have similar values, where a voice has a colour, colours, where the body never is separate from all this. I live in words as cells do in blood.

What interests me are the points of contact, which are nodes of production, of productivity, and thereby produce subjects who act or who can act in the world.
In the world in which I live. In the river. For there is always a river.

Then I spoke with R who said: Don't go.
Later, I spoke with L who talked to me of her situation in relation to art galleries and the industrial system in the visual arts: The work does not want to go there, she says.

Realize I am in a contradiction: what use is there to go to a congress to try to speak only to refuse the frame? In this congress, it won't work. I can survive there only by subsuming myself in the framework. But, as L says, "the work does not want to go there."

The structural problem has to be confronted ALL the time, in acts, and not by talking about it ... it has to be confronted in the actual formulation of the work as it is in process.

Answer: do my talk in Normandy in field May 12 for L's birthday present. And let myself be altered by the field, by whoever comes.

(late mail in from R on 1 maio [día do traballador]:
you must do yr paper for L birthday party).

(later mail in from K on 2 maio)
and then you can perhaps do your paper here! (markdale, ON, field as well)

Finally, I talk to R2 1045pm, May 2
I tell him the structure is too "big theatre," and it seems I am asked to speak as counter-presence: already defined by institution as just that. Paradoxically, to speak at all, I must refuse to play that role in its structure. Though I understand those who have always found resources in institutions to do interesting things, I have to consider where I am being positioned in it all. Standing before 150 people, would I foment conversation or just be *maxestrale?* The structure mitigates already against the act that I can most ethically perform. R2 says that this is what is desired, that I work at cross-purposes, that I am welcome. I feel impossibly torn. I don't want to be responsible for assuming this role of dissident in the machine. Rather: to talk in the field. Both of us, L and me, in the field with cows, talking work and practice.

For that is where the work wants to be, and what the work wants to do.

A CODA — BEACONS

▎When I walked in the DIA: *Beacon* in New York State on the day before the winter solstice of 2007, watching light change and darken across the sculptures and following the map or floor plan, I knew I was in a city of America that I could inhabit: a city of art made huge, in the space of a factory that once made packaging.

Later, looking at the floor plan of the DIA: *Beacon*, I saw it as musical notation, or as a spatial poem, making space and language to represent the city in which I had walked. Besides, on the map, there was also a stream, so necessary to a city.

I thought a poet too could be portrayed by such a map, that a poet too could be a city, that a person could thus keep walking.

Late in Chus Pato's *Charenton*, two pages outline her literary lineage (82–83). To make a poem using the names of her literary ancestors is, to Chus, a political and civic act. I decided to take her names from her poem and translate them into the cellular arrangement of the floor map of the DIA: *Beacon*. Then, because I am Chus Pato's translator, from Galician and Galiza to English and Canada, across an ocean, I made a map of my own lineage too.

These are maps of cities that can be inhabited, I think, that urge you to walk among the names and leave others yours, sharing your lineage too.

DÍA, day. Beacon, light. Daylight. Names. All the names. Graciñas.

Yes, I have just said: *small graces*.

In English: *thank you*.

POEM BASED ON THE MAP OF THE DIA BEACON 2007

ERÍN MOURE | 308 | *my beloved wager*

CHUS PATO'S LIÑAXE in the form of the MAP of the DIA BEACON 2007

ERIN MOURE'S LINEAGE in the form of the MAP OF THE DIA: BEACON 2007

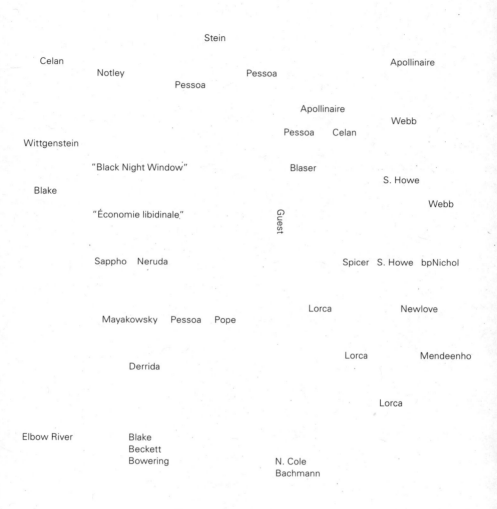

NOTES

READING NEVER CEASES TO AMAZE ME
1   My translation.

AND POETRY
1   This is why, when we learn to drive a motor vehicle, we are trained to keep our eyes in constant motion. Because moving our gaze puts new stimuli in front of it, we move our eyes to remain attentive to the outer world. Otherwise ... that murmur! We daydream.

THE ANTI-ANÆSTHETIC
1   Luce Irigaray refers to this "gaze" in *Speculum of the Other Woman*. Laura Mulvey also has talked about the gaze and its relationship with patriarchal social order in her work on cinema, particularly in a 1973 essay called "Visual Pleasure and Narrative Cinema," published in 1975 in the journal *Screen*. Other writers in the visual arts have talked of the "gaze" in slightly different ways, as a limitation of form and seeing. Irigaray deals with it as part of an economy of representation that objectifies women and perpetuates patriarchal structures in representation — an economy that turns toward origin as "transcendent" and away from any possibility of origin in the mother.
2   Poem read in an issue of *Index on Censorship* from just after Stus's death, but I can't find it now. It could be in "The Death of Vasyl Stus," by Nadia Svitlychna, in *Index on Censorship*, 15, 2, 1986, 34–37.
3   Just ask de Sade.

4   It's as if, at the mirror stage, the mirror shifts and reflects the original relational "non-extension." When reflected, it creates *two*, the distance between *two*—from *zero* to *two*, transgressing *one*, as Kristeva says in *Revolution of Poetic Language*.
5   As different, as marginal.
6   So you can't use it to escape.
7   At the same time, we ought to be careful about creating or enforcing divisions around "masculine" and "feminine," even when we must use those terms. As Derrida said in a 1982 correspondence with his translator, Verena Andermatt Conley, "For reasons of certain structural possibilities, we are as little assured of this economy that you call 'feminine' in what is called 'woman' as that which you call a 'masculine' economy in what is meant to be called 'man'" (*Points* 167–68). He goes on to urge us not to ignore the possibilities of current and future mutations.

DEEPER THAN ANY SILENCE: BRONWEN WALLACE (1945–1989)
1   The quote is from my poem "Seebe," which I read publicly for the first time at an AGM of the League of Canadian Poets, with Bronwen in the audience: she was shocked at the way that the poem chose to insist that "telling a story" was problematic.

BREAKING BOUNDARIES: WRITING AS SOCIAL PRACTICE, OR ATTENTIVENESS
1   Quoted in Barbara Johnson, *A World of Difference* (30) from Mallarmé's essay "L'action restreinte" published in *Divagations*, 1897. The French reads: "Le meilleur qui se passe entre deux gens, toujours, leur échappe en tant qu'interlocuteurs."

POETRY, MEMORY, AND THE POLIS
1   Ingested or inhaled low-level radiation seeks out vital organs like thyroid and bone marrow where it stays, promoting the release of free-oxygen radicals, which damage cell membranes, interfering with white-cell and hormone production. It is an erosion of the immune system. On the other hand, in somewhat higher concentrations of radiation and free-oxygen radical production, the radicals can neutralize each other.
2   "A 1987 study by Ottawa's Laboratory Centre for Disease Control found a 163 percent rise in asthma deaths among people between ages 15–34 from 1970–72 to 1982–84. Among all age groups, the death rate had increased 22 percent for women and

9 percent for men during the same period. Researchers identified a 338 percent increase in asthma deaths among men between 15–24 while the death rate per 100,000 rose to 40 from 8. In men 25–34, there was an 81 percent increase in recorded deaths while the death rate per 100,000 rose to 32 in 1982–84 from 12 in 1970–72. In women 15–24, the rate rose to 52 from 18. For women 25–34, it increased to 34 from 9" (*Montreal Gazette*, June 9, 1988). "Blacks are nearly three times more likely than whites to die of asthma even though asthma itself is only slightly more prevalent among blacks, researchers say. According to one, the death rate is seven times as high as among comparable whites ... According to the National Centre for Health Statistics, the asthma death rate rose from 0.9 per 100,000 in 1976 to 1.5 in 1986. The most recent figures available show the rate among blacks rose from 1.5 in 1976 to 2.8 in 1985" (Janny Scott of the *Los Angeles Times* in *Montreal Gazette*, June 4, 1988). I wonder how much this has to do with availability of public health care and cost of medication. I know from personal experience that when people are poor, they don't get the most modern medications because they can't afford them, and they also end up using expired medications bought under the table outside the industry, or taking medicine improperly in order to conserve it. So these statistics may have less to say about immune system functioning than about the health care system.

3   Michael Hardt and Antonio Negri's *Empire* holds interesting notes on this count, for example, "Imperial rule [which Hardt and Negri contrast with modernist rule or imperialist rule] functions by breaking down. Imperial society is always and everywhere breaking down, but this does not mean it is necessarily heading to ruin" (202). They speak of the perversely generative role of degeneration, which they call "corruption," beckoning to the Aristotelian sense of that word.

4   See Hardt and Negri again: "Imperial sovereignty thrives on the proliferating contradictions corruption gives rise to; it is stabilized by its instabilities, by its impurities and admixture; it is calmed by the panic and anxieties it continually engenders" (202). Perhaps it is a kind of anti-architecture that still uses architectural principles.

5   But is this possible, this "before"? Or is it a trick with mirrors? There is that danger. I think it is possible to be attentive to the "red spade" cacophony that our brain wants to shut down and

"normalize," attentive to what artist Francis Bacon calls the nervous system's capacity to respond directly to paint.

6   See "The Anti-Anæsthetic" in this volume: "Entry into the Law (at Lacan's mirror stage, when the Ego is formed) has an advantage: it reduces anxiety for the organism. Its binding is painful but reduces anxiety. Quite efficiently" (25).

7   "Identification constitutes the act of figuration." Gayatri Spivak, talking about Nietzsche in her preface to her translation of Jacques Derrida's *Of Grammatology* (xxiii).

8   This mathematical term avoids hierarchization of the terms to which it refers (avoids the plus-/minus value inherent in oppositions).

9   "Mouré clearly stands for radical feminism ... her previous books ... marked the lineaments of an authentic talent ... Largely, though, her writing was accessible and universal, exploring themes of predatory domestic strife, mortality, the difficulty of communication.... Now with *Furious*, her fifth book, the talent has gone astray. Most of the poems leave her in a stylistic wilderness beyond the boundaries of usage." From a review of *Furious* by Ken Adachi, *The Toronto Star*, March 20, 1988.

10 "Symbolic" used here in the Kristevan sense as one of the two "modalities of the signifying process." See *Revolution in Poetic Language* (24).

THE MEDIUM

1   I thought I was quoting Simone Weil when I wrote this text in the 1980s, but it is an alteration of a quote from Susan Sontag's essay "Simone Weil" in *Against Interpretation* (50). The quote properly reads "The truth is balance, but the opposite of truth, which is unbalance, may not be a lie" (50).

FOR SCOPING GIRLS

1   Regarding the "exclusion of the feminine from the proprietary discourse of metaphysics" in Irigaray, see Judith Butler in *Bodies that Matter*:

> A constitutive or relative outside is, of course, composed of a set of exclusions that are nevertheless internal to that system...
>
> Irigaray insists that this exclusion that mobilizes

the form/matter binary is the differentiating relation between masculine and feminine, where the masculine occupies both terms of binary opposition, and the feminine cannot be said to be an intelligible term at all. We might understand the feminine figured within the binary as the specular feminine and the feminine which is erased and excluded from that binary as the excessive feminine. And yet, such nominations cannot work for, in the latter mode, the feminine, strictly speaking, cannot be named at all and is not a mode.

Disavowed, the remnant of the feminine survives as the *inscriptional space* of that phallogocentrism, the specular surface which receives the marks of a masculine signifying act only to give back a (false) reflection and guarantee of phallogocentric self-sufficiency, without making any contribution of its own. (38–39)

SPEAKING THE UNSPEAKABLE: RESPONDING TO CENSORSHIP

1. The Little Sisters' Bookstore's legal battle against the Canada Revenue Agency and its censorship of gay and lesbian material at the US/Canada border received extensive news coverage. For a well-documented history of this astounding case, see http://www.littlesisters.ca/docscc/index_court.html (accessed July 9, 2009). The censorship laws at the time were absurd; strictly speaking, the way laws were enforced meant that I could cross into the US with one of my manuscripts—containing imagery or description of lesbian sex (it didn't even have to be published) and then have it seized and removed from me upon return to Canada. The CRA was setting frightening precedents, enforcing laws to disproportionately affect gay people, and claiming it was in the name of a kind of freedom: the standards of the community. In the late 90s, just before the case with Little Sisters went to the Supreme Court, there were many public discussions of the effect of censorship. It was in this context that I wrote the essay.

2. In a review of *A Frame of the Book* by Fraser Sutherland in *The Globe and Mail*, July 31, 1999, D12.

A FRAME OF THE BOOK OR THE FRAME OF A BOOK

1. "In experiments, Merzenich and Kaas went on to show that [in the cortex] the essential parameter regulating map representation was the amount of correlated stimulation to the skin. In other words, there is a competition between skin regions to representation in the brain, and skin regions that are repeatedly and most heavily stimulated (fingers, lips and so on) get the largest representations. Conversely, if a region is deprived of stimulation, its representation is competitively diminished, or can be altogether eliminated and replaced by an alternative skin site" (Finkel 399).

2. The full quote in French is: "C'est très serrée et difficile de savoir pourquoi une peinture touche directement le système nerveux" (28). The English translation of the book, which appeared years after this essay was written, restores Bacon's complete original phrase: "It is a very, very close and difficult thing to know why some paint comes across directly onto the nervous system and other paint tells you the story in a long diatribe through the brain." See Deleuze's *Francis Bacon* (32).

A NEW BIRD FLICKER, OR THE FLOOR OF A GREAT SEA, OR *STOOKING*

1. See Konrad Lorenz, *Here Am I — Where Are You?: The Behavior of the Greylag Goose*, 251–54.

2. Interesting that to be "unEasted," disoriented, in English, is to be *desnortado*, "unNorthed," in Spanish and Galician. In French too, "nord perdu" refers to losing one's sense of direction, both literally and figuratively (losing your head, forgetting what you were about to say).

3. One of the wsw pages on Deleuze is a "rhiz-o-mat," combining rhizome with automat; when I first bookmarked it, the title was "there is no way out of this little tiny box." It is now housed at http://www.bleb.net/rhizomat (last accessed May 28, 2009) where the title bar reads simply "Rhiz-o-mat."

THE CAPITULATIONS, A TEXT BY, FOR, AND THROUGH THE ART OF LANI MAESTRO

1. "Capitulation: a set of terms or articles constituting an agreement between governments" (*Webster's Collegiate Dictionary*).

2. From "Seebe," in Moure, wsw, 84.

3   "In a tautology the conditions of agreement with the world—the representational relations—cancel one another, so that it does not stand in any representational relation to reality" (*Tractatus* 4.462).

4   Phrases in italic are from Lani Maestro in conversation with Erín Moure, February 1998; some quotations have been slightly altered (or authored).

5   Lani Maestro, "a wound in the lung," exhibited in Quebec City at La Chambre Blanche, October 24–November 20, 1994.

6   Lani Maestro, "To dream sleep," exhibited in Paris at the Centre for New Media, Canadian Culture Centre, 1998.

THREE NOTES ON LANI MAESTRO'S *CRADLE*

1   This exhibition photo of Maestro's *Cradle* was taken at the National Gallery of Canada, where the work was exhibited as part of the group exhibition "Traversées/Crossings" in 1998. My three notes were made in response to a different exhibition of *Cradle* two years later at the Galérie UQAM in Montreal.

2   All the foregoing, and only the foregoing, permit the entry of the personal possessive pronoun that indicates that the subject was always present here, but now is not occluded.

MORNINGS ON WINNETT: *TRUST MEDITATIONS*

1   The meditation stops here; she has gone off to translate Pessoa—

POETS AMID THE MANAGEMENT GURUS

1   The original Spanish in Goytisolo's *En los reinos de taifa* reads: "Como no te cansas de decir, la única moral del escritor, frente a la que no cabe recurso alguno, será devolver a la comunidad literario-lingüística a la que pertenece una escritura nueva y personal, distinta en todo caso de la que existía y recibió de ella en el momento de emprender su tarea: trabajar en lo ya hecho, seguir modelos aceptados es condenarse a la parvedad e insignificancia por mucho que el escritor consiga así el aplauso del público: la obra de quien no innova podría no existir sin que su desaparición afectara en nada al desenvolvimiento de su cultura" (112). The standard English translation can be found in Juan Goytisolo, *Realms of Strife: The Memoirs of Juan Goytisolo 1957–1982*, trans. Peter R. Bush (95). The quotation in the essay is partly a paraphrase.

PERSON, CITIZEN: SOME CUES FROM A POETIC PRACTICE

1. These are Derrida's definitions of responsibility, articulated by him in a talk in Montreal on April 4, 1997. The wording is from my notes.
2. From a post to the Buffalo poetics listserv describing a reading in Denver by Lyn Hejinian (May 4, 1998).
3. In the sense in which I use it, "americanize" refers less to the nation of the USA than to the superficial recuperation and display of cultural elements that come with transnational capitalism; it just seems American because it has held together that republic for two hundred and thirty-odd years, suppressing many forces, for example, its hispanicity. There is a whole problematic here, a can of worms to open.
4. A reading of Gilles Deleuze's *Logique de la sensation* on painter Francis Bacon, or of Daniel Goleman's *Emotional Intelligence*, for example, would bear this out.
5. Lyotard uses this word in his *Chambre sourde : L'antiesthétique de Malraux*.
6. See "The Anti-Anæsthetic," earlier in this book.

THE PUBLIC RELATION: REDEFINING CITIZENSHIP BY POETIC MEANS

1. See Gilles Deleuze and Félix Guattari, *A Thousand Plateaus* (106).
2. This is not to say the *whole* interior is unregulated; there is also a regulated interior, yes. But there is always something in excess to regulation in this interior ... something that cannot even be its "supplement" *for the order of the unregulated cannot be discussed in the frame of the regulated.*
3. The word in Portuguese, *aproximação*, does not translate exactly as "approximation," though this is one of its meanings. It can be "approach," or "moving closer," "moving into proximity."
4. Robert Majzels, in a letter to Erín Moure, 2001.
5. See *French, a Language for Everyone: A New Strategic Approach Centred on the Citizen in Society. Summary of the Final Report (English)* of the Commission des États-généraux sur la situation et l'avenir de la langue française au Québec (Quebec: 2001). Later, however, the government announced it would not implement the recommendations of the états-généraux cited here.

6   As in Jacques Parizeau, the Quebec premier, blaming the loss of the 1995 referendum on "money and the ethnic vote." "C'est vrai, c'est vrai qu'on a été battus, au fond, par quoi ? Par l'argent puis des votes ethniques, essentiellement." http://archives.vigile.net/ds-souv/docs2/95-10-30-discours-parizeau.html (accessed January 21, 2009).

7   (Translation from Galician.) I believe that, in a movement that is paradoxical, the exceeding of frontiers, the crossing of frontiers without eclipsing them, frontiers of countries and of languages (and of mentalities), is urgent in order to defend local cultures. Yes, it's paradoxical, but (I believe) we need paradoxes in our time. I believe that without poetry, we are unable to think these paradoxical movements. Analysis and logic leave us far from paradox. In smoothing out paradox, in the end, we blind ourselves.

THE EX*H*ORBITANT BODY: TRANSLATION AS PERFORMANCE

1   Sonorous/tonal/noisy/sound frictions/rubbings/chafings/scuffs and co/incidences/impacts/effects/implications or simultaneous occurrences: to merely say "sound effects and frictions" would flatten the phrase Huston uses. *Coïncidence* is not exactly coincidence; it is technical, not a startling randomness.

2   In translation parlance, this refers to making the work seem as if it had been written in English. See Lawrence Venuti, *The Translator's Invisibility: A History of Translation* (page 5 onward).

3   In Canadian English it's worse; we rely primarily on translations embodied in cultures and values outside ours, cultures that may not fully reflect ours.

4   British translator and publisher Andrew Winnard, in an article called "Books Translated into English: Why so few?", wrote that "Of the 70–80,000 books published in the UK each year, only 3 percent are translations. The figure for the US is even lower: 2.5 percent." Later, he says: "In France, translated books as a percentage of total books published have remained steady at approximately 22 percent during the last few years, up from 18 percent in 1991" (232). The figures in Canada are probably slightly higher than American and UK figures, but I doubt they reach 5 percent, and of course most translations published in Canada are from Canadian French to English or vice versa, not translations of books written outside the country. See also *To Be Translated or Not to Be*: PEN/IRL

    Report on the International Situation of Literary Translation, Ed. Esther Allen (Barcelona: Institut Ramón Llul, 2007). Available at http://www.centerforliterarytranslation.org (accessed January 31, 2009). The whole report is sobering and essential reading.

5   While a pseudonym is an alternate name for a writer, heteronyms are fully fledged characters having their own biographies, physical stature and eye colour, educations, æsthetics, and bodies of work. Pessoa created at least seventy heteronyms; many of them know each other, influence each other, and criticize each other's works. The three main ones are Alberto Caeiro, Ricardo Reis, and Álvaro de Campos; the latter two consider Caeiro their master. There are semi-heteronyms too, whose biographies partly merge with Pessoa's and who write in prose; Bernardo Soares is the most important of these. There is also an orthonym, Fernando Pessoa, who also considers Caeiro his master.

6   See Homi K. Bhaba, *The Location of Culture*.

7   I spent a lot of time in the house watching the cat, as I had torn ligaments in an ankle, so my observations were excessively detailed and repeated.

SUBJECTIVITIES: AN APPROACH THROUGH CLARICE AND FERNANDO

1   Gestures, of course, are movements of a part of a body, seen apart from their effects.

2   Surpass, overcome, exceed: the word has all these registers.

3   "Clarice gives time(s). She is a receptivity that gives itself. Making possible the giving-receiving [relation]" (my translation).

4   Here one must not confuse the "être" with the "person" for a person may be multiply inhabited and digressed by êtres.

5   Those "frottements" again!

6   See Mário Saraiva and Luís Duarte Santos, *O Caso Clínico de Fernando Pessoa*.

7   To feign / pretend / dissimulate = to move / moult / change.

8   A literal, fluent translation of the original text would read:
        Some lady has a piano
        Which is pleasant but isn't the current of rivers
        Nor the murmur made by the trees...

> Why would you need to have a piano?
> The best is to have hearing
> And love Nature.

9   "To take my leave" or "Before I leave" or "One more thing."
10 In the introduction I had said: "This is my simple book."
11 Given all this: *Why would anyone have a piano? What if you want to play a show tune no one likes?*

FIDELITY WAS NEVER MY AIM (BUT FELICITY)

1   I translate mostly from French to English in Quebec, and mostly in the fields, broadly speaking, of finance and fine arts, though I also do some fine arts translating from Galician to English. Otherwise, I translate poetry from Spanish, Portuguese, Portunhol, French, and Galician toward English; this is part of my poetic practice and thinking in poetry.

2   See Fernando Pessoa, *The Keeper of Sheep*, trans. Edwin Honig and Susan M. Brown.

3   Foreign works of poetry, when they do appear in English, often just appear cut up in anthologies. The entire breadth of a poet's expression is rarely allowed space.

4   I'd been studying Galician using workbooks at home in Montreal, without hearing it spoken. Galician and Portuguese both stem from medieval Galician-Portuguese.

5   "Babysitters" is a word first documented in English in 1947; Pessoa died in 1935.

6   Some would argue that this is not "chance." Fortuity, yes, but not hazard!

7   By "readerly relationship" I mean that I wanted to be affected solely by the Caeiro lines, by my experience as reader, not by what I'd already translated, by my experience as translator. The two are normally quickly conflated when one translates.

8   To echo the word "fervent" here, coining a word that points to the verb *ferver*. *Fervindo* would mean "boiling," literally, and, figuratively, "ebullient."

9   Do we still read Pope's translation of Homer's *Iliad?* It's in print, but I think we study it only for Pope. If we want to read the *Iliad* we turn to other translations.

TRANSLATION AS ABSENCE, BOOKENDED AS GIFT

1. The second edition of the book has the author's name on the cover and title page.

2. In fact, they restrict literature, and in a way are not accepted as intelligent internationally. To quote from Esther Allen's essay "Translation, Globalization and English," "Literary scholars notoriously find it difficult to agree, but if there is one point on which they do converge it is the crucial importance to literature of traffic among different languages. The Russian literary theorist Mikhail Bakhtin viewed what he called 'polyglossia'—the interaction of different languages—as fundamental to the origins of literary thinking itself, and particularly crucial to the development of that most heterogeneous of modern genres, the novel: 'Only polyglossia fully frees consciousness from the tyranny of its own language' (17–33). Other critics from Raymond Williams to Jorge Luis Borges have had other ways of putting it, but all agree that circulation among different languages via translation is the very lifeblood of literature. 'Left to itself,' Goethe went on to say to Eckermann, 'every literature will exhaust its vitality if it is not refreshed by the interest and contributions of a foreign one'" (22). [Note: Allen attributes the Goethe quote to Johann Peter Eckermann. *Gespräche mit Goethe in den Letzten Jaren seines Lebens* (1835), as cited in Damrosch (7).]

3. These are two different nationhoods. To delve into this is beyond the scope of this essay, but I will just say that there is a lot more translation from foreign poetries into French published in Quebec with institutional support from Quebec. There is some sign in Quebec that welcoming work across borders into the language is important.

4. The Griffin Prize for Excellence in Poetry is an exception; it has an international prize that admits works of poetry translated into English on the same basis as it admits other works in English: as poetry in English. Here the foreign does enter the native language and is allowed to alter it.

5. Here I am not advocating a *nationalist* practice, but a heterogeneous one, sited in Canada: Canadian idioms should be present and mark the field too, but they don't.

6. The initial reason given me for leaving the information off the book cover was that it was too much text. I think though that the

press originally considered the work to be merely mine, and not to be translation. The Canada Council, however, considered it translation of a foreign author, and the book did not qualify for subsidy. Still, the publisher's website does not list Fernando Pessoa in its list of authors, though other translated authors are so listed. The blind spots continue!

STAKES, POETRY, TODAY

1. Poetry *in* language can be diagrammed as a dot *in* a circle: as such, poetry is always in language, and language is always outside, as well as inside, poetry.
2. It is not necessarily *what we have heard.*
3. Our access to the domain of the possible is already limited by what we *are.*
4. Because the possible, which we don't have access to, always interferes with "what we *are.*"
5. The e of Erín, of transelation.
6. See Chus Pato's Galician poetry, *A Ponte das poldras* (Santiago de Compostela: Noitarenga, 1996).
7. The English translation is mine.
8. *Lani Maestro: Chambres de quiétude / Quiet Rooms* (94).

RE-CITING THE CITIZEN BODY

1. This is, yes, a reference to Kafka's *In the Penal Colony*, which might suffice as a theory of the nation today.
2. (Translation from Galician.) Borders also admit passages.
3. "O único bo que teñen as fronteiras son os pasos clandestinos" (12; the English version is my translation).
4. Edward Said, "La muerte lenta: un castigo minucioso" *El País*, August 12, 2002, 9–10.

ONE RED SHOE: NARRATIVE AS A PRACTICE OF POSSIBILITY

1. See Thomas Kuhn's *The Structure of Scientific Revolutions*. I saw the film at work in the late 1980s and don't remember its name now; it cited Kuhn to talk about how new ideas come about, and how hard it is to think outside the dominant paradigm.
2. See pages 65, 78–79, 84, and 112 for some examples.

CO-TRANSLATING "NICOLE BROSSARD": THREE-WAY SPECTACLE OR SPECTRE DE TROIS?

1   Most of this essay refers to Nicole Brossard's *Notebook of Roses and Civilization*, translated by Robert Majzels and myself, one of three Majzels/Moure translations of Brossard.

2   See Judith Fitzgerald, "Back to Galicia," review of *O Cadoiro*, in *The Globe and Mail*, June 30, 2007.

3   Forthcoming in 2010 from Anansi, Toronto.

4   What if this were a description of translation? "La complexification des transformateurs, théoriques et pratiques, a toujours eu pour effet de déstabiliser l'ajustement du sujet humain à son environnement. Et elle le modifie toujours dans le même sens : elle retarde la réaction, elle multiplie les réponses possibles, elle augmente la liberté matérielle, et en ce sens, elle ne peut que décevoir la demande de sécurité qui est inscrite dans l'humain comme dans tout vivant. Autrement dit, on ne voit pas que le désir, appelons-le ainsi, de complexifier la mémoire puisse relever de la demande d'équilibrer la relation de l'homme avec son milieu. Pragmatiquement, ce désir opère en sens contraire, du moins tout d'abord, et l'on sait que les découvertes ou les inventions scientifiques ou techniques (ou artistiques) sont rarement motivées par une demande de sécurité et d'équilibre" (Jean-François Lyotard, "Matière et temps" in *L'inhumain: Causeries sur le temps* 54).

CROSSING BORDERS WITH A GALICIAN BOOK OF POETRY: TRANSLATING A REALIST POET

1   This essay was originally written in Galician with a wee bit of English. In translating it into English for this publication, I deliberately maintained certain constructions that give rise to a Galician cadence, that *mark* the text as unEnglish. I also altered the construction of the first sentence by subordinating the first part of the thought, so as not to start with "I." In Galician, because the verb is marked, the pronoun is unnecessary unless an emphasis is required: "Son tradutora, pero sempre afirmo que a tradución é imposíbel." My preference is for the Galician weighting that does not emphasize the "I."

2   "Source" and "target": it interests me how we use the vocabulary of shooting here. In Galician, the trope is that of a voyage: we go from the language of departure to the language of arrival.

3   In one of those friendships that will last a lifetime.

4   María Xesús Nogueira, "Escribir despois de m-Talá," 2005, found on LG3, part of culturagalega.org at http://www.culturagalega.org/lg3/ (accessed February 9, 2009).

SHAGGY MAMMAL INTERVENÇÃO

1   This essay was first written in a combination of English, French, and Galician. (I gave it as a talk in English, translating spontaneously and, in doing so, bringing an awkwardness and hesitation into the English.) I have translated most of it into English for this publication; however, I must note that the thinking process in the essay would have been impossible for me had it taken place only in English. In removing the other languages from the text to make it "readable" in English, heterogeneity has been sacrificed, and part of the very crisis of thinking which prompts me to write has been silenced. I leave it to readers to decide if they are willing to assume responsibility for this crisis of thinking by learning another language, or if they are content to have all thought doled out to them in English, thus accepting a homogeneity that diminishes the possibility of new discursive formations in English itself.

2   "La question de l'archive n'est pas, répétons-le, une question du passé. Ce n'est pas la question d'un concept dont nous disposerions ou ne disposerions pas *déjà* au sujet du *passé, un concept archivable de l'archive.* C'est une question d'avenir, d'avenir même, la question d'une réponse, d'une promesse et d'une responsabilité pour demain. L'archive, si nous voulons savoir ce que cela aura voulu dire, nous ne le saurons que dans les temps à venir. Peut-être" (Derrida, *Mal d'archive* 60).

3   And this process is not necessarily a conscious one: it is the red spades again. See p. 228 of this book.

4   Because we are secular, and scientific, the soul does not exist, so we avoid it at all costs. I avoid it at all costs! Lévinas did not though. In his book *Of God who Comes to Mind*, he thinks out a secular and reasoned spacing in us as humans for these transcendent notions.

5   "A discursive formation does not occupy all the possible volume that the systems that form its objects, enunciations, and concepts

rightfully open to it. It is riddled with gaps, due to the systems that form its strategic choices. From this comes the fact that a given discursive formation, when taken up again, placed, and interpreted in a new constellation, may reveal new possibilities ... There is a modification in the principle of exclusion and of possibility of choice that results from the insertion into a new discursive constellation."

This is my translation, as I find the standard English translation (on page 75 of *Archeology of Knowledge*, tr. Alan Sheridan. NY: Routledge, 2002) to be laborious, whereas the French proceeds smoothly. Somehow in the French structure, as well, the dual use of the word "formation" remains clear, a clarity that can only be produced by altering "systèmes de formation" to "systems that form" in English. I append my translation as an endnote here rather than using it in the text of my essay, as it was the French original that spurred my thinking. And I was only able to make my translation after my thinking had been spurred.

O CADOIRO: THE CATARACT

1. Zenith's 115 *Galician-Portuguese Troubadour Poems* is, alas, out of print. It holds the most extensive selection in English of the 1163 poems. I'm hoping it will one day come back into print again.

2. "An Unsung Literature: Galician-Portuguese Troubador Poetry." July 1, 2004. Accessed at http://www.poetryinternational.org/ (link via Portugal, then Troubador) on February 9, 2009.

3. This hokey and historically inaccurate American science-fiction television show that ran in 1966–67 had a great hold on me as a child. Lee Meriwether was playing me, of course, though on *my* clipboard, I wrote poetry.

4. The first Portuguese grammar, by Fernão de Oliveira, dates from 1536. The first Galician grammar in Galician, *Grámatica do idioma galego*, by Manuel Lugrís Freire, appeared in 1922.

5. "Reconhecemos o típico desinteresse medieval pela sequência cronológica, substituída amiúde por uma visão simultânea e pictórica dos acontecimentos" (120; the English version is my translation). See Stephen Reckert and Helder Macedo.

6. And this is entirely possible. Before the expulsion of the Jews from Spain in 1492, Galicia had thriving Jewish communities.

STAGING VERNACULARS

1. Agamben explains that this is the name of a Christian community founded by the French Arabist Louis Massignon whose "members took a vow to live *substituting themselves* for someone else" (*Coming Community* 22). This is also translation's movement. "According to Massignon, in fact, substituting oneself for another does not mean compensating for what the other lacks, nor correcting his or her errors, but *exiling oneself to the other as he or she is* in order to offer ... hospitality in the other's own ... taking-place. This substitution ... is irrevocable hospitality." (My elisions here allow me to create my own sentence in the midst of Agamben's.)

2. All the love poems in *O Cidadán*, which are poems of private life, are called "Georgette."

3. "The Shekinah is the last of the ten Sefirot or attributes of the divinity, the one that expresses the very presence of the divine, its manifestation or habitation on earth: its 'word'" (Agamben, *Coming Community* 80).

4. In his 1971 talk "Signature, événement, contexte" Derrida argued against aspects of J.L. Austin's speech act theory in Austin's *How to Do Things With Words* which provoked sharp responses from philosopher John Searle (an Austin follower and author of *Speech Acts*, 1969) in 1977 when Derrida's talk was published in English translation in *Glyph*. One summary of this famed debate can be found in Ian Maclean, "Un dialogue de sourds? Some Implications of the Austin-Searle-Derrida Debate," in *Jacques Derrida: Critical Thought*, ed. Ian Maclachlan (49–66).

THE POLITICS OF PRACTICE: ARTISTS AND INSTITUTIONS (MY ASSIGNED SUBJECT)

1. This essay was originally written in Galician. My translation.

2. These last three words are all contained in one Galician word: *achar*.

WORKS CITED

Agamben, Giorgio. *Ce qui reste d'Auschwitz*. Paris: Rivages, 2003.
———. *The Coming Community*. Trans. Michael Hardt. Minneapolis: U of Minnesota P, 1993.
———. "The Dictation of Poetry." In Giorgio Agamben, *End of the Poem: Studies in Poetics*. Trans. Daniel Heller-Roazen. Stanford, CA: Stanford UP, 1999. 76–86.
———. *The End of the Poem: Studies in Poetics*. Trans. Daniel Heller-Roazen. Stanford, CA: Stanford UP, 1999. 76–86.
———. *Le temps qui reste*. Trans. Judith Revel. Paris: Payot and Rivages, 2004.
Ajens, Andrés. *Quasi Flanders, Quasi Extramadura*. Trans. Erín Moure. Victoria, BC: Mano Izquierda, 2007.
Allen, Esther. "Translation, Globalization and English." In *To Be Translated or Not to Be: PEN/IRL Report on the International Situation of Literary Translation*. Ed. Esther Allen. Barcelona: Institut Ramón Llul, 2007. 17–33. http://www.centerforliterarytranslation.org (accessed January 31, 2009).
Anderson, Benedict. *Imagined Communities: Reflections on the Origin and Spread of Nationalism*. NY: Verso, 1991.
Baert, Renee, et al., curators. *Lani Maestro: Chambres de quiétude/Quiet Rooms*. Montreal: Galerie de l'UQÀM, 2003.
Bhabha, Homi K. *The Location of Culture*. London, UK: Routledge, 1994.
Blaser, Robin. *The Holy Forest: Collected Poems of Robin Blaser*. Ed. Miriam Nichols. Berkeley: U of California P, 2006.
Brossard, Nicole. *Cahier de roses & de civilisation*. Montreal: Éditions d'art le Sabord, 2003.

———. *Notebook of Roses and Civilization*. Trans. Robert Majzels and Erín Moure. Toronto: Coach House, 2007.

Buci-Glucksmann, Christine. "Le plissé baroque de la peinture." *Magazine littéraire* 257 (Automne 1987): 54–56.

Bueno, Wilson. "From Mar Paraguayo." Trans. Erín Moure. In *The Oxford Book of Latin American Poetry: A Bilingual Anthology*. Ed. Cecilia Vicuña and Ernesto Livon Grosman. New York: Oxford UP, 2009.

Butler, Judith. *Excitable Speech: A Politics of the Performative*. New York: Routledge, 1997.

———. *Bodies that Matter: On the Discursive Limits of Sex*. New York: Routledge, 1993.

———. *The Psychic Life of Power: Theories in Subjection*. Stanford, CA: Stanford UP, 1997.

Castelao, Alfonso Daniel Rodriguéz. *Sempre en Galiza: Antología*. Ed. Xosé Ramón Pena. Reprint, Vigo, Spain: Galaxia, 2001. Written between 1937 in Barcelona and 1943 in exile, and first published in 1944 in Buenos Aires.

Cixous, Hélène. "Aproximação de Clarice Lispector. Deixar-se ler (por) Clarice Lispector — A Paixão segundo C.L." Trans. Pina Coco. *Revista Tempo Brasileiro* [Rio de Janeiro], 104 (1991): 9–24. Appeared in original French as "L'approche de Clarice Lispector: se laisser lire (par) Clarice Lispector." *Poétique*. Paris: Seuil, 1979. 408–419.

Cole, Norma. *Spinoza in Her Youth*. Richmond, CA: Omnidawn, 2002.

Commission des états-généraux sur la situation et l'avenir de la langue française au Québec. *Le français, une langue pour tout le monde: Une nouvelle approche stratégique et citoyenne*. Quebec: Government of Quebec, 2001.

Conley, Verena Andermatt. "Betrayed." In *Joyful Babel: Translating Hélène Cixous*. Ed. Myriam Díaz-Diocaretz and Marta Segarra. NY: Rodopi, 2004. 39–44.

Damrosch, David. *What Is World Literature?* Princeton, NJ: Princeton UP, 2003.

Dante Alighieri. *La Vita Nuova*. http://digilander.libero.it/letteratura_dante/alighieri_dante_vita_nuova.html in Italian, or http://www.adkline.freeuk.com/TheNewLife.htm in A.S. Kline's English version (both accessed February 2, 2009).

Deleuze, Gilles and Félix Guattari. *Notes on Kafka: Toward a Minor Literature*. Trans. Dana Polan. Minneapolis: U of Minnesota P, 1986.

———. *A Thousand Plateaus*. Trans. Brian Massumi. Minneapolis: U of Minnesota P, 1987.

Deleuze, Gilles. *Francis Bacon: Logique de la sensation*. 4 ed. Paris: Éditions de la différence, 1996.

———. "Letter to a Harsh Critic." In *Negotiations, 1972–1990*. Trans. Martin Joughin. New York: Columbia UP, 1997. 3–12.

———. *Logic of Sensation*. Trans. Daniel W. Smith. Minneapolis: U of Minnesota P, 2003.

———. *Negotiations, 1972–1990*. Trans. Martin Joughin. New York: Columbia UP, 1995.

———. *Spinoza: Practical Philosophy*. Trans. Robert Hurley. San Fransisco, CA: City Lights, 1988.

Derrida, Jacques. *Adieu à Emmanuel Lévinas*. Paris: Galilée, 1997.

———. *Mal d'archive: une impression freudienne*. Paris: Galilée, 1995.

———. *Of Grammatology*. Trans. Gayatri Chakravorty Spivak. Baltimore, MD: Johns Hopkins UP, 1976.

———. *Points... Interviews, 1974–1994*. Trans. Peggy Kamuf et al. Stanford, CA: Stanford UP, 1995.

———. *Positions*. Trans. Alan Bass. Chicago, IL: U of Chicago P, 1982.

———. *Schibboleth, pour Paul Celan*. Paris: Galilée, 1986.

———. "Signature, Event, Context." In *Limited Inc*. Trans. Samuel Weber and Jeffrey Mehlman. Evanston, IL: Northwestern UP, 1988. 1–23.

———. *Writing and Difference*. Trans. Alan Bass. Chicago, IL: U of Chicago P, 1978.

Durif, Eugène. *Meurtres Hors Champ*. Theatre Program from Théâtre Espace GO. Montreal, Spring 2006.

Edelman, Gerald. *The Remembered Present: A Biological Theory of Consciousness*. New York: Basic Books, 1989.

Encarta World English Dictionary. Microsoft Corporation, 1999.

Finkel, Leif H. "The Construction of Perception." *Incorporations*, ed. Jonathan Crary and Sanford Kwinter. New York: Urzone, 1992 (Zone 6). 393–405.

Fireweed. "Canadian Women Poets." Special Issue 23 (August 1986).

Fitzgerald, Judith. "Back to Galicia." Review of *O Cadoiro*. *The Globe and Mail*, June 30, 2007. D12.

Foucault, Michel. *Ditos e escritos III — Estética: Literatura e pintura, música e cinema*. Trans. Inês Autran Dourado Barboda. Rio de Janeiro: Forense Universidade, 2001.

———. *L'archéologie du savoir*. Paris: Gallimard, 1969.

———. *L'ordre du discours*. Paris: Gallimard, 1971.

———. *O que é um autor*. Trans. Antônio F. Cascais e Edmundo Cordeiro. Lisbon: Vega, 1992.

Goleman, Daniel. *Emotional Intelligence.* New York: Bantam, 1995.
Goytisolo, Juan. *En los reinos de taifa.* Barcelona: Seix Barral, 1986.
———. *Realms of Strife: The Memoirs of Juan Goytisolo, 1957–1982.* Trans. Peter R. Bush. San Fransisco, CA: North Point, 1990.
Haraway, Donna. "The Ironic Dream of a Common Language for Women in the Integrated Circuit: Science, Technology, and Socialist Feminism in the 1980s or A Socialist Feminist Manifesto for Cyborgs." 1983. http://www.egs.edu/faculty/haraway/haraway-the-ironic-dream-of-a-common-language.html (accessed January 29, 2009). Revised and reprinted as "A Cyborg Manifesto: Science, Technology, and Socialist-Feminism in the Late Twentieth Century." In Haraway, *Simians, Cyborgs and Women: The Reinvention of Nature.* New York: Routledge, 1991. 149–81.
Hardt, Michael, and Antonio Negri. *Empire.* Cambridge, MA and London, UK: Harvard UP, 2000.
Harris, Claire. *Fables from the Women's Quarters.* Toronto: Williams-Wallace, 1984.
Hilderley, Bob, and Ken Norris, eds. *Poets 88.* Kingston, ON: Quarry, 1988.
Howe, Fanny. *On the Ground.* St. Paul, MN: Greywolf P, 2004.
Huston, Nancy. *Nord perdu.* Paris: Actes Sud, 1999.
Irigaray, Luce. *Speculum of the Other Woman.* Trans. Gillian C. Gill. Ithaca, NY: Cornell UP, 1985.
Johnson, Barbara. *A World of Difference.* Baltimore, MD: Johns Hopkins UP, 1988.
Kristeva, Julia. *Language, The Unknown.* Trans. Anne M. Menke. New York: Columbia UP, 1989.
———. *Revolution in Poetic Language.* Trans. Margaret Waller. New York: Columbia UP, 1984.
———. *Language and Desire: A Semiotic Approach to Literature and Art.* Ed. Leon S. Roudiez. New York: Columbia UP, 1980.
Kuhn, Thomas. *The Structure of Scientific Revolution.* Chicago, IL: U of Chicago P, 1962.
Lévinas, Emmanuel. *Of God Who Comes to Mind.* Trans. Bettina Bergo. Stanford, CA: Stanford UP, 1998.
Lorenz, Konrad. *Here Am I — Where Are You? The Behavior of the Greylag Goose.* Trans. Michael Martys and Angelika Tipler. New York: Harcourt Brace Jovanovich, 1991.
Lyotard, Jean-François. *Chambre sourde: L'antiesthétique de Malraux.* Paris: Galilée, 1998.
———. *Libidinal Economy.* Trans. Iain Hamilton Grant. Bloomington: Indiana UP, 1993.

———. "Matière et temps." In *L'inhumain: Causeries sur le temps*. Paris: Galilée, 1988.
Lyotard, Jean-François, and Jean-Loup Thébaud. *Just Gaming*. Trans. Wlad Godzich. Minneapolis: U of Minnesota P, 1985.
Macherey, Pierre. "Lire *L'Éthique* aujourd-hui." *Magazine littéraire* 370 (Novembre 1998): 35–40.
Maclachlan, Ian. ed. *Jacques Derrida: Critical Thought*. Farnham, UK: Ashgate, 2004.
Maestro, Lani. *Chambres de quietude/Quiet Rooms*. Curated by Renée Baert, et al. Montreal, QC: Galerie de l'UQÀM, 2003.
Malherbe, Jean-François. "Du terrorisme comme symptôme: Face à la violence, penser est toujours un devoir." *Le Devoir* (Montreal) September 15, 2001.
Miki, Roy. *Broken Entries: Race, Subjectivity, Writing*. Toronto, ON: Mercury, 1998.
Mouré, Erin. *A Frame of the Book (The Frame of a Book)*. Toronto, ON: Anansi and Los Angeles: Sun and Moon, 1999.
———. *Furious*. Toronto, ON: Anansi, 1988.
———. *Search Procedures*. Toronto, ON: Anansi, 1996.
———. *Sheepish Beauty, Civilian Love*. Montreal, QC: Véhicule, 1992.
———. *WSW (West South West)*. Montreal, QC: Véhicule, 1989.
Moure, Eirin. *Sheep's Vigil by a Fervent Person: A Transelation of Alberto Caeiro / Fernando Pessoa's O Guardador de Rebanhos*. Toronto, ON: Anansi, 2001.
Moure, Erín. *Little Theatres*. Toronto, ON: Anansi, 2005.
———. *O Cidadán*. Toronto, ON: Anansi, 2002.
———. *O Cadoiro*. Toronto, ON: Anansi, 2007.
Moure, Erín, and Sampedrín, Elisa. *O Resplandor*. Toronto, ON: Anansi, forthcoming 2010.
Mulvey, Laura. "Visual Pleasure and Narrative Cinema." *Screen* 16,3 (Autumn 1975): 6–18.
Nancy, Jean-Luc. *La Création du monde ou la mondialisation*. Paris: Galilée, 2002.
———. *The Sense of the World*. Trans. Jeffrey S. Librett. Minneapolis: U of Minnesota P, 1998.
"Noisy Space." *Postmodern Spacings*, a processual text/discussion project at http://jefferson.village.virginia.edu/~mplanet/submit/, February 1997 to end of 1997, appeared online only. Participants were Paul Bains, Vic Bancroft, Angela Hunter, Paul Mathias, Mark Nunes, Laurent Oget, Ariosto Raggo, Bjarte Rekdal, Martin Rosenberg, Harry Smoak, Heather Wagner but no text is credited. The project

is described at http://htc.spsu.edu/nunes/samla.htm (accessed January 30, 2009).
Pato, Chus. *A Ponte das poldras*. Santiago de Compostela, Spain: Noitarenga, 1996.
———. *Charenton*. Trans. Erín Moure. Ottawa: BuschekBooks and London, UK: Shearsman, 2007.
———. *m-Talá*. Trans. Erín Moure. London, UK: Shearsman and Ottawa: BuschekBooks, 2009.
———. *Secesión*. Vigo, Spain: Galaxia, 2009.
Pessoa, Fernando. *Aforismo e afins*. Ed. Richard Zenith. Lisbon: Assírio & Alvim, 2003.
———. *Fragments d'un voyage immobile*. Ed. and trans. Rémy Hourcade. Paris: Rivages, 1990.
———. *The Keeper of Sheep*. Trans. Edwin Honing and Susan M. Brown. Riverdale, NY: Sheep Meadow, 1997.
———. *Sheep's Vigil by a Fervent Person: A Transelation of Alberto Caeiro / Fernando Pessoa's O Guardador de Rebanhos*. Trans. Eirin Moure. Toronto: Anansi, 2001.
Reckert, Stephen, and Helder Macedo. *Do Cancioneiro de Amigo*. Lisbon: Assírio & Alvim, 1996.
Rivas, Manuel. *O Lapis do Carpinteiro*. Vigo, Spain: Xerais, 1998.
Robertson, Lisa. "The Device." In *Lisa Robertson's Magenta Soul Whip*. Toronto, ON: Coach House, 2009.
Sacks, Oliver. *The Man Who Mistook His Wife for His Hat*. London, UK: Duckworth, 1985.
Said, Edward. "La muerte lenta: un castigo minucioso." *El País*, August 12, 2002. 9–10.
Saraiva, Mário, and Luís Duarte Santos. *O Caso Clínico de Fernando Pessoa*. Lisbon: Referenda, 1990.
Semprún, Jorge. *Mal et modernité: le travail de l'histoire*. Castelnau-le-Lez, France: Climats, 1998.
Serres, Michel. *Le Tiers-Instruit*. Paris: Éditions François Bourin, 1991.
Sontag, Susan. *Against Interpretation*. New York: Dell, 1996.
Stănescu, Nichita. *Occupational Sickness*. Trans. Oana Avasilichioaei. Ottawa, ON: BuschekBooks, 2006.
Stein, Gertrude. *Narration*. Chicago: U of Chicago P, 1935.
Tarkos, Christophe. "The Train (Excerpts)." Trans. Erín Moure. In *Ma langue est poétique: Selected Work*. Ed. Stacy Doris and Chet Weiner. New York: Roof, 2001.
To Be Translated or Not to Be: PEN/IRL Report on the International Situation of Literary Translation. Ed. Esther Allen. Barcelona:

Institut Ramón Llul, 2007. http://www.centerforliterarytranslation.org (accessed January 31, 2009).

Vallespín, Fernando. "Nacionalismo y Constitución." *El País*, December 9, 2000.

Venuti, Lawrence. *The Translator's Invisibility: A History of Translation*. New York: Routledge, 1995.

Vişniec, Matei. *Théâtre décomposé, ou, L'homme-poubelle: textes pour un spectacle-dialogue de monologues*. Paris: L'Harmattan avec l'Institut français de Bucarest, 2000.

Wah, Fred. *Diamond Grill*. Edmonton, AB: NeWest P, 1996.

———. *Faking It: Poetics and Hybridity, Critical Writing 1984–1999*. Edmonton, AB: NeWest P, 2000.

———. *Music at the Heart of Thinking*. Red Deer, AB: Red Deer College Press, 1987.

Wallace, Bronwen. *Common Magic*. Ottawa, ON: Oberon, 1985.

Watten, Barrett. "The Conduit of Communication in Everyday Life." *Aerial 8: Contemporary Poetics as Critical Theory*. Ed. Rod Smith. Washington, DC: Edge, 1995. 32–38.

Wittgenstein, Ludwig. *Tractatus Logico-Philosophicus*. Trans. David Pears and Brian McGuinness. London, UK: Routledge, 1974.

Wolf, Christa. *Accident: A Day's News*. Chicago, IL: U of Chicago P, 2001.

Winnard, Andrew. "Books Translated into English: Why So Few?" *LOGOS: Journal of the World Book Community* 7,3 (1996): 232–36.

Zenith, Richard, trans. *115 Galician-Portuguese Troubadour Poems*. Manchester, UK: Carnacet, 1995.

ACKNOWLEDGEMENTS

Since my first book of poetry appeared in 1979, thirty years ago, I have been thinking about my writing practice, and this thinking has been an integral part of my practice. In 1984, prompted by my move to Quebec and my encounters with Quebec feminists, I began to write critically and philosophically about poetic practice, as part of my engagement with poetry and with other women and men writing it.

The essays in this book follow a more or less chronological trajectory through a pattern of thought, loci of thought, and praxis in poetry. They have been revised but not substantially altered; my understanding and interests have changed over time, and my own constructions of thought developed, and I think this is clear in the arc of the book.

I'd like to thank all those who commissioned talks and articles from me since 1984, including: Janice Williamson and Rob Gray (Edmonton), Kim Fullerton (Toronto), Liba Scheier (Toronto), Ana Bringas López and Belén Martín Lucas (Vigo, España), Xosé María Gomez Clemente (Vigo, España), Caroline Bergvall (London, UK), Jack Stanley (Montreal), Dianne Darby and Keith Jafrate (Huddersfield, UK), Otília

Martins (Aveiro, Portugal), Glen Lowry (Vancouver), Pauline Butling (Calgary), David Kennedy (Sheffield, UK), and Sharon Kivland (Sheffield, UK).

I thank, warmly, all those whose various conversations, long and short, have encouraged me and enriched my own thinking at many points and in many ways over the past thirty years, particularly: Andrés Ajens, Oana Avasilichioaei, Caroline Bergvall, Robin Blaser, Anthony Burnham, Pauline Butling, Susan Clark, Norma Cole, Chris Daniels, Kim Fullerton, Emeren García, Barbara Godard, Xavier Gómez Guinovart, Phil Hall, Guillermo Iglesias, Liz Kirby, Emma M., Lani Maestro, Robert Majzels, Daphne Marlatt, Belén Martín Lucas, Ashok Mathur, Roy Miki, Bill Mouré Jr., Ken Mouré, Lou Nelson, Miriam Nichols, Chus Pato, María Reimóndez Meilán, Lisa Robertson, Susan Rudy, Heidi Schaefer, Gail Scott, Vida Simon, Jack Stanley, Cheryl Sourkes, Colette St-Hilaire, Fred Wah.

I would also like to acknowledge small Canadian presses like BuschekBooks and La Mano Izquierda who publish translations of non-Canadians without funding, thus enriching who we are as a people.

And the book would never have appeared and been readable without the commitment and fierce labour of my publisher, NeWest Press, their fab designer Natalie Olsen, and — last but not least — my editor, Smaro Kamboureli, who despite her rigour in making me connect my ragged phrases into English sentences, will probably let me start and end this run-on sentence with "and."

Earlier versions of some essays were first published or prepared as talks:

"Reading Never Ceases to Amaze Me." *Independent Weekly*, U of Toronto, January 2000.

"And Poetry." In *Sudden Miracles*, ed. Rhea Tregebov (Toronto, ON: Second Story, 1991).

"The Anti-Anaesthetic" was written in May, 1988 and appeared in *Open Letter*, 9 Series 3 (Summer 1995).

"It Remained Unheard" was developed from a footnote to a text published in *dANDelion* 15, 2 (Fall/Winter 1988) that bore the same title (the rest of this text was later developed into "The Anti-Anaesthetic").

"Breaking Boundaries: Writing as Social Practice" was published in a pamphlet prepared by Roy Miki in 1992 for his SFU class. It was originally written for the Maritime Writers' Workshop, July 1990.

"Poetry, Memory, and the Polis" In *Language in Her Eye*, eds. Eleanor Wachtel, Sarah Sheard, and Liba Scheier (Toronto, ON: ECW, 1990).

"The Medium" appeared in *Fireweed* 23 (August 1986), the Canadian Women Poets issue.

"Notes on Poetry and Knowing" was my response in April 1996 to Tim Lilburn's questions: What does poetry know? And how does it know? They were notes toward an essay for a book to which I did not, in the end, contribute, so fierce was my hesitation about knowing anything at all.

"I Learned Something about Writing from You in the Sports

Pages of the Montreal *Gazette*" first appeared in the University of Victoria student magazine *Susurris*, 1994.

"My Relation to Theory and Gender" was written on January 16, 1991 in response to a query about the relationship of my writing with my gender (though I forget for whom, why, where).

"For Scoping Girls" was prepared as a talk for the Toronto Photography Workshop exhibition of the work of Shonagh Adelman, January 1997.

"Speaking the Unspeakable: Responding to Censorship" was first written for a panel discussion at Video In, Vancouver, August 1996.

"On *The Frame of a Book* or *A Frame of the Book*." *Tessera* 27 (Winter 1999).

"A New Bird Flicker, or The Floor of a Great Sea, or Stooking" was prepared for a panel called "Sexing the Prairie" at the conference De:Scribing Albertas, University of Alberta, Edmonton, September 1996. It was published in Open Letter, 10th Series, 3 (Summer 1998).

"*The Capitulations*, on Lani Maestro" was prepared to accompany Lani Maestro's exhibition "La Rêve de l'autre" at Galerie La Centrale, April 25 to May 1, 1998 and was published in *Multiplier. Points de vue sur l'art actuel des femmes.* (Montreal, QC: La Centrale and Éditions du remue-ménage, 1998).

"Three Notes on Lani Maestro's *Cradle*." *dANDelion* 2002.

"Mornings on Winnett: *Trust Meditations*." *Arc* 48 (Summer 2002).

"Poets amid the Management Gurus" appeared in *The Globe and Mail*, commissioned by Carl Wilson, August 10, 1998.

"Person, Citizen: Some Cues from a Poetic Practice" was commissioned as a talk by Belén Martín Lucas and Ana Bringas López, and appeared in *Challenging Cultural Practices in Contemporary Postcolonial Societies*. (Vigo, Spain: Universidade de Vigo: 2001. 225–33).

"The Public Relation: Redefining Citizenship by Poetic Means" was commissioned as a talk by Belén Martín Lucas and Ana Bringas López, and appeared in *Global Neo-Imperialism and National Resistance*. (Vigo, Spain: Universidade de Vigo, 2004).

"The Exhorbitant Body: Translation as Performance" appeared in *Matrix* 60 (Fall 2001) and in *Performance Research* (UK) 7,2 (Summer 2002), eds. Ric Allsop and Caroline Bergvall.

"Fidelity Was Never My Aim (but Felicity)" appeared as "O meu obxectivo nunca foi a fidelidade (senón a felicidade)," trans. into Galician by Laura Sáez Fernández, in *Viceversa*, 6. (Vigo, Spain: Universide de Vigo, 2000, 277–82).

"Subjectivities: An Approach through Clarice and Fernando" appeared in *Portugal e o Outro: Uma relação assimétrica?* Ed. Otília Martins. Aveiro, Portugal: Univ. de Aveiro, 2002.

"Translation as Absence, Bookended by Gift" is a reworked version of my notes for a talk at the annual conference of ACCUTE (Association of Canadian College and University Teachers of English) in Quebec City in 2001.

"Stakes, Poetry, Today." *Open Letter*, 12th series, 2 (Spring 2004), eds. Frank Davey, Nicole Markotic, and Susan Rudy.

It was prepared as a talk to open the Alley Alley Home Free conference in Calgary in May, 2003 (honouring the work of Fred Wah and Pauline Butling) and was originally drawn as a six-sided cube. Each section title of the talk bears the title of a conference session. All beckon to potencies in the work of Fred Wah, a major figure in Canadian poetry, in experimental endeavour, in critical writing, in raced writing, and in writing practices that draw from music and visual art to speak a world "deserving of this name." The photographs in the text are my own, and were originally in colour. The colour versions can be found online at http://www.newestpress.com.

"Re-çiting the Citizen Body" was prepared for a workshop on citizenship and creation of poetry organized by Ashok Mathur at the Emily Carr Institute of Art and Design in Vancouver, August 2003.

"One Red Shoe: Narrative as a Practice of Possibility" was given as a talk at Sheffield Hallam University, Sheffield, UK, February 12, 2003, organized by Heidi Schaefer and Sharon Kivland.

"Staging Vernaculars." *West Coast Line*, 50, 40.2 (Fall 2006). The photographs are my own and are part of the thinking of this text. Though they are printed here in black and white, the original colour versions can be found online at http://www.newestpress.com. Thanks to Oana Avasilichioaei and to Robert Majzels for reading earlier versions and offering comments that helped me finish the text. This essay stages the vernacular through a very personal reading of Giorgio Agamben's *The Coming Community*; Agamben's book is other to this text and recommended on its own.

"Co-Translating 'Nicole Brossard': Three-Way Spectacle

or Spectre de Trois?" was first published in *dANDelion*, 33,
2 (December 2007), the "Radical Translation" issue, and in
Translating Translating Montreal (Montreal, QC: Pressdust, 2008).

"Crossing Borders with a Galician Book of Poetry" was
given as a talk at the Centro dos Estudos Galegos at Bangor
University in Bangor, Wales, October 2007.

"Shaggy Mammal Intervençaõ" was given in a panel discussion
at the State University of New York at Buffalo's Poetics
Program in May 2004.

"O Cadoiro: The Cataract" appears as a pdf on the House of
Anansi Press' web page for *O Cadoiro*: http://www.anansi.ca

"The Politics of Practice" has some itineraries of presence that
need noting: L is Lani Maestro, Lignières-Orgères, France;
R is Rachel Levitsky, Brooklyn, NY; K is Kim Fullerton,
Markdale, ON. R2 is Roy Miki, Vancouver, BC. It was
commissioned by Roy Miki as a talk at the first TransCanada
conference, Vancouver, June 2005, which I was not able to
attend.

"A Coda—Beacons" first appeared in *West Coast Line*, 59, 42.3
(Fall 2008), "Citizenship and Cultural Belonging" issue.

PERMISSIONS

The quotations from Nicole Brossard's poems in *Notebook
of Roses and Civilization* on pages 237 and 238 are reprinted with
the permission of Coach House Books (for the English)
and Nicole Brossard (for the French).

The quotation from the poem by Claire Harris is taken

from her *Fables from the Women's Quarters* and is reprinted with the permission of Gooselane Editions.

Joshua Lovelace's questions and interventions in "I Learned Something about Writing from You in the Sports Pages of the Montreal *Gazette*" on pages 79–86 are reprinted with the permission of Joshua Lovelace.

The photograph of Lani Maestro's installation *Cradle* (1996) on page 127 is a black and white version of a colour photograph by Lincoln Mulcahy and appears courtesy of Lani Maestro. All other photographs were taken by Erín Moure.

Quotations from the poems of Erín Moure, and the essay "O *Cadoiro*: The Cataract" appear with the permission of House of Anansi Press (http://www.anansi.ca).

The quotation from Lisa Robertson's poem "The Device" on page 90 is reprinted with the permission of the author. As well as appearing in the magazine *Hole*, it was later collected in *Lisa Robertson's Magenta Soul Whip* (Toronto, ON: Coach House, 2009).

INDEX

A

Adelman, Shonagh, 90, 91, 92, 94
Africa, 290
African, 35
Agamben, Giorgio, 254, 261, 277, 278, 327n1; *The Coming Community*, 281, 283, 288–89, 292–94, 298
Ajens, Andrés, 241
Alberta, 37, 63, 106, 113–17, 133, 154, 186
Allen, Esther, 322n2
Anderson, Benedict, 167
Arbus, Diane, 42
Auerbach, Frank, 74
Augustine, Saint, 161
Auschwitz, 93, 158, 261

B

Bacon, Francis, 22, 92, 108, 110, 314n5, 316n2, 318n4
Badalona, 289, 290
Baudelaire, Charles, 84, 309
Berlin, 49, 141
Bernhardt, Thomas, 234

Bhabha, Homi, 176
Blanchot, Maurice, 123
Blaser, Robin, 141, 278, 310
Borges, Jorge Luis, 248, 322n2
Brassens, Georges, 116
Brossard, Nicole, 21, 235–41, 243, 250, 324n1
Bueno, Wilson, 241
Butler, Judith, 122, 153, 161, 169, 179, 283, 314–15n1
Butling, Pauline, 212

C

Caeiro, Alberto, 198, 199, 247, 320n5; translation of, 173, 176–77, 182–86, 188–93, 248, 321n7. See also Moure, Eirin; Pessoa, Fernando.
Calgary, Alberta, 37–39
Calgary Herald, 38
Campos, Álvaro de, 188, 320n5
Canada Council, 323n6
Canada / Canadian, 133, 191, 220; Chus Pato in, 251–59, 307; English, 154, 163, 188, 189,

345

247, 322n5; poetry, 46, 98, 161, 312n1; state, 170, 184, 185, 196, 315n1; translation in, 195–98, 241–43, 263, 276, 319n3, 319n4
Canadian Broadcasting Corporation (CBC), 37
Cantonese, 208
Castelao, Alfonso Daniel Rodriguez, 170
Celan, Paul, 152, 160, 161, 310
Chernobyl, 59
Cixous, Hélène, 168, 180, 235
Cole, Norma, 161, 278
Conley, Verena Andermatt, 235, 312n7
Cowan, Hélène, 82–83
Cunqueiro, Álvaro, 257

D

Dante Alighieri, 147, 275
Deleuze, Gilles, 92, 97, 161, 316n3, 318n1; Deleuzian, 109, 164, 175; *Francis Bacon: Logic of Sensation*, 92, 110, 316n2, 318n4; *Negotiations*, 14–15, 126
Derrida, Jacques, 170, 282, 294, 312n7, 318n1; *Of Grammatology*, 25, 45, 314n7; *Mal d'archive*, 242, 262, 264, 267, 274, 276, 278, 325n2; *Schibboleth, pour Paul Celan*, 152, 153, 160; "Signature, événement, contexte," 294, 327n4; *Positions*, 33–34; *Writing and Difference*, 269
Durif, Eugène, 282

E

Edelman, Gerald, 104
English (language), 155, 164, 168, 174, 182, 195–99, 205, 248, 264–65; Canadian, 154, 163, 188, 189, 247, 319n3, 322n5; Chus Pato in, 251–59, 307; effects on, 273, 276, 292; in Quebec, 170, 219, 220, 251, 252; translation into, 175, 177, 191–93, 207, 208, 210; US, 188
Europe, 59, 155, 159, 246, 259, 271, 287

F

Ferrín, Xosé Luís Méndez, 257
Fireweed (journal), 46
Foucault, Michel, 126, 261, 263, 271, 302; *Archéologie du savoir*, 267, 274, 326n5
France, 266, 272, 319n4
French (language), 154, 164, 168, 170, 195, 196, 205, 247, 264, 287, 321n1, 325–26n5; in Canada, 196; in Quebec, 155, 219–20, 252, 322n3; and translation, 237, 242, 282, 319n4

G

Galicia, 154, 170, 254, 259, 263, 273, 275, 326n6
Galician (language), 161, 182–84, 208, 219–20, 241, 261; and Latin, 287; translation of, 163, 241–42, 245, 249–59, 266, 271, 307, 324n1; in *Little Theatres*, 263–64, 292; and Portuguese, 188, 242, 247, 265, 271, 276, 285, 321n4
Germany, 272
Glenbow Museum, 37
Globe and Mail, 100, 145, 315n2
Goto, Hiromi, 161
Governor General Awards (Canada), 197
Goytisolo, Juan, 148, 162, 317n1

Griffin Prize for Excellence in
Poetry, 322n4

H

Haraway, Donna, 91, 94, 104, 153, 161
Hardt, Michael, and Antonio Negri, 217, 313n3, 313n4
Harris, Claire, 31–32
Hebrew (language), 276
Hejinian, Lyn, 158, 318n2
Hobbes, Thomas, 171
Homer, 207, 321n9
Howe, Fanny, 278
Howe, Susan, 310
Husserl, Edmund, 67
Huston, Nancy, 174, 196–97, 319n1

I

Irigaray, Luce, 25, 28, 311n1, 314n1
Italy, 272, 273

K

Kafka, Franz, 161, 207, 255, 259, 323n1
Kant, Immanuel, 161
Kim, Myung Mi, 161
Kristeva, Julia, 52, 74, 314n10; *Desire in Language*, 67; *Language, the Unknown*, 50; *Revolution in Poetic Language*, 24, 312n4, 314n10
Kuhn, Thomas, 229, 323n1

L

Lacan, Jacques, 25, 208, 314n6
Lautréamont, Comte de, 259
Ledger, Heath, 175
Lévinas, Emmanuel, 156, 168, 170, 325n4

Lisbon, 272, 276, 296
Lispector, Clarice, 168, 180, 184, 207, 233, 320n3
Little Sisters' Bookstore (Vancouver, BC), 315n1
London, UK, 36
Lorca, García, 187, 310
Lorenz, Konrad, 153, 316n1
Lyotard, Jean-François, 104, 106, 116, 122, 155, 161, 179, 211, 318n5; *Économie libidinale*, 184, 248; *Just Gaming*, 110; *L'inhumain: Causeries sur le temps*, 324n4

M

Macherey, Pierre, 14
Maestro, Lani, 121–30, 213, 317n4
Majzels, Robert, 156, 161, 169, 235, 240, 241, 243, 318n4, 324n1
Malherbe, Jean-François, 165
Mallarmé, Stéphane, 53, 269, 309, 312n1
Mandarin (language), 208
Mankiewicz, Joseph, 175
Mathur, Ashok, 161
Meriwether, Lee, 272, 326n3
Miki, Roy, 154, 161, 184
Milton, John, 161
Montreal, Quebec, 51, 190, 219–21
Montreal Gazette, 79, 83, 313n2, 317n1, 318n1, 321n4
Moure, Eirin, 173, 177, 182, 185, 190, 214; *Sheep's Vigil by a Fervent Person*, 175, 185–88, 190–93, 195, 198, 199, 323n6. See also Caeiro, Alberto.
Mouré, Erin, *A Frame of the Book (The Frame of a Book)*, 94, 104, 109–11, 157; "12 Descriptions of Trees," 232–33; *Furious*, 25, 29, 34, 43, 46, 47, 64, 66, 87,

314n9; "The Acts," 23, 79, 81–82, 84, 104; *Search Procedures*, 103, 104, 157; "Morphine, or the Cutting Stone," 228; "Tales of the Sumerians (Auburn, NY)," 228; *Sheepish Beauty, Civilian Love*, 79, 80; *WSW (West South West)*, 29, 43, 60, 79, 82, 316n3; "Seebe," 84–85, 312n1

Moure, Erín, *Little Theatres*, 263, 265, 292, 296, 297; *O Cidadán*, 155–60, 162–69, 183, 205, 207, 217–19, 263, 265, 291; "Document 13 (porous to capital)," 230; "Eighth Catalogue of the *in jure* of Harms," 231; "Second Catalogue of the Substitution of Harms,*" 232; *O Resplandor*, 242

Mulvey, Laura, 311n1

N

Nancy, Jean-Luc, 161; *La création du monde*, 203, 207, 209–11, 217; *Sense of the World*, 151, 162, 164, 165

Neruda, Pablo, 36, 310

Nietzsche, Friedrich, 122, 314n7

Nissei, 184

North America, 59, 154, 159, 258

O

O'Connor, Flannery, 47

Olympic Arts Festival (Calgary, Alberta), 37, 38

Ontario, 41

Ourense, Galicia, 254, 255

P

Pato, Chus, 241, 259, 278, 323n6; *m-Talá*, 249–51, 253, 263; *Charenton*, 253–58, 307

Pessoa, Fernando, 173, 176, 177, 180–90, 241, 247, 253, 310, 320n5, 321n5; *O Guardador de Rebanhos*, 262; *Sheep's Vigil by a Fervent Person*, 175, 185–88, 190–93, 195, 198, 199, 242, 317n1, 323n6; *Fragments*, 165. See also Caeiro, Alberto.

Petit, Philippe, 42

Plato, 24, 31, 32

Pope, Alexander, 310, 321n9

Portugal, 177, 180, 273, 326n2

Portuguese (language), 164, 188–89, 190, 195, 199, 221, 242, 247, 265, 266, 271, 273, 286, 318n3, 321n1, 326n4

Probyn, Elspeth, 161

Provence/Provençal, 271, 272, 275, 289

Q

Quebec, 82, 154, 155, 160, 170, 195–97, 219, 251, 319n6, 321n1, 322n3

R

Reagan, Ronald, 52

Reckert, Stephen, 274

Red Deer, Alberta, 63, 133

Reimóndez, María, 249, 250, 255

Reis, Ricardo, 188, 320n5

Ritsos, Yiannis, 36

Rivas, Manuel, 171, 208, 220

Robertson, Lisa, 90, 95, 161, 278

Romanian, 242, 297

Royal Canadian Mounted Police (RCMP), 35

Rwanda, 159

S

Sacks, Oliver, 27, 36, 225, 226
Sade, Marquis de, 311n3
Said, Edward, 221
Sampedrín, Elisa, 242, 297
Santiago de Compostela, 133, 250, 251
Sappho, 266, 310
Saramago, José, 186, 234
Semprún, Jorge, 152, 161, 217
Serres, Michel, 99
Shakespeare, William, 285
Shklovsky, Viktor, 158, 234
Soares, Bernado, 320n5
Somalia, 159
Sontag, Susan, 314n1
Spain, 167, 256, 259, 326n6
Spanish (language), 36, 220, 231, 241, 247, 316n2, 317n1, 321n1
Spinoza, Baruch, 14, 97, 98, 105, 161
Spivak, Gayatri, 314n7
Stănescu, Nichita, 297
Stein, Gertrude, 227, 233, 310
Stus, Vasyl, 23, 24, 311n2

T

Tarkos, Christopher, 241
Taylor, Elizabeth, 175
Toronto, Ontario, 51, 176, 177, 185–86, 188, 189–91, 198–200, 247, 296
Tostevin, Lola Lemire, 208

U

UK/Britain, 145, 198, 251, 319n4
Ukrainian, 23, 207
USA, 197, 198, 220, 255, 263, 318n3

V

Vallespín, Fernando, 165
Venuti, Lawrence, 185
VIA Rail, 55, 147, 148, 263
Vigo, Spain, 249
Vișniec, Matei, 93

W

Wah, Fred, 207, 208, 209, 212, 278
Wallace, Bronwen, 42–47, 312n1
Watten, Barrett, 90, 91
Weil, Simone, 314n1
Weiss, Peter, *Marat/Sade*, 253, 256, 257, 259
Winnard, Andrew, 319n4
Wittgenstein, Ludwig, 91, 122, 153, 155, 161, 227, 281, 317n3
Wolf, Christa, 234

Y

Yevtushenko, Yevgeny, 36
Yugoslavia, 159

Z

Zenith, Richard, 272, 326n1

Erín Moure is a Canadian poet and translator who lives in Montreal. Since releasing her first book in 1979, she has published several award-winning English poetry collections and translated the poetry of several acclaimed writers, including Nicole Brossard from French (with Robert Majzels), Chus Pato from Galician, Fernando Pessoa from Portuguese, and Andrés Ajens from Spanish. Moure has published poetry and translations in over 150 journals and anthologies in several countries, and her poems have been translated into eight languages.

In 2008, Moure was awarded an honorary doctorate (D.Lit.) from Brandon University in recognition of her contributions to poetry. Her most recent collections are *O Cadoiro* (2007) and *Little Theatres* (2005). Her translation of Chus Pato's famed *m-Talá* was released simultaneously in Canada and the UK in spring 2009, and a book of collaborations with poet Oana Avasilichioaei, *Expeditions of a Chimæra*, was published in the fall of 2009. Moure's next solo book of poetry, *O Resplandor*, will be released in February 2010.